KNOW THE TRUTH

EXTENDED EDITION

By Danyell J. Elder

TRILOGY
PROFESSIONAL PUBLISHING MEETS POWERFUL PROMOTION
A wholly owned subsidiary of TBN

Know the Truth Extended Edition
Trilogy Christian Publishers A Wholly Owned Subsidiary of Trinity Broadcasting Network
2442 Michelle Drive Tustin, CA 92780

Rights Department, 2442 Michelle Drive, Tustin, CA 92780.
Trilogy Christian Publishing/TBN and colophon are trademarks of Trinity Broadcasting Network.
Cover design by: __
For information about special discounts for bulk purchases, please contact Trilogy Christian Publishing.

Manufactured in the United States of America
10 9 8 7 6 5 4 3 2 1
Library of Congress Cataloging-in-Publication Data is available.
ISBN: 978-1-63769-844-0
E-ISBN: 978-1-63769-845-7

Words Given to Danyell by God
for the edification and exhortation of God's people
and the salvation of all mankind

THE TABLE OF CONTENTS

Timeline:

2013…………………………………… Pg. 7-10

2015…………………………….. Pg. 11-34

2016………………………..Pg. 35-46

2017……………………..Pg. 47-64

2018………………..Pg. 65-76

2019…………..Pg. 77-151

2020……...Pg. 153- 211

2021…Pg. 213-394

Conclusion…395

YEAR 2013

October 15, 2013

Every day I look at the sky, every morning, I see the sun, and every night I see the moon and the stars shine. Just by looking at it relaxes me. Sometimes I close my eyes and think about the beauty of this world, but at the same time, it's so corrupt because of how we all make choices. I don't know about you guys, but my eyes are so open, and I see a lot of things happening to this world, to this society, to the governments, and to the people. I wisely tell you all this, make good choices not just with your mind but also with your heart, soul, and spirit.

October 24, 2013

Aw, life! Have you ever wondered if there's more to it than just this (money, big house, nice cars, and fame)? Have you ever wondered whether there is still something missing? Well, there is. Many people believe that being rich and having more than what other people have is true success. Others believe that being famous and adored by many people around the world is too. But I tell you this: true success is knowing who you are, knowing what your calling is by God, and accomplishing that very thing that many can't. Everyone (and I mean everyone) has a destiny and a talent to help them achieve it. So, believe in yourself because, with God, you have more power than you think. Know who you are and achieve wonders because that is what I'm going to do.

November 15, 2013

We are what we think and believe we are, so believe in yourself and know that you can do anything you put your mind to with the power of the living God in heaven. Always think positive and never negative about yourself and other people around you because the curse of your words that you say to people can always come back on you tenfold, and the negative words that you say unto yourself will even curse you as well. Words are powerful and have been given to us by God, so use them wisely.

YEAR 2015

January 13, 2015

Every day, we all make mistakes and don't even realize it sometimes. Maybe you have spoken something wrong and painful to someone that was not right nor respectful or have done things that you're not proud of. Please, I tell you this: be respectful to thy neighbor and love on your elders, for we would not have been here were it not for their choices and the sacrifices they have made for the comforts that we all love and enjoy. Everyone in this world deserves respect even if they do not look, talk, or walk like you. Even if they do not deserve it, still, I tell you, give respect and show that you are more than how society acts. Learn to love, and you shall be loved.

January 26, 2015

Some people in this world that we all live in believe that if you repent unto God for the sins that you have committed, you shall be forgiven, for that is true, but please understand that if you are not sincere within your heart while repenting unto God, the sins that you have prayed for shall not be forgiven and denied, and you will still be accountable for that sin on judgment day. For I tell you on behalf of my Father who is in heaven, repent with a sincere, humble, and true heart and do not sin again.

February 10, 2015

Why cry in the midst of tests and trials when God our

Father has already given you the victory? Why cry when you already know that God has you covered? Why cry when you already know that Jesus died on the cross for our sins so that you may have life? Why cry when you can just believe, have faith in Him, and rejoice, knowing that God will make a way out of no way? Not just for some things (the devil is a liar!) but for all things. Believe in Him, and you shall see His wonders and miracles manifest!

February 10, 2015

As sons and daughters of God, He gave us an inheritance, and that inheritance is power, the Word of God (the Bible). We are more powerful than we believe we are. He has given us the power to speak life in times of trouble and show people the light (Jesus) when there is nothing but darkness and hurt. For God's glory will rain on us, and He will use us, and when the time comes, there will be no demon in hell that can stop us. Read the Bible, learn from it, live it, hear God's voice, and follow it. All gifts and abilities are given by God, who is in heaven and no other. Within John 10:4-5 (MEV), Jesus Christ said, "When he brings out his own sheep, he goes before them. And the sheep follow him, for they know his voice. Yet they will never follow a stranger, but will run away from him. For they do not know the voice of strangers."

June 15, 2015

There are so many people in this world that want God but do not want to accept Jesus Christ as the Son of God and the Savior that died on the cross for our sins. Truly I tell you this, Jesus (as seen in John 14:6) is the way, the truth, and the life, and no man cometh unto the Father (God), but through Him (Jesus Christ). Before you can get to God, you must believe in Jesus Christ. For Jesus Christ said,

> Verily, verily, I say unto you, He that believeth on me, the works that I do shall he do also; and greater works than these shall he do; because I go unto my Father. And whatsoever ye shall ask in my name, that will I do, that the Father may be glorified in the Son. If ye shall ask anything in my name, I will do it. If ye love me, keep my commandments.

John 14:12-15 (KJV)

August 2, 2015

Though life is hard sometimes, and it seems like you don't know where to go or what to do, all you can do is wait on the Lord and hear His voice. For God is my guide and my light in dark places, my source of strength, my healer in the time of hurt and pain, my joy because He makes the sun shine and the birds sing a new melody of praise unto Him. He shall walk with me, talk with me, and create change in my lifetime, and we shall be one (*I in him as he is also in me*), for Jesus Christ declares it within John 14:20 (KJV) for all of them that truly abide in Him. And His light will shine through me as bright as the sun. And many will bear witness to the power and glory of God. Who am I? I'm one of the children of God, a prince in my Father's house, and through me, He shall do wonders. I must not forget who I am. I love You, God, my Father, for You are my heart and my reason for living. I must not forget who I am.

August 22, 2015

For I do not praise and give glory unto man but praise and give all the glory unto the Lord, for man did not give me the breath of life, created, anointed, nor birthed me with the Spirit that I have been given by God from the womb of my mother. Woe unto them that praise and worship a man just because of the anointing and mantle that God has placed on his life, for God's wrath and anger shall be upon them lest they amend their ways, and woe unto the man that is praised as a god by many. For the anointing and mantle that God has given him, He can also take it away! You would be wise to heed the warning, God's people, for He is a jealous God, and there shall be no other gods before Him.

September 25, 2015

When you are in a place where God is preparing you for something great, He starts to grow your maturity level, and your mindset starts to broaden to where you gain more wisdom, knowledge, and understanding. But I tell you this, if you do not speak and pray unto your Father (God) in your private time, night and day, to build your relationship with Him, it will become tremendously difficult to stay within that place of nurturing until the development is finished. For the devil, since you are weak, will try to send you distractions and confusion to drive you away from the place of development. Knowledge of God will only get you so far, but with the relationship of God comes wisdom, understanding, power, and the greatest one of all is the path. Truly I tell you this, it is impossible for one to do the will of God without the relationship of God, and if one believes that he is doing the will of God, but without the relationship with God, then he is not being led by God but only of the flesh, for he is a false prophet.

October 6, 2015

I shall be righteous because my Father in heaven is righteous, I shall be holy because my Father in heaven is holy, I shall love and show mercy because my Father in heaven loves me and shows me mercy also, and I shall stand upright and be slow to speak on the words that I say unto others, for my Father in heaven is with me. And because we are in His image (sons and daughters of God), why not walk and talk like Him also? Truly I tell you this: when you build a relationship with God, it will often happen that He starts using you as His vessel more and more when the time is right. Let go of your worldly desires and fears and let God use your spirit to show forth His light within you unto the world so that they may be saved from hell beneath.

October 6, 2015

Oh, ye hypocritical Christians, how long will you falsely accuse others with your judgmental mouths and corrupt minds? How dare you falsely speak against your own brother and sister without knowledge of anything? For your brother has done nothing wrong, yet you plot corruptly with the devil to seek a downfall and to speak his sin throughout the congregation. Oh, ye hypocritical Christians, for even the Pharisees did the same. After all the sin that you have done in your lifetime, that you made God deal with, what gives you the right to judge others? Ye snakes, have you not read when Jesus Christ said that before you can take the speck out of your brother's eye, you must take the log out of your own eye first, and to not judge lest ye be judged? Truly I tell you this: if you keep walking in that way of a hypocritical accuser the evil and false accusations that you speak unto your brother and sister, even greater sin will you do. Truly, for your sake, I pray God does not wipe you off the face of this earth, for even the devil is an accuser of man, and surely even his time is almost up. Please repent so that God may forgive you and remember to love your neighbor as you love yourself. Many use the word "love" in vain too many times over; watch it because even God is love.

October 13, 2015

Why, oh corrupt generation, saved and unsaved, just and unjust, good and bad? Why are you so blinded by the ways of this world that you know not what you do? Can you not see the error of your ways? Has God not given you signs time and time again warning you of your actions? You call the people around you brothers and sisters, yet you treat them as the lowest of lows. You disrespect who they are, you curse their name, talk wrong about them to others, and dishonor the way they dress, and then say, "Oh, I'm just joking, man." Why, oh ye corrupt generation, do you let the devil use you to tear down your brother and sister so easily? Truly I tell you this, a foolish man is he that is forward with his tongue and his doings, for he lacks maturity and his name will be in shame unto all that know him but wise is a man that respects, loves, and honors the people around him, for he shall gain favor.

October 14, 2015

One that is of the world acts just like the world and does as they do. But one that is a son or daughter of God does what the Father in heaven shows them to do, for they lead by the example of Christ.

October 20, 2015

Oh, this generation of churches, have you lost your way? What has happened to saving souls that are lost and loving

God with all your heart, mind, soul, and strength, and loving Him more than anything? And pastors, prophets, and preachers, what has happened to your ears that you have not been heeding to the voice of God? Have you been so influenced by money, popularity, and the number of followers that you have lost your way also? Why are God's sheep not being fed the way that He desires? Why have they been under your teaching for many years and yet have been stuck under "religion" not gaining anything? For most of your members were supposed to be there only for a season and not decades. Is it not in our Father's will to teach them so that they also may go out and be used by God to teach others also? For I tell you all this, do not be as the hypocrites, false prophets (self-serving leaders), and religious people (also known as church folk) are, for they are under the world's system and control. Therefore, they are of the world and not led by God. God has more in store for you than just sitting in a seat in church every Sunday, for I tell you, do not be deceived by the world's standards on what a "Christian" is. For there is truly more of what God wants you to do.

October 21, 2015

A man that argues to prove himself better knowledgeable than his brother is foolish and prideful of himself, but wise and humbled is he that avoids arguments and debates, for he shall keep his joy and peace. But as for the foolish, he stormed off in anger, for the devil has robbed him of his joy.

October 25, 2015

I warn you all, do not follow women but follow God with all your heart, soul, mind, and strength, loving the Great "I Am" more than anything and anyone. Those of you that follow your desire will be bound because of it, and you will not hear the voice of God clearly, and you will do just as Adam did in the beginning, but those that love God turn away from the strange women and stay in the will of God and your reward will come from heaven and not from the devil to take you out of the will of God. For I tell you all this, women and men of God, if what you do takes you out of your relationship with God, then you are not in the will of God. Keep God as your first love now and forever. Please do not let the devil deceive you so easily. Let him and her that has an ear, let them all hear. Stay in the will.

November 5, 2015

Unto you who are wise, I say unto you, correct with brotherly love, an understanding heart, and the wisdom of God. With those three attributes, you are correcting without condemning. And remember to make sure the correction that you are giving your brother or sister is from God and not from your own opinion because you may be wrong. I tell you this, woe unto them that misguide others for the path they walk may be in the hands of the misguider. For Proverbs 3:5-6 (KJV) says, "Trust in the Lord with all thine heart; and lean not unto thine own understanding. In all thy ways acknowledge him, and he shall direct thy paths."

November 6, 2015

Oh, Father, for I love all of my brothers and my sisters equally, saved and unsaved, unknown and known. For there is none that I despise. Truly I tell You, oh Abba, there is none that I hate at all. For my unsaved brothers and sisters, known and unknown, truly sometimes I weep for them because I do not know how much time left they have to find You and truly get to know You, Jesus. For my greatest dream is for every soul on this earth to be saved from the doors of hell and be delivered into eternal life in heaven where there is no more pain, trials, and suffering. But only they can make that choice and seek You for their salvation. And for my saved brothers and sisters, known and unknown, I pray that we only get stronger, wiser, and grow in maturity as we stand within the will of the Lord, remaining in the love of God in Jesus Christ. And as for the ones that have left You, oh Abba, because of the tests and the trials that they had to face against the devil, my greatest dream is that they return unto You because they must see that tests and trials are the very things needed to make us stronger.

For how can a baby run before it can crawl, then walk, for truly it cannot until it strengthens itself by the tests of trying to stand, and when the baby falls, it gets back up and tries again. Therefore, the test and trials are essential for our growth. And Father, I pray that all my brothers and sisters, saved and unsaved, remember who the enemy truly is. For it is not one another nor You Abba, but only the devil that deceives us all. For even in the beginning of humanity, it was as this, oh, my beloved Father, my God, my life, and my heart, Amen. Unto you, my unsaved brothers and sisters, Jesus Christ is saying, “Come unto me so that you may live and not die, for hell is trying to take in whomever it can devour for eternity.” And unto you, my saved brothers and sisters, God is saying,

> Stand stronger and keep staying focused within me, spread the gospel of Christ and do not be afraid, for I shall walk with you and talk with you, and I will be with you even until the ends of this world.

November 8, 2015

Bless the Lord, oh children of God, and give Him all of the glory and praise, for He has woken us up this morning with breath in our bodies. He makes the sun rise and shine unlike any other light in this world. Sing praises unto Him, oh Zion, as the birds do. For great and wondrous are His works and love! I love You, Father, Abba, for just being with me in my ups and downs, and just because of that, You will always have my heart. It is in Your hands; mold it as You will, for in You my soul, spirit, and heart trust. And I give all of me unto You, continue to use me as Your vessel, take control of me, make me more like You every day, and shine through me as bright as the sun so that man may see Your glory and rejoice in Your name. For I submit unto You completely, I am in You as You are in me.

November 11, 2015

The ways of the righteous are pure, and they walk in the path of the Lord, and victory is what the righteous shall obtain. But as for the ways of the foolish, they are corrupt and lead to nothing but their own destruction.

November 11, 2015

Many have wondered, what is the thing that maketh one great? Is it wealth, the ability to preach and teach, popularity, having a church, fame, objects, your appearance, or maybe it's having someone's love and affection? I tell you, none of these things maketh one great, nor will they get you into the kingdom of heaven. But it is better for one to be poor and have nothing to offer this world but still love Jesus Christ with all of their heart, obey His voice, and have a relationship with God, for I say unto you, that one is called great and the kingdom of heaven shall they inherit.

Therefore, for this reason, Jesus Christ said,

> Take heed and beware of covetousness. For a man's life does not consist in the abundance of his possessions.

Luke 12:15 (MEV)

November 15, 2015

Why listen to what people say when you may already know that the devil himself is speaking through them to stop you from what God is telling you to do? I say unto you, rebuke Satan and continue in the will of God.

November 17, 2015

They that obey the will of God will prosper and flourish in spirit, but as for the ones that walk in their own understanding, they will drain their spirit and fail.

November 17, 2015

Live to be loved by God and not man.

November 18, 2015

The life of man is only for a moment, but the life of a soul lasts forever; where shall you lead it? Wise are they that choose eternal life instead of eternal condemnation.

November 21, 2015

Cruel words to your brother or sister can cut deeper than any heated blade or knife to where it can kill any relationship or friendship. This I say unto you, watch the words that come out of your mouth so that the devil shall not tear apart something that God has drawn together. Speak with love.

November 22, 2015

People that you hang out with will always betray you and curse your name. But blessed by God is one that has a friend that truly sees them as a brother or sister, for they will always stand by their side, never talk negatively but positively about them to others, and correct them with love if need be. For that is a true friend.

November 24, 2015

Always give thanks to God for every day that you live, for the days are not promised to us. This is the day that the Lord has made, and I will rejoice and be glad in it. I shall be joyful because He is still with me, and I love Him because He never left me. For what greater love is it that God sent His Son to die on the cross for our sins and took a beating for our transgressions? For the true purpose of thanksgiving is to thank God for everything that He has done in and for your life.

November 25, 2015

Yes, cherish the beautiful life that you have built with your families, but do not forget who has given it to you, for without God, no matter how successful you are now, your life now and after you die physically will be meaningless, for you will miss the point of you truly being alive.

November 25, 2015

To all my unsaved brothers and sisters, known and unknown, I say this with love, for in the life of the flesh you hold on so dearly to is nothing that comes out of it but death: choose eternal life of peace instead. For I say unto you, at the end of this life, there is nothing but heaven or hell, and I tell you, hell is real and a place of torment and torture forever, for there is no end to it as there is in this life. It is not a fun place. In the beginning, hell was only meant for fallen angels, but because Adam and Eve ate of the tree of knowledge, the evil of the flesh entered us. But before that, only good was in us, and we were perfect "like" our Father in heaven, but because of the tree, we became eligible for hell because only evil is sent there, and evil entered us, which opened hell's gates for humanity as well. But since we have "free will," we have the right to choose our destination. For this life is nothing compared to where you are going to go. So, I say again; I'd rather see you choose eternal life, for even Peter said, "The Lord is not slow to fulfill his promise as some count slowness, but is patient toward you, not wishing that any should perish, but that all should reach repentance" (2 Peter 3:9, ESV).

Truly I say this unto all: even the cruelest person can redeem themselves and their ways to God because of mercy and grace. When Jesus Christ died on the cross for our sins, it was so. Heaven you can inherit; life eternally shall be yours. For Paul said, "That if thou shalt confess with thy mouth the Lord Jesus, and shalt believe in thine heart that God hath raised him from the dead, thou shalt be saved" (Romans 10:9, KJV). You don't need to be in church to become saved; you can be saved from hell beneath anywhere. Truly that is what he meant by "saved," redeemed from hell beneath. Believe with your heart and confess with your mouth that Jesus is Lord and that God has raised Him from the dead, and you shall be saved. Now you are able to repent, pray to God for forgiveness of your ways, get baptized, becoming a new creature. Then from there on, pray unto God and read His Word night and day, and day and night so that you may learn from God. I love you all, and I don't want you to reap the eternal death of the soul but instead to receive eternal life with Christ Jesus in Paradise.

November 25, 2015

Before you become a leader, you must be a servant, and as a leader, you are a servant. For if a person becomes a leader without knowledge and understanding of being a servant, then is he truly a leader or a deceiver?

December 1, 2015

They that live without God are like dead plants without water waiting to be thrown away because they are losing their own soul. But they that will call on the name of Jesus Christ shall gain living water that shall always satisfy, and their stem shall grow stronger than before. For radiant and bright shall they become because eternal life they have inherited.

December 2, 2015

The best way of getting through a test and trial is to stay in the counsel of God. Pray, fast, and read His Word so that you may hear His voice and be in control of your flesh. For in Him you shall find rest, and when the test and trial are over, greater will you become. And the greater you become, the greater the tests shall be, but do not waver nor give up because our Father in heaven shall fight for you, and an example in Him shall He make you. Just stay with Him and never leave Him because truly I tell you this, He has never left you, nor will He ever leave you, for you are His chosen.

December 2, 2015

I thank You, God, my Father, for keeping me. The reason why I smile and have joy is because you are still with me, for no matter how hard the tests and trials get, I know that You shall hold me through it all. I love You so much, my Father. I love You so much. You are my reason for living. Without You, there is no purpose.

December 4, 2015

Many do not want to hear the truth, but only something that will make them feel good. But I tell you this, the Word of God does not come to make you feel good but to deliver and bring salvation; it does not come to praise but correct, for the Word is truth, and many will be offended by the truth, but it is not for them but only for the ones that are drawn to it. I tell you this, for the truth is the light, and they that are of light will come, listen, and learn. The ones that are offended by the truth are of darkness and hate the light. For Jesus is the truth, and only His sheep shall know His voice, for truth was sent for the ungodly so that they will see the light and walk therein.

December 5, 2015

Men and women of God, choose ye this day whom you will serve, for you cannot serve God and man at the same time. You either choose yourselves or the one that has created and saved you. Please God or man. Just as you cannot mix clean clothes with dirty clothes, that is the same with light and darkness, God and the devil. I pray that you choose wisely. Separate yourself from the people and things that are unclean, or they will corrupt you and take you away from God.

December 9, 2015

It's not about the test that we all go through but only

God's purpose for it all. Seek Him, and He will bring understanding when the time is right.

December 10, 2015

Make me wiser, Father, so that my face will shine bright; make me stronger, Father, so that I'll be more powerful in You. Work within me, Father, so that You may shine through me as bright as the sun, for in all these things I ask of You, in this let souls be drawn to You. For God, Your light can penetrate through any heart. This is my heart's desire so that You would use me to save many souls throughout the world to be used by You also, for they are my brothers and sisters, and they shall be set free. With me, there shall be no limit on the way You can use me. Show me Your wonders and power. As I am Your son, teach me in Your paths, Father.

December 14, 2015

Oh God, my Father, before You, there is nothing. But with You, You are my everything.

December 17, 2015

Unto you that are steadfast in the will of God, when a door that was meant from God to stay open closes in your face, do not fret, fight, or even get angry. Since you have been humbled throughout the tests and stayed focused on God, an even greater door that is worthy shall you receive. And since the thing that was meant to be a blessing to you turned into a curse, a blessing that is even greater shall come to you instead. And happy, filled with the joy of the Lord shall you be.

December 19, 2015

It is not what people think about you that makes you who you are. It's only about what God knows about you that makes you who you are and how great in Him you are going to become.

December 19, 2015

Everyone that is saved is an example to the people that know them, whether they know it or not.

December 22, 2015

Though you may hate me, I still shall love you as my brothers and my sisters because God, my Father, still loves me as His son. Why then should I not show forth His love to the ones that hate and mistreat me also? Truly I tell you this, for God's love is truly the only love that matters most in this life, so don't expect love given back from the world because we are not of the world but of the Father in heaven sent into the world so that His people may be saved from eternal fire.

December 26, 2015

Everything evil in the sight of God that is hidden in the dark shall always come into the light. No matter how deep in the darkness you tried to cover it, it shall be open in plain sight, as like a light shining on a criminal that's trying to break out of prison. Maybe not now or maybe not later, but soon enough, God's judgment on His people is coming.

December 26, 2015

Wise are they that repent daily unto God, for they bring unto account that their deeds known and unknown did not separate them from the presence of God. But as for the foolish, self-righteous, and blinded, are they that live life believing that they have never sinned and feel no need of repentance. For little do they know that they are driving their souls straight into hell's gates.

December 26, 2015

Wise are they that listen to the wisdom of the elders, for the days of their life shall be lengthened.

YEAR 2016

January 3, 2016

Oh, my brothers and sisters, in everything that you do, do it unto God and before anything that you do, speak unto Him about it so that you know that what you do does not go against God.

January 4, 2016

Many wonder what love is. Love gives something dear to someone without expecting anything in return. Love forgives their brethren, though knowing that what they did to them hurt and was wrong. For love gives mercy to the sinful and blesses the poor. Love never judges neither curses its brethren with harsh words but instead shows compassion to all that it sees. Love brings up and never tears others down. I tell you all this because God is love, and love is God and His love He has put within us to show unto others. So, I say unto you, show it, don't just speak it, but rather live it so that you will not be a hypocrite. If you're going to love one, why not love all? For in love our Father in heaven within us is shown so that they may ask you, "What manner of a person is this that acts this nice and does these things for a person like me?" And you shall say, "For it is not me but God, my Father that shows His eternal love through me, for I am nothing but a vessel of His, and He is love."

January 8, 2016

In everything that is good in your life, thank God and give Him glory for it all. Thank Him for His love and favor. For without Him, it would not have been so.

January 9, 2016

Unto you that say that you love God, I say unto you, then love Him. Don't say and act like you love Him around the believers and then act like you don't know Him around the unbelievers and go to do the things that they do, acting like there is no God in this world. For I say unto you, whosoever be ashamed of God and his Word, shall God also in return be ashamed of those people.

January 9, 2016

Stop worrying and looking at the past when you should be walking in your present, for in the past, there is nothing but death and ashes, but in your present, God shows you life. This is a new year, men and women of God, don't live it in the thoughts of the past, for there are new things that must be shown in the present, preparing you for the future.

January 10, 2016

They that feel the need to correct someone every five

minutes and yearn for the attention of their neighbors, lack confidence and self-esteem within themselves, and still do not yet know who they are. For I tell you this: if your confidence is in God, then why need the approval of man?

January 13, 2016

God put you through tests and trials not because He doesn't trust you but only because He believes you can make it through, and if you make an error, will He not correct you?

January 17, 2016

For there is none greater than the one true living God, the great "I Am." And before Him, there is and was no other God, for He is the God of this world, He had created the birds and the bees, the mountains, and trees, for He guides the winds wherever He sees fit. He is the God of seasons, and time is in the palm of His hands; when He speaks, things change, for He is Jehovah! He is the beginning and the end. There is no other god, for even the breath that we breathe is His. Do you not know Him? Have you not heard of His mighty works and seen His miracles? For yes, I say unto you, yes, He is even the God of the impossible and magnificent. Have you not heard of how He gave His only begotten Son (Jesus Christ) to die on the cross for our sins so that we may have mercy and grace and be drawn back unto Him? God is love, and His Word is truth. For God loves us, and all He seeks of you is your repentance to turn away from your evil ways, your submission, and your obedience, and mainly your love. Seek His face and learn of His ways so that you may know Him!

January 17, 2016

No one can tell you who God is; you must seek Him for yourself.

January 21, 2016

The parable of the great man:

There was once a great man that produced other men, and one workman that worked for the great man knew much knowledge about the great man's business and saw himself worthy of being promoted, but then one day a different hard-working man got promoted instead of him. Therefore, he was furious and went to go speak to the great man, and when he found him, he asked the great man, "Why did he get promoted instead of me? For I know more than he does." And the great man said unto him, "You may know more things than him, but he has a greater relationship with me than you ever had. Therefore, I have set him higher than you. Seek me more, get to know me better, speak to me daily, gain that relationship, and then shall I pour out more unto you." I say unto you, as the great man is unto his workers, that is how God is to His people.

January 22, 2016

Relationship with God:

Building a relationship with God is like building muscles. The more you exercise it, the stronger it becomes, and the stronger it becomes, the stronger you become, and the stronger you become, the more it starts to show unto others. But when you stop doing it, you start to slowly let go of what you have gained, but when you decide to turn away from the path that you put yourself into and dedicate yourself better than you did before, your muscles start to become stronger than they were before, and you become even stronger than before. And the stronger you become, it will show unto others even more than it did before. But I say unto you, woe unto them that stopped for a long period of time. For I say unto you, harder will it be than the beginning of when you started building your muscles to gain back everything that you have let go of.

February 6, 2016

You can know more scriptures than anyone else in the world, but I say unto you, if you do not know the Father in heaven, then it profits you nothing, and you are just memorizing words off of a paper to make yourself look knowledgeable. But I say unto you, if you knew the Father in heaven, the Word of God should be already within you, and the Holy Spirit would give you power in using it. But if there is no relationship with God, then there is no power. Do you think just because you know a lot of words and their location in the Bible that you can cast out demons, heal the sick, and raise the dead? No, you cannot because your head knowledge has no power, but with God and the relationship come power, gifts, and even wisdom. For I say unto you, they that memorize scripture to make others look uneducated, for even the devil and the Pharisees knew scripture but the Spirit of God was not found in them, and their relationship with God was corrupted. Therefore, they had no power.

March 30, 2016

Men and women of God, I say unto you, know who you are and do not let any man tell you otherwise; I say unto you also, do not forget who you are. For many things in time fade away. So, keep in remembrance of the Father within your heart, do not forsake His ways, and do not get tired of right-doing. For you shall reap the rewards of your fruit. So, I say again, remember who you are and know thyself. For are you not sons and daughters of God? Then I say unto you, you are more than conquerors; kings and queens wrapped in the glory of God. So, I declare and decree over your lives if it shall be by the will of God, my Father in heaven, that you shall get through every weapon that the devil tries to throw at you, and you will not only get through it but also become stronger because of it in the name of Jesus Christ! For no weapon that is formed against you shall prosper!

May 12, 2016

My brothers and sisters, I urge you all to serve one another and do not be the one that always yearns to be served, for they gain nothing. Whether from the people around you, your friends, or your family, we should want to serve them all with love. For do you not know, servants are called great in the kingdom of heaven? Therefore, in everything you do, do it unto God, our Father in heaven. And before you do anything, ask Him about it first so that He may be pleased with your work. And leaders, know that serving your followers is your duty so that they may become greater servants than they already are, for great leaders are great servants. Do not serve to be served but instead serve to show love and kindness unto each other, for your reward shall come from God and not man.

June 20, 2016

Many try to find their own perception of power and call it their own. Then use it to control and manipulate the minds of people that are under and below them. But truly, I tell you all, true power comes from the only one true and living God, the great "I Am," and He gives it to whomever He sees fit. They that try to find power shall never obtain it, but they that will pick up their cross and seek after God shall inherit it. And they that use their own perception of power to control and manipulate those that are under them shall lose that little power that they have. For I tell you all this, the days are coming when the weak shall be made strong, and the strong shall be made weak.

August 3, 2016

Never let fear dictate your actions. For God has not given us the spirit of fear but only of love, power, and a sound mind.

August 13, 2016

Within life, many people will not understand some of the things that you do, and because of the lack of understanding, they will judge you by only what they see and hear. Then they gossip behind your back with false accusations. Oh, ye judges and accusers, for who are you to claim yourself as God? I say unto you all, none of us has the right to judge one another, for only the one true living God, Jehovah, has that power, and instead of judging, have love and understanding because they that judge shall be judged.

August 15, 2016

A man that always judges others and never looks at the wrong within himself but instead sympathizes for his actions and always thinks highly of himself is self-righteous and prideful in heart. And when a wise man corrects him in his error, he turns away the reproof and condemns and curses the wise man instead. Woe unto them that are self-righteous in heart, for if they do not turn from their ways, at the end of their life, the judgment of the Lord shall they face.

November 9, 2016

My brothers and sisters, many bad things within this life will happen all around us, and they are even happening now, and it hurts seeing many get killed around the world. But we as sons and daughters of God must all understand, we cannot let fear determine the actions we take but only get through the hard times by trusting in the Lord with all our hearts and not leaning on our own understanding. We must always acknowledge Him in all our ways, and He shall direct our paths. I say unto you all, always remember, this life is not our last, and it's not promised to us either, for we are in the world but are not of it, but only of the one promised to us in the end!

YEAR 2017

March 7, 2017

Where do I see myself in five years? I see myself as a great light shining in the midst of darkness, but the thing is, it is not me as myself nor giving glory to myself, but instead, it is the Father being one with me and me with Him. And wherever He goes, I will follow, and wherever I go, He will be with me and not just with me but as me speaking His words with fire, doing miracles, signs, and wonders around the world. For my works will not be my own, for I am His vessel and one of His true sons, a prince in my Father's house. For I am in the world but truly am not of it but only sent into the world so that chains may be broken, so that those that have no hope find it so that those that are in darkness will find the light. For who is this light that many will see? I say unto you, it is Christ living within me.

August 2, 2017

What we have been taught and raised to eat have been lies, and it has affected our condition greatly! We have been misled and misguided by the enemy to destroy us and take us away from how God truly intended us to be. From the beginning of mankind, we were truly only supposed to eat from the vegetation of the ground, and now we have even forsaken that. The Word of God said, "Out of the ground the Lord God made to grow every tree that is pleasant to the sight and good for food" (Genesis 2:9, KJV). Adam and Eve were vegan!

August 21, 2017

The coming of the Lord is at hand! And it's closer than we think!

Glory be to the Lamb of God!

April 27, 2017

The Parable of the True King:

How does one know the true King if he doesn't spend time with Him?

How does one know a king if they do not know the true King?

How does one hear from the true King if they're listening to other kings instead?

For there is only one thing that happens:

For what happens to a plant when it does not receive living water?

The full revelation from God that was given of this message in a parable was not given until the year 2020, September 8th.

For this is the revelation of the message:

Thank God for everyone that is around you and for everyone that you come in contact with but do not make them in your life greater than they ought to be. Do not see them as gods and change the mindset and heart that God has meant for you to have. For I say this unto you, whoever forsakes the truth to believe in lies instead will indeed perish. Many within this generation have the mindset of the world (Satan) and think of the things of the world, but I rather choose the mind of Christ, for in Him there is living water that always satisfies. To forsake living water is as to forsake life to choose death. For whosoever forsakes the truth for lies and wholeheartedly holds on to lies instead of the truth might as well just claim that they committed suicide of their own soul. Therefore, for this reason, Christ said in Matthew, "The Son of man goeth as it is written of him: but woe unto that man by whom the Son of man is betrayed! It had been good for that man if he had not been born" (Matthew 26:24, KJV).

> Think not that I am come to send peace on earth: I came not to send peace, but a sword. For I am come to set a man at variance against his father, and the daughter against her mother, and the daughter in law against her mother in law. And a man's foes shall be they of his own household. He that loveth father or mother more than me is not worthy of me: and he that loveth son or daughter more than me is not worthy of me.
>
> Matthew 10:34-37 (KJV)

September 9, 2017

Repent! For the kingdom of heaven is at hand!

September 16, 2017

I say unto you all, and take thought of this, they that go after the things of the flesh will be bound by the flesh and will not think of the things that are of God but instead the things that are of this world. But I say unto you, they that will go after the things of God and love Him more than the desires of this world will reap the inheritance of the Lord. Think on the things above and not on the things beneath lest you fall into the pit!

September 19, 2017

Who are they that will give their whole hearts unto the Lord, who shall break free of religion, who shall give up their desires and sin for the glory of God, who shall listen to the voice of the Lord? Blessed are they that do! For the glory of the Lord shall be upon them that truly love Him!

September 23, 2017

Oh, my saved brothers and sisters, why are you so far from the truth that you cannot see? You speak peace, peace, God's love, grace, but indeed do not know the time that we are in! For yes, this is truly a time for consecration, but how will you consecrate if you are not willing to give up your own selfish desires and the wickedness of your evil hearts for God! Pride, control, gossip, judgment, idol worship, jealousy, wrath, lust, sexual immorality, scorning, fakeness, religion, unforgiveness, racism, and everything else that is unlike God must go! We must be willing to crucify our flesh daily (must be willing to change). Love and relationship with God must be at the top of our list right now. Who is willing to give up their own will for the will of God?

September 30, 2017

Disappointments happen when expectations are given. So don't expect anything from anyone unless you are willing to be let down. And when someone does not live up to your expectations, do not think wrongly of them nor be angry because of it. Continue to love them as yourself and just be wise in what you do.

October 3, 2017

How is it that you can try to discern someone else's sins but indeed do not see your own? You hypocrite! Did not the Pharisees do the same? For Jesus Christ said in Matthew 7:5 (KJV), "Thou hypocrite, first cast out the beam out of thine own eye; and then shalt thou see clearly to cast out the mote out of thy brother's eye."

October 6, 2017

Oh, my brothers and sisters, never let unforgiveness reign in your hearts to where it stops you from truly loving one another. For I say unto you, where there is unforgiveness, true love is not present. Let it go and if it takes you to let that person know how you feel to forgive them, then do it quickly. For the longer you hold in unforgiveness, the longer you can hold up what God wants to truly do in you. Love everyone to the fullest but always be careful of who you trust. Trust no man but God alone. For Psalm 118 says, "It is better to trust in the Lord than to put confidence in man" (Psalm 118:8, MEV). And Jeremiah 17 says, "Thus says the Lord: Cursed is the man who trusts in man and makes flesh his strength, and whose heart departs from the Lord" (Jeremiah 17:5, MEV). But Jeremiah 17:7 (MEV) says, "Blessed is the man who trusts in the Lord, and whose hope is the Lord."

October 17, 2017

The good deeds that I do, I don't do it to be seen by others nor to receive a reward, glory, praise, or honor from any man. So, then you would ask me, "Then why do you do all these good things?" For I say unto you, I do my good works not unto man, but unto God, my Father in heaven, and I do not do these good works to even be seen by men but only to be seen by my Abba, for I know whom I serve. And my good works are not my own but only Christ, my eldest brother who lives within me. For I do nothing and am nothing but a vessel, so do not praise me but praise ye the Lord for His wondrous works and thank Him for His kindness and favor! Only He alone is worthy!

October 18, 2017

Please, my brothers and sisters, do not let the fear of the spirit of offense stop you from doing the will of God and standing on the Word of Truth. For this must happen, so that the truth may be spoken with confidence and boldness in the pureness of heart without compromise, revealing, therefore, the truth of all things. But beware that you do not speak out of the spirit of error because of the lusts (desires) of your flesh which brings forth deceit and manipulation, and in turn, offend the righteous because what was spoken or done was not fulfilled in the Spirit of Truth, neither in the Love of God. For this reason, Jesus Christ said in Matthew 18:7 (KJV), "Woe unto the world because of offenses! for it must needs be that offenses come, but woe to that man by whom the offense cometh." This is why one must be purged of all unrighteousness that he may be able to bring forth good fruit by The Holy Spirit.

October 21, 2017

Oh, my brothers and sisters, know and understand the difference between correction and man's judgment. For they are not the same. Correction has love and understanding and will let a person know what they are doing is wrong, and with sound wisdom, it will show you a better path to follow. Man's judgment does not show love at all and does not know understanding. It accuses without knowledge of the truth. It curses the people that do wrong and remembers their faults so that it may have something against them. There is no justice in man's judgment; it only knows error, condemnation, shame, and death. But within correction, there is mercy and compassion.

October 26, 2017

Do not play with vows unto God. For the Word of God spoke through Solomon saying in Ecclesiastes 5,

> When you make a vow to God, do not delay in fulfilling it because He has no pleasure in fools. Fulfill what you have vowed. Better it is that you do not make a vow than you make a vow and not fulfill it.

Ecclesiastes 5:4-5 (MEV)

October 26, 2017

My unsaved brothers and sisters, if you love justice, truth, purity, and freedom, in Christ you can find all these things and more. For there is only one true living God, and besides Him, there is no other. He is not a religion nor even a practice. He is the way, the truth, and the life. In Him, you can find true peace and joy. You seek, and you cannot find, and you fill your soul with the things of this world and count it all as joy. But I say unto you that enjoyment is only for a moment and will soon fade away. But look, God and His Word will last forever. You cry, and you weep because of the weight of this world. You say that you are happy, but truly your heart is filled with sadness. But look, Christ is calling you and is saying,

> Come unto me, all ye that labour and are heavy laden, and I will give you rest. Take my yoke upon you, and learn of me; for I am meek and lowly in heart: and ye shall find rest unto your souls. For my yoke is easy, and my burden is light.
>
> Matthew 11:28-30 (KJV)

He wants you and hears your heart. When you have wept, so has He. When you were hurt, so was He also. You try to find love but yet do not know that He is love. He will fill you with His loving embrace. Seek Him, and you shall find Him. Knock, and the doors will be open unto you. For in Him, you will find purpose and truth. Your eyes have been blinded from the truth, and religious people have condemned you instead of loving you through your pain. For the religious people indeed do not know Him but mock and blaspheme His Word all day long. But I say unto you, God loves you. He knows your mistakes and sees your wrongs, but if you come unto Him, He will forgive you of them all and make you as white as snow, cleansing you for His good purpose. Just believe in your heart and confess with your mouth that Jesus Christ is Lord, and you shall be saved. All He wants is you; it doesn't matter what you did in your past, you can be forgiven, but the question is, what will you do now? Will you continue after reading these words a life that will lead to death, or will you pray on your knees unto God for forgiveness and begin to speak to Him and grab a Bible to know His Word? Who is the Word? Jesus Christ is the Word and truth, and He will bring upon you His Holy Spirit.

October 27, 2017

They that are of the world are controlled by the world and will be forced to do unholy things in the sight of the Lord. But those who are true sons and daughters of God are not of this world and know no other god. Therefore, we are not bound by the control of the enemy. Who is the enemy? Is it not the devil that deceives us all? Look and know who it is that whispers abominable deeds in your ear and makes you feel like wrong is right and right is wrong. For the leaders and kings of this world are in bed with the one that wishes to condemn us all. People of this world, know by whom you are deceived; open your eyes and see the truth!

November 3, 2017

This is what the religious churches are deceived by, and they do not see it:

> Beware lest anyone captivate you through philosophy and vain deceit, in the tradition of men and the elementary principles of the world, and not after Christ.

Colossians 2:8 (MEV)

November 7, 2017

Oh, my brothers and sisters, why do you not heed correction and go back to following the wickedness of your own hearts? For I say unto you, correction is from the Lord, not to harm you but only so that you may live and be fruitful. But instead, you have turned away from Him and His reproof. Are you that hell-bent on your own desires that you would go to hell for it? You seek to find that which is good in your own eyes, and all you found was more grief, sorrow, and pain. The Lord said to you, "Come here so that you may have rest." But you said "no" and rejected Him. You seek for rest and find no rest, you seek for love and only found betrayal and hate, you seek for peace, but there is no peace, you seek false gods, but there is none that will heal your pain nor can they answer you because you are not going to the only one that can give it all.

Seek the only one true living God, the great "I Am," Jehovah, and Christ, His Son, who is calling out to you, and you shall find Him! Seek the Lord thy God who is thy strength, and He will answer, and He is able to heal all your pain. For the Lord God, our Father in heaven is the only one true and living God. For He breathes, He hears, He sees, He knows, He answers, and He has created you, and beside Him, there is no other God! Come unto Jesus Christ, and you shall find Him! This is the only way that leads to life and your salvation!

November 22, 2017

May we all pray for one another (for the saved and unsaved) and share each other's burdens, helping to pick up a cross that someone is carrying so that they may get back up and be strengthened. We ought to love our brothers and sisters (the people around us, those that we do not know, and those of all and any race without partiality) as we love ourselves. To not speak with harmful and scornful words. To not love to hate and bring people down but only love to love and lift people up. Truly I tell you this, people (saved and unsaved) that love to hate indeed do not know in whom they are being used nor by whom they are controlled!

November 22, 2017

Scorners, do not let yourself become happy when you hurt someone emotionally, physically, and mentally, nor become joyful and laugh when others get hurt. Do you believe that is funny? Do you even see or know the spirit that you are of? We all need to look deep within ourselves daily and fix our wrongs, being of a pure heart.

November 22, 2017

Love them that even hate you. For if you only love them that love you, then you have already received your reward, but if you love them that hate you, then your reward will come from the Father in heaven. But also, be aware of snakes. Still love them as yourself but also guard your heart so that on the day they betray you, you will not be shaken but be able to love them and forgive them through the pain. For with God, all things are possible, but with man, it is impossible. Look within yourselves, brothers and sisters. Why do you do the good that you do? Do you love people to please God, or do you love people to please man?

November 25, 2017

My brothers and sisters, you should have been taught this in your youth. Just because someone does wrong unto you, it does not make it right to do wrong unto others, nor is it right to do wrong unto the person that did wrong unto you. For if you do wrong to the person that does you wrong, you will be held accountable for your deeds and will reap an even greater judgment than the person that did you wrong if you already knew not to do wrong to them that do wrong unto you. So, I say this unto you, when someone does wrong unto you, go on and tell them of their faults privately, and if he receives you by saying he is sorry and does not do that evil again, then you have won yourself a brother. But if he does not receive and only curses you, then forgive him instead, and go on your way, not holding a grudge against him. For if you do not forgive your brother or sister of wrongdoings, then you will not be forgiven of yours when your time comes.

November 27, 2017

The devil will try to make you believe and bring people to tell you that love is a weakness, but I come to tell you with the voice of the Holy Spirit, walking into the midst of darkness saying, "Love is not a weakness but strength!" For love will keep you humbled, it knows no hate and has no jealousy; it keeps you patient and teaches you how to be kind. It does not get angry quickly nor curses people with its mouth. Love helps you to endure all things, bear all things, believe all things, and hope all things. And many will try to take advantage of you because of this but remember who you are doing this for, and bear your cross. You become weak when you stop believing in God and stop loving everyone. For I say this unto you, if you put down your cross (turn away from God) and give yourself into the evils of this world, then you would have lost the great fight of faith. It is when you give up living for God and not staying in truth is when you lose not only your will and your drive but also your life (your soul) lest God has mercy upon you and brings you back into truth.

> So, I say unto you with the Word of God and the Holy Spirit,
>
> Be not conformed to this world: but be ye transformed by the renewing of your mind [praying, fasting, and reading the Bible], that ye may prove what is that good, and acceptable, and perfect, will of God.

Romans 12:2 (KJV)

Do not give up on loving one another, and keep on the good fight of faith, my brothers and sisters!

November 29, 2017

You who are accusers, why do you seek to know the sins of others so that you may have something against them? Do you not know whom you are serving? For the devil speaks in your ear, and you gladly do his bidding with laughter that is unholy, bringing down true men and women of God because you know your deeds are ungodly. My brothers and sisters, wise are they that listen and hold their words unto people like these. For Christ speaks of them frequently, for they come in as wolves in sheep's clothing and as snakes within the grass. For I say this with the sound wisdom of Christ my brothers and sisters, "Do not cast your pearls before swine, lest they trample them under their feet, and turn again and rend you." For even Christ was aware of them, and so am I by my Father's help. Who is this Father of mine? Do you not know Him? He is the King of kings and Lord of lords, Abba the Father and Creator of all, the great "I Am," Yahweh! For He is Christ's Father also and whoever else that loves the Lord, so is God their Father also. For we are His sons and daughters! So, I say unto you all, if you love God, do what is pleasing in His eyes and love one another as He also loves you.

December 8, 2017

Instead of trying to find the bad in others, try to find the good, and love the good that you find in them so that you may speak good things out of your mouth, instead of trying to find ways to scorn someone, speaking all kinds of evil. For the same measure that you give unto others is the same measure that you will get back.

December 17, 2017

He who works out his own salvation will grow in maturity and flourish in spirit, and will be able to change nations. But he who feels that his calling is to judge others, never looking at the wrong within himself, and never seeking to change will be stuck in his own ways (never growing). And the people that he had judged will even surpass him in maturity and spirit because they looked upon themselves while he was looking upon others.

YEAR 2018

January 8, 2018

God does not need you to find your mate. God needs you to find Him!

January 9, 2018

Oh, my saved brothers and sisters, listen and hear me well. The Word of God is not just limited to the scriptures but existed long before the Bible was even written. The Word of God was a Spirit that came upon the sons of men. The Word was here before Christ (who is still the Word) died on the cross for our sins and resurrected Himself on the third day after His death. The Word was here even in the times of Solomon, David, Elijah, Daniel, Jeremiah, Ruth, Isaiah, Joshua, Moses, Abraham, Noah, Enoch, and down throughout all the ages of history. The Word was alive even from the beginning of time itself. For truly I say this unto you, the Word was with God and was God. Though the Bible is the Word of God and still is truth, do not limit the Word of God and all that He is and can do. The Word is too big to fit all of itself into a book created by man. Moses had the Word within Him without even having scriptures. For the Word used him to write most of the beginning stages of the scriptures.

For the Bible even bears mysteries within itself that are untold unto the ears of man that only the Holy Spirit can bring unto revelation. And that is only if God even sees fit to burden us with some of the untold and unknown. For only

God (who is also the Word) knows all things and shows mysteries to whoever He sees fit, from the saved to even some of the unsaved (and some don't even realize, the revelations that they have figured out themselves were given to them by Him).

January 11, 2018

What the world (Satan) believes is normal, that is not normal. But what the world believes is crazy, weird, and insane, that is normal. The people of this world only believe and know what society and the governors of this world have taught them. For little do they know, they are being manipulated and are blinded from the truth. For even the History that society has long taught are lies and deceit. You who are of this world, if you come unto the Lord and repent turning away from the evils of your ways and your hearts, the Lord will show you truth, and the truth shall set you free!

For we have been slaves of this world, and we realized it not. But may the blind eyes be opened and deaf ears to hear, oh Father in heaven. It's time for the sons and daughters of God to wake up from our sleep as roaring lions with the power of the Holy Spirit. For the supernatural power of God is normal and real! For our spirit that was in chains shall be set free to prevail against the kingdom of darkness. For the kingdom of heaven is at hand, and who shall withstand the glory of the Lord?

January 11, 2018

Mercy and grace are only here to help us reach after eternal life without condemnation on earth by God, but we must take the steps with determination, patience, and endurance to ensure eternal life in the land that our Father in heaven promised us by giving up what we want to do (flesh) and pursuing what God wants us to do (Holy Spirit)! For only with Christ Jesus is this possible, and all things are possible unto them that believe in Him, our Risen King!

January 11, 2018

God is looking for people that are after His own heart, who walk not after the flesh but after His Spirit!

January 11, 2018

For the time is coming for the separation of the kingdom of darkness from the kingdom of God because it's looking too similar. But in these last days, you will see and know the difference!

September 5, 2018

Love is not true love without discipline, correction, and sacrifice.

September 11, 2018

Repent quickly, for the kingdom of heaven is at hand, and every tree that's not bearing forth good fruit shall be cast out!

September 30, 2018

A healthy amount of positivity is good but never let it blind you from the truth.

October 14, 2018

My brothers and sisters, why do you say, "You haven't been through what I've been through, so you don't know how I feel"? For I say unto you, everyone has been through many hurts and pains within this life, and some suffer more than others depending on the measure of their strength to overcome. So, listen, and listen well: just because someone has not been through what you went through doesn't mean they do not understand your pain. Therefore, know that you are not alone and do not let your heart be hardened, stand strong within God, overcoming the trials that you face, not giving up on doing that which is good in the sight of the Lord God our Father who is in heaven. So, I say again, "Don't give up but overcome!" May God bless you.

October 24, 2018

My brothers and sisters, why have you seen the correction of the Lord as judgment and do not take heed to His reproof? For do you not know that God corrects and warns them that He loves. Therefore, since you have believed that which is good is bad and that which is bad is good, you shall know and see what God's true judgment looks like. For the seven bowls of God's wrath are coming for the generation that has turned away from God's corrections and truly denied Him within their hearts. For not even I would wish for those woeful days. For God shall not strive with man always. So, repent turning away from your evil ways, not out of fear but only because you know the truth and you know you need to change. Come back into the light of God from out of the darkness in which you have placed yourself.

November 5, 2018

In man's intelligence, there is nothing but foolishness, but with God's wisdom, you will find truth in all things.

November 20, 2018

Without God, there is no purpose, only but a vain life that accomplishes nothing for things to come after death. For it is a fear to them that do not believe in God.

December 6, 2018

I say unto you, man's judgment is flawed, but God's judgment is right and just. For He sees all things, knows all things, and hears all things from the mouth of man even to the thoughts of them. For He examines the heart, and nothing is hidden from the Lord.

December 12, 2018

Oh, my brothers and sisters, do you not know that loving the Lord is to keep and live by all His commandments? And to live by them in all righteousness, holiness, and purity? Oh, this generation, why do you love that which is evil so much? We may not be slaves to the law, but in Christ Jesus, we should want to desire to live a life that is worthy of pleasing God. For I say unto you, do you not know that living a life in holiness and truth unto God is the true worship that He requires? For the Word of God in Mark 7 says,

> He answered, "Well has Isaiah prophesied of you hypocrites, as it is written: 'These people honor Me with their lips, but their hearts are far from Me. In vain do they worship Me, teaching as doctrines the precepts of men.' For laying aside the commandment of God, you hold the tradition of men—the washing of pitchers and cups, and many other such things you do." And He said to them, "You full well reject the commandment of God so that you may keep your own tradition."

Mark 7:6-9 (MEV)

Hypocrites, how can you worship God with praise, shouting, and dancing but do not worship Him with your whole heart (obeying God's commandments) first? My brothers and sisters, understand. Before you do anything in life, first evaluate yourself and see if this is pleasing in the sight of God. Watch yourself (your words and your deeds) so that it may line up with the Word of God. For in Exodus 20, Matthew 5-7, Genesis 1-2, and all throughout the Word of God, He speaks on what He requires from us and what is pleasing in His sight for us to do. This is why God said to meditate on His Word day and night, and night and day so that we may be able to know that which is pleasing to the Lord and walk in that way. God is looking for people that would worship Him in spirit and in truth, not just on Sundays but in all of their actions and speech throughout their days. Therefore, love the Lord your God with all your heart, soul, mind, and strength. Honor Him with your whole life.

December 12, 2018

Do not forsake the commandments of the Lord, for in it we show our love unto the Father.

December 15, 2018

For it is a dangerous thing for an evil man to believe that his ways are pure and good. For he is blinded by confusion inspired by ignorance of that which is true.

December 16, 2018

Oh, my dearest beloved brothers and sisters in the Lord, I know you feel like I have left you and don't want to have anything to do with you and that I have forgotten you. But I say unto you, none of these things are true. Though we are not near, my soul and my heart have not forgotten you. I'm not angry with you, nor do I hold you unto any account. We had to separate so that our Father in heaven may grow us in maturity and flourish us in spirit. For the season has changed, and those that do not bend to its purpose will cease to grow until the next season opens again. If it is in the Father's will, we will see each other again, and I say unto you it will be to rock the kingdom of darkness back to the pit of hell from where it came.

For God has made us lights within this world, to heal the sick and raise the dead, to bring the people that are in darkness into the Lord's marvelous light, to break the chains off of them that are bound and are enslaved. And to preach the good news of the Lord unto all that will hear it, for we are the children of God and heirs in the kingdom to come. Therefore, I say unto you, let your heart be healed and your mind set free, my beloved family in the Lord. May God bless your hearts. Be ye at peace concerning me.

December 18, 2018

Whosoever twists the Word of God for their own benefit will not be so innocent!

December 25, 2018

For it is better for an evil man to know his mistakes and change his ways to do that which is good in the sight of the Lord and to walk in holiness all the days of his life than it is for one who is "called" a good man who is corrected so that he may do well, yet disregards and rejects the corrections of God and continues in sin and wickedness. For I say unto you, the evil man that changed his ways will be forgiven of his past sins by the Lord, but the one who rejects the corrections of God and continues in sin shall be considered guilty until he changes his ways also.

YEAR 2019

February 2, 2019

My brothers and sisters, know that coming unto Christ and becoming saved is a signification stating that we are accepting God's will and no longer that of our own. So, I say unto you, don't just come unto Christ just because you want to go to heaven but come unto Christ to receive God and all that He is, to become more like Him, receiving His Holy Spirit. In doing this, you're throwing away all that you have known to believe before and are now receiving truth. But this I say unto you, if you just become saved just to go to heaven and don't want His will, then truly within your heart you have not received Jesus Christ. For Christ said in Matthew 10:38 (KJV), "And he that taketh not his cross, and followeth after me, is not worthy of me." To take your cross is to do the will of the Lord. They that have gotten saved but do not want the will of the Father are not believers of the faith but are masqueraded as deceivers sent by the devil to corrupt them who truly are of the faith. For they are like wolves in sheep's clothing. Brothers and sisters of the faith, beware, do not receive from everyone who cries out, "Lord, Lord," for they have denied God, so He has denied them. For Christ said in Luke 9:23 (MEV), "Then He said to them all, 'If anyone will come after Me, let him deny himself, and take up his cross daily, and follow Me.'"

February 21, 2019

My brothers and sisters, saved and unsaved, known and

unknown, let brotherly love continue and do good unto one another. Though others filled with the spirit of hate, anger, wrath, and jealousy may try to come and test you, you yourself do not combat them with the same spirit that they are in. I say unto you, combat them with the Love of Christ, not out of anger, but out of the humbleness and pureness of heart. For I say unto you, know understanding with the fullness of wisdom. For you do not know the troubles that they face daily. So, I say unto you, let love reign. Do not let yourself contribute to their pain but instead be a relief unto them by love. For do you not know that our enemy is not one another? Open your eyes, you who are without knowledge of truth and are blinded by Satan from noticing the spiritual world that you cannot see. In the Word of God of Ephesians 6:12 (KJV), Paul spoke, saying, "For we wrestle not against flesh and blood, but against principalities, against powers, against the rulers of the darkness of this world, against spiritual wickedness in high places." My brothers and sisters, open your eyes and uncover your ears.

Wars, fights, battles, arguments, debates, politics, and everything dealing with controversy and chaos are because of this. And it begins with the selfishness of someone's heart to let an evil spirit in. But I say unto you all, you can either be a contributor of hate and despair hurting everyone that passes you by, or you can be one being used by God to ease the suffering of others, bringing life and not death unto all. Love, not hate; peace, not destruction; understanding, not ignorance; compassion, not heartlessness; forgiveness, not retribution. Fight in love. For who is love? God is love.

March 3, 2019

The History and Mindset of Satan:

Unto you who wholeheartedly believe the devil is a friend and the hero of this story, I say unto you: truly you are utterly deceived by the devil himself. For do you not know how greatly jealous the devil is of the connection we have with the Father? Before the beginning of mankind, Satan's true name was Lucifer (meaning son of the morning). He was a beautiful angel; his wings were so big it was able to cover the whole throne of God. And his voice, when he sang, it was unmatched. He was loved by God and adored by the angels and was one of the greatest angels in the kingdom of heaven, and held a great position. But because of his pride and greed, he wanted more. He wanted to become God. So, he deceived and led a third of the angels to rebel against God. And because Lucifer had gone against God, he and the third of the angels that betrayed God were kicked out of heaven.

Satan lost everything, his title, his position, and power, and instead of being adored and loved, he gained shame and guilt. And the worst part is that he was disowned by the Father (God), no longer being in full of light but now full of utter darkness and lack of purpose. And then, when he bore witness to God creating mankind, he noticed that God gave us all His love. He noticed that God gave us all His power and light. He noticed the bond that we had with God. He noticed that God gave us something that he didn't even get, and that was dominion over the whole earth and everything in it. When Satan saw this, he was enraged with anger, jealousy, and indignation towards God and humanity. Because of this, Satan hated God and mankind. For the devil is like an ex-wife of a groom who is getting ready to marry his beautiful and beloved bride before the wedding day. But the ex-wife saw how great her ex-husband adored and loved his fiancée. So, then the ex-wife says within herself, "He never gave me that kind of love that he is giving her." So filled with rage and jealousy, she goes to the bride and speaks all kinds of evil and lies against the groom to deceive the bride and make the bride leave and separate from the love of her life forever. Unto them that have an ear, let them hear what the Holy Spirit is saying to the church and to them that are of the world.

For those of you who lack understanding, the ex-wife represents Satan, the groom represents God, and the beloved bride represents us, mankind. Open your eyes, you who are of the world. You have been deceived. You who left God, you have been deceived. Even yes, some of you who claimed to be saved have been deceived. The reason why I do not only call the saved in Christ brothers and sisters but also the unsaved (people who don't believe in God nor have a relationship with him) is because we are all His people and His children! Though those that are of the world do not have the Holy Spirit (yet!), they still have the essence of God inside of them. We all saved and unsaved, good and evil, visioned and blind, still bear the same DNA signifying mankind. For I say unto you, is it not the breath of God that we all breathe with, and do we all not have the power to create change in the world because of the dominion God has given us, whether to do good with it or bad?

So, therefore, you who are of the world, do not be deceived. God does not hate you. The devil hates you. God does not want you to go to hell. The devil wants you to go to hell because he knows he is. They that come unto the Father and believe in Christ will be resurrected into eternal life; they will never die again after the death of the flesh. But they that keep believing the lies of Satan, he will guide them not into just one death but two deaths (one of the flesh, then one of the soul). You who are of the world and serve Satan, do you not see? Satan wants to kill you and use you to send others into the lake of fire also. He is not a hero. He is and was a liar and a deceiver from the beginning. He hates us all with strong jealousy and fury. My unsaved brothers and sisters who deal in witchcraft, you who kill in the name of Satan, you who believe God hates you and is controlling and is evil, you who believe in false gods, you who believe there is no god, you who are in sexual immorality, you who do sexually abominable acts of homosexuality, bestiality, adultery, incest, and other forms of sexual wickedness. You who have done very evil and wicked things in your life, you who know you have done wrong in your life and need relief of the guilt and pain, you who are just living life, you who have left God. All of mankind, I say unto you, it is not too late. Repent turning away from your evil ways and come unto Christ and into a new life quickly, come back into the light from out of darkness, for you are God's people, and He has created you. All of your past sins can be forgiven. And God will remember your sins no more, for they will be washed away in the blood of Christ.

Come into the narrow gate and receive the Holy Spirit along with eternal life.

But please do not wait! For the time is coming and is now here where the separation of the godly and the ungodly happens. For the mark of the beast has come, and the beast is deceiving many in taking it. For that chip is the broad gate into hell! For it's the mark of the kingdom of darkness. Do not open that broad gate of no return. Choose the Father who loves you dearly and has a place prepared for all of them that love Him! For the Lamb of God comes for His people! Praise be to the Lamb of God! For indeed He is worthy above all!

March 18, 2019

These are the two greatest lies Satan has made humanity believe. Yes, even most of the believers in Christ. This is the first, "Nobody's perfect," and the second is "We are only human."

March 18, 2019

We can overcome sin because, with Christ, all things are possible. For the Apostle John said, "Ye are of God, little children, and have overcome them: because greater is he that is in you, than he that is in the world" (1 John 4:4, KJV).

March 18, 2019

Temptations will always be there, but sin should not.

March 25, 2019

Love shines brightest when it is tested.

March 26, 2019

Brothers and sisters, saved and unsaved, known and unknown, stop boasting in yourselves and "your anointing" but remain humbled with all meekness. Beware, for boasting leads to pride, and pride leads to idol worship, and idol worship will lead to your destruction. For all power and authority is given by God Himself. And every good work, miracle, sign, and wonder is done by the Holy Spirit, who is also God Himself. Yes, even Christ, who is the Word, who is also God Himself. For they are three but yet are one. Therefore, do not boast in yourself neither think of yourself so highly but boast and praise in God in every good work that is done. For we do nothing, but it is God who works through us. Without Him, we are nothing and can do nothing, nor even exist, let alone breathe. Therefore, let God's light shine within you that man may see His good works through you, then glorify the Father who is in heaven unto all that bear witness to His glory. And be ye joyful in God, for His work was made perfect in you.

For all praise, glory, and honor belongs to God, who is

the creator of all creation, even of mysteries and unknown wonders we know not of nor understand and comprehend.

March 30, 2019

Serving the Lord is not about how huge a church building can get, nor is it about how many people attend service, but it is about getting people saved from the lake of fire. Serving the Lord is not about performance, nor is it about appearance, but it is about seeking the Lord's face. Serving the Lord is not about imitating a pastor, nor is it about kissing the ground they walk on, but I say unto you, let Christ be your example to follow, and imitate Him with the fullness of the Holy Spirit. Look up to God, who is your Father and not a man. Follow and trust God with all your heart and not man lest you be led astray. The Lord our God speaks, but who will spend time with Him and listen?

April 4, 2019

Some of you leaders of God's people have become so prideful and greedy in your position that you have taken over what was meant to be God's church and made it yours. You have taken God's people and made them your people, binding them to your own will and oppressing them. You have made yourselves false gods. Therefore, you are cursed, you bear great weight, gaining no sleep nor rest day and night, and great sicknesses and illness shall plague your bodies, and shall reap great judgments, and will each fall one after the other as like the grass in the field. You have become even worse than the Pharisees and have done worse than Saul. Oh, how the mighty have fallen!

For Satan has deceived your minds greatly, and because of your wicked desires, you have fallen into his traps. And the prayers that many pray concerning you will not be answered. For God has warned you. God is a jealous God, and there shall be no other gods before Him. For they all will fall, and the fall shall be great! The house of God is meant to be for the Holy Spirit, of the Holy Spirit, and by the Holy Spirit. But you have made it into a haven of demons to run freely. Repent, turning away from your wicked ways. For the kingdom of heaven is at hand!

April 4, 2019

The reason why many people in the body of Christ are not of like-minded faith (think alike, being of one mind, the mind of Christ) is because many are led by their own desires and not by the will of God.

April 5, 2019

Without correction, there is no accountability, and without accountability, one becomes reckless in their ways.

April 5, 2019

Wise are they that listen to sound wisdom, for they are being guided by the Lord. But woe unto them that turn away good counsel, for they are not aware of who speaks through the messenger.

April 5, 2019

Patience can open up blessings for you that you are not aware of.

April 6, 2019

A society that depends on itself will not survive and slowly decay. But a society that depends on God for all their needs will outlast generations, lest they go astray.

April 7, 2019

Your mistakes are not what makes you imperfect but only that which is in your heart.

April 8, 2019

My brothers and sisters, conceal the vessel God has put His Spirit within, for you never know whom you will attract, neither the spirits that come along with them.

April 9, 2019

It is not food, nor even the body that can sustain us but only the Word of God, for His Word is what brings life.

April 9, 2019

It is a sad thing for a person to go through life never knowing who they truly are nor what they are called to do.

April 10, 2019

The Truth about Holidays:

Just because you put the name Christ in front of a worldly holiday, it doesn't mean that it is good to participate in it. For many are deceived because of this abominable deceit and deception. For truly I say unto you, they do not know whom they're serving nor worshipping. My brothers and sisters in Christ, be a peculiar people set aside for the Lord and the Lord alone and do not be like the world nor do the things that they do. All of these holidays are corrupt and give no glory unto the Father. Therefore, do not participate in things just because the majority rule it in their eyes as "good." But I say unto you, do that which is right in the sight of the Father not in the sight of man. For there are things that seem right to a man, but in the sight of God, they are the ways of death. For even Christ spoke about the people that do and created these things in Mark 7, saying,

> He answered and said unto them, Well hath Esaias prophesied of you hypocrites, as it is written, This people honoureth me with their lips, but their heart is far from me. Howbeit in vain do they worship me, teaching for doctrines the commandments of men. For laying aside the commandment of God, ye hold the tradition of men, as the washing of pots and cups: and many other such like things ye do. And he said unto them, Full well ye reject the commandment of God, that ye may keep your own tradition.

Mark 7:6-9 (KJV)

April 11, 2019

Brothers and sisters, do you not know that your identity is in God our Father? When you seek Him, in time, you will find it.

April 13, 2019

A time is coming when God does away with temples, and He Himself will be the temple.

April 22, 2019

When you have God, you are never alone.

April 22, 2019

What many see as isolation, I see as spending time with the Father. What many see as being shy and reserved, I see as being set apart, not doing that which the world does, nor doing that which is sinful or corrupt just because of the many that are. The world may not be simple, but that does not give us the right to do that which is evil in the sight of God. When God said, "thou shalt not kill," He meant what He said, do not kill (everything that has a heartbeat and breath in its body) no matter the circumstances. But I say this unto you, should not our faith be in the Lord and not within objects and ourselves? Trust ye in the Father and not in yourselves! Believe in Him and believe in Christ also in all things and not just some! For truly, truly, I say unto you, you either choose heaven or hell, for the grey area is still hell. Choose ye this day whom you will serve, God or the devil.

There is no grey area; choose truth or lies, eternal life or eternal damnation, light or darkness. Blessed are they that choose God, for you are written in the Lamb's Book of Life. For them that suffer with Christ will reign with Him. Therefore, the reign of them that love evil is now but unto them that have hope in the Father and have been humbled unto death as a lamb fed to the wolves, I say unto you, our salvation is near! Remember, stay humble and meek, being as wise as a serpent and as harmless as a dove resisting no man, give unto them that ask of you, bless them that curse you, do good unto them that hate you, and pray for them that persecute you and use you hatefully with ill intent. For the first shall one day be last, and the last shall one day be first.

Therefore, be patient, my brothers and sisters in Christ, and in all these things, know whom you serve. Though we are all things unto all flesh, know in doing so we are serving the Father in heaven, not man.

April 22, 2019

My brothers and sisters, do you not understand that, in the love of Christ, we are made perfect? Therefore, perfect yourselves in love. And know that perfection is from the Father and not from ourselves, neither from the flesh.

April 22, 2019

Love is perfection.

April 27, 2019

Always have love within your hearts but do not compromise truth for a lie for no man, but let the truth be the truth, and the lie be a lie.

April 27, 2019

Woe unto you who see that which is bad as good and that which is good as bad. For I say unto you, be ye transformed by the renewing of your mind through the Word of God and know the truth with fasting and prayer.

May 7, 2019

I don't fear the darkness, but the darkness will fear me because I bear my Father's light.

May 21, 2019

The wrath of the Lord comes for the generation that has rejected Him and His corrections. Who shall survive it? Repent!

May 21, 2019

America is going to have a great awakening; do not be one that is caught sleeping.

May 21, 2019

Do not fear, but repent and turn away from the wicked ways that this world has taught you from your youth and awaken to the truth!

May 21, 2019

The warnings of God come to save, not to kill; to correct, not to condemn; to create a way of escape, not to close off and cast away. But beware. This I tell you, warning comes before destruction. For this is a time for mercy, but truly I tell you this, do not abuse nor take advantage of mercy in this time of grace that we have now. For them that love to do so, the wrath of God is near unto them, and when it comes upon them, though they have heard the warnings of God, they will know it not, but instead, their end will be established.

May 21, 2019

The narrow gate is open and whoever comes through it, come quickly, for the time of the Lord is near, and the reign of Satan and those that follow him is coming to an end!

May 21, 2019

Many will perish, and only a few will be left!

May 21, 2019

Protect the hearts and minds of your children, for the devil wants their lives. Teach them in the ways of the Lord and to beware of the ways of the world so they may do good and not evil, to speak with purity and truth, filled with innocence and not corrupt, defiled, wicked, and abominable language filled with lies, deceit, and manipulation. For the dirty tongue comes from the evil one.

May 24, 2019

The world has taught you to stand up for yourself, or you will always be taken advantage of. But I say unto you, the Word of God says to endure long-suffering and to bear your cross daily. Pray for them that misuse and persecute you. For those that suffer with Christ will reign with Him. For I say unto you, why do you feel the need to fight against adversity? Is it not because of the pride you bear within your heart to not look weak in front of an audience? For do you not know that in your weakness, God is made strong? Therefore, let the Lord fight your battles. And you, hold your peace and trust in the Lord, having faith that He will deliver you and your family from the hands of the enemy. For in the book of Isaiah 40:31 (KJV), it said, "But they that wait upon the Lord shall renew their strength; they shall mount up with wings as eagles; they shall run, and not be weary; and they shall walk, and not faint." Also, remember, my brothers and sisters in the faith that of which Christ has spoken, did He not say in John 15,

> If the world hate you, ye know that it hated me before it hated you. If ye were of the world, the world would love his own: but because ye are not of the world, but I have chosen you out of the world, therefore the world hateth you.

John 15:18-19 (KJV)

We who are in Christ and children of God will always face adversity by the devil, but I say unto you remember, this world is not our own. For our lives lie in the place that our Father in heaven has promised us from the beginning and even now. Therefore, be ye humbled having faith, hope, and confidence in God, knowing that all that He has promised shall be fulfilled and is already done.

May 24, 2019

Trust in the Lord your God!

May 25, 2019

If the angels of heaven can be humbled in their positions giving all glory, honor, and praise unto God, so can we.

May 29, 2019

My unsaved and saved brothers and sisters, known and unknown, seen and unseen, related and unrelated, many of you ask this question, "Who is God?" Some of you ask this question to insult the truth, but yet you do know the truth; you just rather stay blind to the truth. You would rather believe in anything else that are false idols/gods (yes, even your family, your holiday idols, and entertainment idols) than come unto Christ and know the only one true living God. From your youth, Christ has called you, but you have denied Him and have chosen the lies of Satan over truth. Come back unto the arms of the Father, and He will heal all of your hurt and your pain. Yay, indeed He will restore you. And then there are you who have heard of so many false gods you do not know what to believe in nor know that which is the truth. Some of you have been trying to look for Him, but yet the devil has been driving you to the wrong places going from false god to false god, and some of you have found some sort of happiness in your morals but yet have not found peace in your souls and you still feel like you are missing something. I say unto you, there is only one true and living God, and besides Him, there is no other God.

He goes by many names, the great "I Am," "Jehovah," "The Lord of Hosts," and many more do man call Him. He is the beginning and the end, the First and Last, the Alpha and the Omega; He is from everlasting to everlasting (He lives and reigns forever, He has no weaknesses, He cannot die nor can He be killed), He is life incarnate. His Word is truth and lasts forever. He is the creator and Father of all. He is God and Judge over all. He is all things and can do all things. He is the one who gives life and takes it away. He created the story of humanity from the beginning to the end. He knows all things and sees all, and He is the past, present, and future. His ways are unsearchable. His knowledge, understanding, and wisdom are never-ending. He does not make mistakes, and what many may see in their eyes as a mistake concerning God, I say unto you, they know nothing and see as eyes of man with many errors and not eyes of God. Everything He does and everything He made to be, happens for a reason and for the good of His people (reasons we as humans may never understand or comprehend, but He as God can).

No one can tell Him or show Him things He does wrong. I say unto you, learn from Job's mistakes and do not make the same. If I continue to speak of who God is, what He can do, and what He is, it will never end. Therefore, I say unto you, seek to know Him for yourself, and you will find Him, and with Him is your purpose and identity. As He is a God who sees, listens, knows, and understands. He is also a God who speaks. And your relationship with Him (if you will it) will never end but will forever grow stronger going from glory to glory. Therefore, seek His face. For the pure in heart shall see God. Find Him in His Word. For no one goes unto the Father except through Christ. Who is Christ? Christ is God's Word. To know God, you must first become saved. If you believe in your heart and confess with your mouth that Jesus Christ is Lord and Savior and believe that Christ died on the cross for your sins and rose again on the third day after His death, then you shall be saved.

May 31, 2019

Quickly, come. Come into the narrow gate before it is too late. For Christ calls for you.

June 20, 2019

Some of you need to really take a good look at some of the pastors and leaders you are under. For I say unto you, are you sure they serve the same God that you do? Watch what they teach and what they do, testing the spirit by the Holy Spirit. And know their fruit, is their fruit the works of iniquity or the fruit of the Spirit? For some of them are not serving the Lord our God in heaven (who is the King of kings and Lord of lords) but instead the "gods" of this world—teaching you the ways of this world instead of teaching you the Word of God! Beware of your adversary, the devil, lest you are persuaded to practice the same abominations as the world does. Open your eyes and listen with your ears and see the truth so that it may set you free from the oppression of the enemy! Run to God, your only Father, and Christ, who is your Lord, Savior, and eldest brother in God!

June 20, 2019

Many leaders in God's kingdom have given up their right to the tree of life, selling their souls to live greatly in this life. But I say unto you, they have no gain, for their end is near and also of all their materialistic vanities, their objects, wealth, clothes, fame, vainglory, and furnishings that they love so much. And they shall take their portion with the beast and Satan in the lake of fire because they loved their lives more than they loved God. For God will shut the mouth of the false prophet! For its idol worship shall be heard no more!

But, this I shall speak and cry out unto the mountains, on top of the tallest building in the world, in the cities, on the streets, and from every corner to every corner of the world so that all may hear this magnificent and wonderful good news, "All glory, honor, victory, and praise be unto the Lamb of God who sits upon the throne, for in His appearance shall bring forth a whole new life, making all things new!"

June 27, 2019

Armageddon is coming, and the seven bowls of God's wrath are almost at hand. Repent, For it will come upon those who receive the mark of the beast. For Babylon the Great shall fall because it did not take heed of God's corrections nor did ye repent but instead mocked and insulted the name of the Lord as you increased in abominable deeds against God. Therefore, it shall reap the judgment of the Lord, and the evils of its sexual immorality and sorcery have reached unto heaven, and God has remembered its abominations! Therefore, the warnings of natural disasters that many have been dreaming about shall come to pass. For the judgment that is going to happen to this nation shall be worse than it was for Sodom and Gomorrah. Repent and turn away from your evil ways! For in this, you shall know that there is only one true living God, and besides Him, there is no other!

July 2, 2019

Religiosity would keep one from seeing the truth and knowing it. Those who are of a religious mindset will serve religion. But those who have a mindset of Christ will serve truth, know truth, see truth, believe truth, and listen to truth without ignorance. The devil uses religion to blind God's people from the path in which we are supposed to walk, deceiving them to believe they are truly serving God, but instead, they are serving the devil, keeping bound them who are trying to get closer to God. Religion is a facade, but the truth shall set you free.

July 2, 2019

My brothers and sisters, saved and unsaved, did you not know that warnings and corrections that come from God come from love?

July 3, 2019

Unto you leaders who are of a religious spirit, you preach lies, deceitfully saying, "The Lord is not angry, nor does He get angry, but He is only joyous, peaceful, loving, graceful, and merciful." But I say unto you, do you not know the Word and that which was spoken of in the Old Testament? For in the times of old, there were many that pushed the Lord our God (who still is the God of Abraham, Isaac, and Jacob) to anger. And did you not read what God did to them because of the evils and wicked abominations that they have done and submitted themselves to in His sight? For truly, truly, I say unto you, "He is still the same God today, yesterday, and forever, for God does not change." Only because of His love for us, He gave mercy and grace in time to get ourselves right in the Holy Spirit. For I say unto you, this is truly a generation that has not known the fear of the Lord, but warning unto you who deal wickedly, the time of the Lord is at hand, and all those who worship the beast and have done evil in the sight of God shall have their portion in the lake of fire.

Therefore, repent and turn away from your evil ways. Do you think that God desires you to endure this kind of judgment and suffering that is indeed everlasting without an end? God forbid, if that were so, He would not have sent Jesus Christ to die on the cross so that you may have mercy and grace for your sins. He did that to show His love for us all, for He does not wish to see you perish but to save you from the day of judgment. For the judgment was meant for Satan and those who follow him. For God loves you, and His love comes with a promise so that you may prosper in a whole new life in the place which He called paradise that bears no more weeping, no more pain, no more suffering, no more torment, and no more death unto all of them that love Him. Come unto Christ, for you are all His people, and He is your God. For He calls weeping loudly out for you saying,

> "Look, I am coming soon! My reward is with Me to give to each one according to his work. I am the Alpha and the Omega, the Beginning and the End, the First and the Last." Blessed are those who do His commandments, that they may have the right to the tree of life, and may enter through the gates into the city.
>
> Revelation 22:12-14 (MEV)

July 3, 2019

There's more to gain to deliver someone from an evil spirit than to kill someone that has an evil spirit.

July 9, 2019

Do not trust in witchcraft (also known as magic), but trust ye in the power of the Holy Spirit!

July 10, 2019

Oh, my brothers and sisters in Christ Jesus, don't get so overwhelmed by a church building to where you're trying to make it be something you should already be. For I say unto you, are you not the temple that houses the Holy Spirit? For are you not supposed to be the lamp that shines within a house? For if the lamp has light, then the entire house would radiate its light also. Therefore, I tell you this, get closer to God; fasting in prayer is the key, and let your motives for doing it be just. For many ask and don't receive because they ask amiss to spend their desires on their own passions. But do not try to make a building become what you are supposed to be and to do what you are supposed to do. For you are the church, therefore wherever you go, there the church will also be. For if you want more of the Spirit of God, spend more time with Him fasting and praying. Knock, and the door will be opened unto you. Seek, and you shall find.

July 10, 2019

Unto you who believe you're doing God's will by having a church, I say unto you, did God tell you that or did the world teach you that through the means of religiosity and the traditions of men?

July 10, 2019

Many are lost because of religion, and they see it not. Jesus Christ and God are not a religion, nor is He in the bounds of religion. But I say unto you, He is the way, the truth, and the life. He is even the resurrection.

July 13, 2019

Satan, as you take, I shall give. As you command servants to do as you wish, I shall be a servant to God, to do as He wishes. As you live comfortably, I shall labor. And as you do great evil, I shall do great good. So, tell me, at the end of this life, who shall gain more? Me or you?

July 13, 2019

Beware of Satan's devices, but never fear him, for Christ who lives in you is greater than even him.

July 14, 2019

Woe unto some of you who call yourselves pastors, prophets, and apostles, for when the Lord sent correction unto you, you did not incline your ear to listen, nor repent, nor did you amend your ways unto the Lord, but instead you took offense and judged, scorned, and condemned God's messengers so that you may feel comfortable in your own sins and evil ways. For I say unto you, beware, lest you judge and condemn an angel of the Lord, and be cursed by the wrath of God. Therefore, I say unto you, yes, even pleading with you: repent and turn away from your evil ways. Give up your own will and worldly desires for the will and plan of God for His people. Break out of the bounds of religion and tear down the wall that has been keeping you from the true purpose in your life to do. Do not follow the will of religious men and women, for they are the blind leading the blind. But I say unto you, do the will of the Father and hear His voice and go unto Him for guidance for all things. Spend time with the Lord and listen so that you may hear!

July 16, 2019

Religiosity brings ignorance, seeking to prove and never listen, having eyes to see and ears to hear but are blind and deaf, always learning but never coming into the revelation of truth.

July 17, 2019

God Is the Father of All Creation:

Oh, my dear sisters and brothers, saved and unsaved, known and unknown, many of you take God our Father for granted, and when you sin or love your evil ways, you say, "Oh, God loves us all, and He is merciful, He will forgive me." But woe, you have not known the fear of the Lord, I say unto you and unto you religious people who use this line to heal the brokenness of the Father's people superficially saying "peace, peace," when there is no peace. God indeed does love us all, but when you love your evil ways and sin so much to where you do not heed to the correction of the Lord, then He sends discipline for your actions by much suffering to save you from your own destruction. For I say unto you, just as a parent disciplines their children, when they do not heed to correction and are disobedient, so is God to us, hoping that by discipline you may be saved from the day of destruction. And if you do not heed to the discipline of the Lord, then you'll be laid up for destruction. For does not Ephesians 6:2-3 and Exodus 20:12 say to obey and honor thy father and mother so that thy days may be long upon the earth the Lord has given you? And because God is our Father, this Word applies to Him also.

If you do not take heed to correction and instead see the correction as judgment, then you must take heed to discipline, and if you do not take heed to discipline, then (God forbid) you're laid up for destruction. For I say to you, do not blame God if that day comes upon you. For God has sent warnings and corrections time after time unto you so that you may listen to prevent that day from arising. Therefore, heed the corrections, for obedience is better than sacrifice. His corrections lead you in the way of the narrow gate. If you walk in it, His yoke will be easy, and His burden will be light. But if not, you will be as the children of Israel who walked in the wilderness for forty years and died there because of their disobedience and ignorance towards the will of God. He wishes to save you because He loves you, but will you let Him?

July 18, 2019

Never confuse love with lust and lust with love. Beware, for many are deceived thereby.

July 18, 2019

Religiosity limits you, but with Christ, all things are possible!

July 18, 2019

My brothers and sisters, do you not know that if you harbor offenses, it would keep you from receiving the truth? Woe unto you.

July 26, 2019

The Holy Spirit Is the Only Weapon:

You cannot kill a demon by any weapon nor fists, but only by the power of the Holy Spirit can it be cast out. Because of the influences/sorceries of this world (TV, games, music, false teachings), many are deceived by the devil to think otherwise. Those who believe they can kill a demon will only kill the vessel (human, animal, objects, and any other thing in which it manifests) of the demon and not the spirit itself. For flesh could only kill flesh, and spirit only can torment spirit. Therefore, the Word of God (Christ) said in John 3:3-6 that you must be born again (saved) in spirit and water and obtain the Holy Spirit (which Christ paraphrased as "a sword" in Matthew 10:34) to fight in spiritual warfare. For besides this, with prayer and fasting to put your flesh under subjection of the Holy Spirit and by believing in the name of Jesus Christ, there is no other power that a man can obtain against demons. For in Ephesians 6:12, Paul explains that we wrestle not against flesh and blood but against the spiritual evils of this world that possess many. And do not forget your adversary, the devil, who deceives us all. Peter spoke of him well in 1 Peter 5:8.

July 30, 2019

Oh, my brothers and sisters in Christ, do you not know that our weapons of warfare are not carnal but are spiritual and mighty through our Lord Jesus Christ? Therefore, do not trust in man for defense nor worldly weapons to protect yourself. But trust in the power of the Holy Spirit, who indeed is the sword, as well as an advocate of them who are of the faith. For if you have faith as the size of a grain of a mustard seed, you would tell a mountain to move, and it shall be moved. For our war is not against one another but against demons and spiritual evils of this world that are in high places. Stop arguing and fighting against one another but see the demons that are within that you face and cast them out. Cast away the wickedness and sins within you and repent.

July 30, 2019

God gives to us so that we may give unto others, especially towards them that curse and do evil unto us.

July 31, 2019

Love not the ways of the world nor the world itself (Satan) but only the people in which God is trying to save from it.

July 31, 2019

Perfect love casts out all fear.

July 31, 2019

My brothers and sisters, do you not know that God is love? For if you do not have love, then you do not have God. And if you do not love your brother (everyone), how is it that you can love your Father (God)? Therefore, I urge you all to love one another and perfect yourselves in love. For true love does not operate in partiality but sees everyone equally. For there is no difference from the poor to the rich, from the evil to the good, from the crippled and deformed to the well looking and healthy, the young nor to the old, neither from the male to the female nor from races to nations. For all are worthy of love (brotherly love). Therefore, give it freely, seeking nothing in return. For this is the will and command of God unto all people, unto whom are your brothers and sisters that you have not known. Greet and respect one another in the love of God.

August 1, 2019

My brothers and sisters, please understand, Jesus Christ sat with the sinners not so that He could partake in their wickedness nor listen to their council but only so that they may hear and know truth reaching unto repentance, coming into salvation.

August 2, 2019

Let those who love evil and deal wickedly bear great riches in this world that lasts only for a moment, but let us who are written in the Lamb's Book of Life bear great treasures in heaven that last for eternity.

August 5, 2019

Oh, my brothers and sisters, saved and unsaved, it is a grievous thing for one to go through life, fighting to keep their peace of mind and joy with a broken heart and have tried everything, but yet have not considered coming unto Christ who gives it all, along with a promise of a whole new life unto them that endure in His will until the end. Therefore, the question is, would you rather go through much for vanity that shall not last or for eternal life of no more pain, sorrow, torment, and confusion, finally being able to see and be with the one who created you?

August 7, 2019

For darkness comes before the dawn, but when dawn breaks it, the sun shall radiate its glorious light. Stand strong until that time comes with endurance and patience, beloved saints.

August 7, 2019

You keep trying to look for love when God is saying, "I am right here, come unto me."

August 7, 2019

You really do not know how much God loves you, do you? And you have not seen all that He has done for you, for He has done much.

August 8, 2019

Whosoever Claims God Has Done Nothing for Them Is a Liar:

Did God not keep you from the hands of death, and did God not wake you up this morning with breath in your body? Did God not keep you in the right mind? Did He not bless you with a home to sleep in and a car to get you from place to place? Does He not keep you fed and satisfy your stomach when there are many that go hungry many nights without a place to rest their head nor a car to travel in? But yet how is it that you complain while in the meantime they find a reason to thank God anyhow? Did God not save you from getting hit by a car or from being in a car accident? Did God not heal and strengthen your heart when you were hurt and abused by many?

Did God not send His only begotten Son to save you from your own sins so that you might get closer to Him? Did God not stop the devil when you were sleeping from letting someone creep in the night to break into your house and kill you unaware? Did God not cover you with His blood, hiding you from the demons that are tormenting and possessing the people in this world that many have called crazy, insane, psychopath, mentally ill, and unstable? Truly, truly, saved and unsaved brothers and sisters, there are many things that you have not known that God has done for you and saved you from spiritually and physically, from things that have happened and have not happened, from things that are seen and are not seen.

Therefore, don't make yourself into a liar, saying to yourself and believing that God has not done anything for you. Do not be in ignorance nor of an ungrateful heart. For because He has loved you, He protected you and is still protecting you now. He comforts you and is still comforting you now, He gives you strength, and He still strengthens you now. He loves you, and He still loves you now. All He wants from you is for you to come unto Him and have a relationship with

Him so that you may be with Him in paradise. Therefore repent, turning away from your evil ways, and have a relationship with the Father that shall last for eternity.

August 9, 2019

Days may go by in a flash, but even time itself knows when to hold its peace concerning the will of God.

August 10, 2019

Darkness Knows Not Love:

If you seek love, then come unto Christ. For I say unto you, you will not find love from the world. For the world only knows hate and evil, and its love is hate. Therefore, the world only loves them that hate because in hate and evil do they love. For the world only "loves" that of its own. Hate does not know love but is against it. Hate and love are opposites of one another, for they cannot coexist. Hate hates love, and love hates hate, for only one can stand. Either love overcomes hate, or hate overcomes love. Therefore if you have love, how great is it in you? Or if you have hate, how great is it in you? For if you have love, you have light, but if you have hate, you have darkness. If you have light, then how great is that light? And if you have darkness in you, then how great is that darkness? For I say unto you, you cannot have two masters. You are either a part of the kingdom of light or the kingdom of darkness. You either love or succumb to hate; there is no gray area. But woe unto you who wholeheartedly give into hate, for you forfeit your inheritance of God being your Father and embraced Satan as your father as well as his mind. For those who are of the kingdom of darkness are like-minded (the mind of Satan), as like them who are of the kingdom of light are of like-mind (the mind of Christ). The sheep will know their father's voice, and that is of whom they shall follow. Therefore, choose you this day whom you will serve. For those who have chosen not to choose, unwise and foolish are they, because by not choosing, they have denied Christ. Therefore, they are of darkness because they have denied the only begotten son of God. Therefore repent ye sinners, and turn away from your evil ways you double-minded, coming unto Jesus Christ as your Lord and Savior.

August 10, 2019

For it takes hate to kill, but it takes love to give forgiveness.

August 10, 2019

The world practices hate so that their deeds may be made manifest unto every evil work. But sons and daughters of God practice love so that their deeds may be made manifest unto every good work so that they may be perfect even as the Father in heaven is perfect, not so that man may glorify them, but only so that many may come unto Christ glorifying God.

August 11, 2019

The Depths of Love:

There are three depths of love by which we must operate. The first is "brotherly love," for this love we give freely unto all in charity, compassion, mercy, and grace with all forgiveness without partiality. Treating even one another as you would treat yourselves and would want to be treated. Know also indeed, beloved, that there is *no greater* love that has been shown than this: that a person lays down their life for a friend.

The second goes deeper than the first, and that is "companionship love," for companionship love should only be operated in marriage. This love should not be taken lightly but rather with all seriousness, for whoever you choose will change your life forever. For when one woman and one man come together in marriage, they go in a deeper love that should not be given to anyone else (only the one you are married to). Your mate must be your best friend, should always be close, and you two are one, thinking alike (having the mind of Christ) and agreeing with one another in every decision you make. When you are joined with your companion in marriage, you're no longer for yourself but for your companion, and do not deny them anything of you, whether in mating or in helping. There is no room for selfishness in companionship love, for both must be selfless. The only one greater than your companion should be God and His will for both of your lives. For in this love, a husband and wife alone can operate in romantic interactions and mating together that should not be operated with anyone else or anything else.

For this is the gift of God for those who are in lifetime companionships (marriage) until judgment day. You two are made one, and it must stay that way. And what God has joined together, let no argument or debate, no man or woman, no devil or evil spirit put asunder (split apart). For you two are in a battle against everything unholy and unlike God. You must be strong together. For if one of you falls, quickly pick them back up, and if the other falls, pick them back up also, so that no borders of your wall may be defenseless and come to destruction. For you would ask me, "So what if my companion does not listen to me about an opinion or a solution for a problem, or even about what God has told me to do but yet do not listen and do not agree? Should I then go to talk to someone else about my disagreement or problem I have with my companion for some sympathy or comfort?" I then say unto you, even warning you, *no,* lest the devil uses that as an open door to tempt you to do something that is out of the will of God. But you should rather go pray to your Father who is in heaven (God) and tell Him of your concerns concerning your companion. For if you are right, then God will correct your companion to put them in agreement with you, but if you are wrong, God will correct you to put you in agreement with your companion, and if you are both wrong in your opinions, then God will correct you both in that which ye err making the crooked places straight and rough places smooth so that you may walk together as one in the will of God with all prayer and supplication unto God without ceasing.

If you do not have a companion to love this way yet, then I say unto you wait on the Lord your God, for He will send you the right mate when the time is right and when you are ready. Do not try to find them nor even think about a companion, for God needs you to seek Him. But a warning unto you who are waiting, be not anxious for anything and do not rush God's timing. For if you do, you may send your life in the wrong direction and in a place that you do not want to be. Do not rush into marriage, lest you set the wrong one as your companion, for that is the trap and deception of the devil.

And the third love goes deeper than the first and the second, and that is the "'All-in-all' love." For this is the *most important* love of them all because it reigns over all love, and in this place, only God must reign. In God is where your entire life is constructed and where your decisions should be made, for there should be no one greater than your love for God. Brotherly love and companionship love needs and depends on your love for God. For you must love God with all your heart, mind, soul, and strength, loving Him more than anything in this life. For you cannot love everyone if you do not love yourself, and you cannot love yourself if you do not love God, and you cannot love God if you do not love everyone.

Therefore, you must love God with all that you are so that He may enable you to love to the fullest in perfection. But I say this to you, you cannot love God if you do not love Christ, believing that He is Lord of all and that He is the Son of God who came and died on the cross for our sins so that we may have life, and that He rose from the dead on the third day after His death. For I say unto you, become saved by believing with your heart and confessing with your mouth that Jesus Christ is Lord of all and truly is the Son of God who came and died on the cross for our sins so that we may have life, and that He rose from the dead on the third day and you will finally be saved by faith. For this is the beginning of the love of God, now do His will by keeping His commandments and pray without ceasing and humble yourself into fasting in the Word of God, and then you will be able to love with godly love to fulfill brotherly love and companionship love rightly and purely in the sight of God.

Therefore, the three depths of love are love for all people (brotherly love), love for your companion in marriage (companionship love), and the most important of them all, love for God (all-in-all love). Whoever does not operate in all three depths of love sins. Only those who have never been wedded are exempted from the companionship love but should still be operating in brotherly love and love for God more than anything with all their heart, soul, mind, and strength. For whoever is not married and does not operate in these two depths of love, sin and anyone who has sex without marriage (fornication) still yet sins. Now, everyone has sinned and fallen short of the glory of God, but by His mercy and grace in salvation, we can all reach to do better in our Lord Jesus Christ because we love Him, and in loving Him, we love God. Therefore let us keep His commandments, for we believe in Jesus Christ.

August 12, 2019

Those who are alive in Christ but dead to the ways of the flesh walk by faith and not by sight, but those who are of the carnal mind cannot understand nor comprehend that which we see, speak, and do by faith because faith in God they lacketh.

August 12, 2019

Those who walk by faith in the will of God are Abraham's seed, and Abraham's seed is God's children.

August 12, 2019

Do you not know that it takes faith to receive salvation? Therefore, believe in the only begotten Son of God, who indeed is Jesus Christ.

August 13, 2019

It's better to be a humbled and pure lowly servant that sees his mistakes and fixes them than a wealthy and proud corrupt king who does not see when he does evil but instead thinks that his ways are pure and good with no need for correction. For blessed is that servant, for he shall be brought high. But woe unto that king, for he shall be brought low and great shall his fall be.

August 13, 2019

Humility and meekness are better than pride and arrogance.

August 21, 2019

Flee from Adultery:

My brothers and sisters, I say this not to judge but only so that you may have understanding and know the truth to do that which is right in the sight of God. If one has sex before marriage (even kissing and touching sexually and perversely), it is indeed fornication. If one has sex with someone else while being married to another, it is also indeed adultery. And if one was married and then divorced and had sex with someone else, it is still indeed adultery and fornication. And if someone divorces and then marries another, it is still indeed adultery. And if someone marries someone else while being already married to another, it is still considered adultery.

> "Yet you say, "Why?" It is because the Lord has been a witness between you and the wife of your youth, against whom you have dealt treacherously. Yet she is your companion and your wife by covenant. Did He not make them one, having a remnant of the Spirit? And why one? He seeks godly offspring. So take Heed to your spirit, that you do not deal treacherously. For the Lord, the God of Israel, says that He hates divorce; for it covers one's garment with violence, says the Lord

> of Hosts. Therefore take heed to your spirit, that you do not deal treacherously."
>
> Malachi 2:14-16 (MEV)

Therefore, if you get married, don't just marry to test the waters but marry to stay with one another forever and fight through the storms together until Jesus Christ returns.

But if you are not able to do so, then do not get married at all nor rush into marriage until you are ready. And do not fornicate but build your relationship with God as being celibate. And I say unto you also beware, do not watch pornography nor look at any type of being to lust. For Jesus Christ does explain in Matthew chapter 5:28 that whoever looks upon someone to lust after them commits adultery with them already within their heart.

> "If you will not listen, and if you will not take it to heart to give honor to My name, says the Lord of Hosts, I will send a curse on you and I will curse your blessings. Yes, I have cursed them already, because you do not take it to heart. I rebuke your descendants, and spread refuse on your faces, the refuse of your solemn feasts, and you will be taken away with it. And you will know that I have sent this command to you, that My covenant with Levi may remain, says the LORD of Hosts."
>
> Malachi 2:2-4 (MEV)

Therefore, I say unto you that pornography is a sin because you commit adultery with your eyes and with your heart against God. And I say unto you also do not masturbate, for when you spew out your seed, you are spewing out life. Therefore, my brothers and sisters, saved and unsaved, let us be holy and acceptable unto God to be used for His glory, and let our vessels be cleansed for His good purpose.

For in Hebrews 13:4 (MEV), The Word of God said, "Marriage is to be honored among everyone, and the bed undefiled. But God will judge the sexually immoral and adulterers."

August 21, 2019

To be "boyfriend and girlfriend" is nothing but an excuse and a lie from the devil to do that which is not right in the sight of God. Just stay as close friends until marriage. Hold on until then, beloved, for patience is a virtue.

August 22, 2019

I say unto you also beware, do not watch pornography nor look at anyone or anything to lust. For Jesus Christ does explain in Matthew chapter 5:28 that whoever looks upon someone to lust after them commits adultery with them already within their heart. Therefore I say unto you, pornography is a sin because you commit adultery with your eyes and with your heart against God.

August 22, 2019

I say unto you also do not masturbate, for when you spew out your seed, you are spewing out life. In Exodus 20:13, in the Ten Commandments, God says, "Thou shalt not kill." For indeed, this commandment coincides with masturbation because it's killing off life that God put within your body to produce a living vessel. For masturbation is murder to your seed. Therefore, my brothers and sisters, saved and unsaved, let us be holy and acceptable unto God to be used for His glory and let our vessels be cleansed for His good purpose.

August 24, 2019

Do not believe and trust in what the world says, lest you be a part of the kingdom of darkness. But I say unto you, trust and believe in the Word of God, being a part of the kingdom of heaven. For in our Lord Jesus Christ, there is life without an end. Though we may die, we yet still live. But those who believe and trust in the world wholeheartedly reap death. And death indeed without an end because they did not believe in the name of Jesus Christ, who indeed is life.

August 24, 2019

God does not need you, but because He loves you, Jesus Christ cries out, saying, "Repent and come unto me, for I come quickly and all those who endure in my will until the end will reap eternal life with me in paradise!"

August 25, 2019

It is by grace and mercy that we are forgiven of sins, but it is by believing in the Word of God that we overcome the temptation of sin.

August 25, 2019

I say unto you, who is it that tempts you to do evil? Indeed, it is not God, but only Satan who is the accuser and deceiver of all men. Beware of the devices of the enemy, for he plays on your desires to get you to lust and then to act upon that which you coveted after.

August 25, 2019

Remain in the Word of God:

It's not just enough to be freed from sin, but you must maintain your freedom by meditating on the law of liberty (the Ten Commandments) in Jesus Christ. For it is now temptation you must overcome daily. For in this, you crucify your flesh, feeding your spirit through the Word of God. And through fasting and prayer, you are putting your flesh under submission to the Holy Spirit. Always speak to your heart so that you may stay in line with God's will, hiding His Word within your heart so that you may not sin when temptation comes.

August 28, 2019

Endure Unto the End:

Therefore, what shall I say then, shall I stop doing the will of my Father when adversity comes? Shall I stop preaching truth unto them who know it not? Because of the attack of the enemy, shall I lose faith and stop walking with boldness into the midst of darkness, showing forth my Father's glorious light? Shall I give in to fear and lose my salvation? God forbid, for greater is He that is within me than he that is of this world. For I am called to tread on serpents and not get bitten, go through flames of fire, and not one flame shall kindle upon me. To tell a mountain to move, and it shall be moved. Though I may die a thousand times, I shall still yet have life, for I am a king wrapped in the glory of God in my Father's house.

In the name of Jesus Christ, get thee behind me, Satan. For Christ is even greater than you, for your time is almost up, and the kingdom of heaven is at hand. For your defeat was written even before the beginning of time and is sealed in truth. And blind eyes shall be opened in Jesus' name; death ears shall hear right now, in the name of Jesus Christ. Chains shall be broken, and every yoke of bondage shall be destroyed. Those who are asleep in Christ shall be awakened, and those who were left for dead in darkness shall live and not die as the light of God shines forth before them. For there is hope for them who believe in Jesus Christ and come into the salvation of the Lord. You who are in the world shall know the truth, and the truth will set you free. Glory to the Lamb of God who sits upon the throne, for in His coming shall bring forth a whole new life. Blessed are they that believe in Him.

August 30, 2019

When there are two opposites of a thing, one will either corrupt the other, or the other will corrupt the one, but if there is no agreement between the two, then there is only opposition between both. For light and darkness cannot coexist. Only one can dominate the other.

August 31, 2019

Believe indeed in Jesus Christ, for He is the only way that leads into your salvation and freedom!

September 7, 2019

One who believes in lies lives in lies, and with it comes death, but one who believes in truth lives in truth, and with it comes life.

September 7, 2019

My beloved brothers and sisters, saved and unsaved, believing in Jesus Christ is not just accepting Him and who He is, but it also means believing in His Word and living it. For if you believe in Jesus Christ, then you believe in the Word of God to do the will of our Father in heaven. For your belief will show in your works and speech. For believing in Christ is to have faith in Him also. And your faith will influence your works.

September 7, 2019

For darkness comes before the dawn, and when it breaks, the sun shall radiate its glorious light.

September 10, 2019

Message to the World:

To tell you about myself would be to tell you about my Father, and before you can know my Father, you must know my eldest brother. For my eldest brother is Jesus Christ, for He was the one since the day that I came out of my mother's womb who taught me how to love and to be kind, to give without asking for anything in return, to be a helpful hand without making people owe me anything. And God is my Father, for whatever my Father does, my eldest brother also does, and whatever my eldest brother does, my Father also does. For they are one, and whatever I see them do, I also do because in doing my Father's will, I show my love unto my Father. For I have many siblings, but the greatest and oldest of all of us is Jesus Christ. Some of my siblings seek to do my Father's will to please Him just as I do, but most of my other siblings left my Father because they desired their own will and not the will of our Father, for they are indeed a rebellious and ignorant bunch.

But because my Father loves His children, my eldest brother went to go look for them, and when He found them, He began crying out, "Come back unto me, for our Father misses you dearly and look, our Father has prepared a new home for all of us so that we may live comfortably in His house, so come back home with Me." Some listened to Him and came back home, and the Father forgave them for all the evil they had done. But the others did not come and refused our eldest brother because, filled with lust, greed, and desire, they loved their own lives more than they loved their own Father. But little did they know that their path will lead to their own destruction, for our Father was trying to save them from their own end.

September 13, 2019

Did you not know that through the Holy Spirit, we can teleport? For in Jesus Christ, we have transportation.

September 18, 2019

What Satan gives is a false life, and all of it is vanity, but what God wants to give unto you is real, and with it comes eternal life. Just come into the revelation of truth, and you will be set free from that of which you were blinded from seeing. Your eyes will be open, and your ears will finally hear the truth of life you have been missing. For you were in darkness, but now you've come in light. Know the truth.

September 19, 2019

How is it that one can say, "Well, this is your truth, and this is my truth." For I say unto you, how can truth be a lie? For it cannot, lest you are blinded from seeing the truth and believe ignorantly in a lie. For there is only one truth and under Him follows everything that is true. For then, you would ask me, "Who is the truth?" And I would say unto you, "The truth is Jesus Christ, of whom you have heard but never knew but I tell you, He knows you."

September 19, 2019

For I hate sin, but I love the person of whom you are meant to be in God our Father. Therefore I say unto you, my beloved unsaved brothers and sisters, break free from the mentality of the world that binds you. And come into truth knowing your true self and what you are meant to do in this life. For God still loves you, and Christ is calling for you. Come into your salvation. For in Christ Jesus, there is purpose and destiny.

September 21, 2019

So many of you have lives like the people in The Matrix, so blinded and wholeheartedly dependent on the system and are not ready to be unplugged from it because you were deceived by Satan to believe in it (even from your youth), but not in the truth that comes to save you from it. It is to where some of you would even die to protect a system that was made to enslave, control, manipulate, and condemn you to eternal fire. But in this case, what binds you is not a computer but instead the kingdom of darkness. And what's after you is not secret agents, but instead, it is the rulers of darkness that are of this age, principalities, powers, demons, and evil spirits of wickedness that are in high places. You who are of the world, do you not understand? They want to possess your vessels like the virus in the system taking over many hosts.

But do not be afraid; look, God did not leave us helpless. For Jesus Christ shows you the way of escape and your freedom by believing and receiving Him as your Lord and Savior so that you may see and know the truth. And along with salvation is a sword, who is the Holy Spirit to help us fight and prevail against the wiles of the enemy. Therefore I say unto you, repent, turning away from your evil ways and come unto Jesus Christ who is your only Savior, the only way to eternal life.

September 24, 2019

Sound the Alarm, for the Trumpet Has Been Blown:

There was once a great kingdom, and it is still alive even to this day, for it is arrayed in glory and has a great light. One third of its population turned against it, causing a civil war against its own. The one third that waged war against it was defeated and was kicked out of its kingdom. At that time, that one third roamed around the earth, going from nation to nation seeking to dominate, reign, and rule. And when the one third found their places and dominated them, they became comfortable and relaxed in their new homes for a time. But then the army of the kingdom that they came from followed them and took over the nations that the third had enslaved and dominated, freeing the inhabitants from the chains that bound them. And the one third yet again tried to fight the army of the kingdom that they came from, and their efforts came to naught.

Yet again, they were kicked out of the nations that they lived in. So, then the one third tried to look for a place of refuge roaming the earth, seeking a place to dominate, reign, and rule. And then they came and saw this huge nation that was rich, fulfilled, ripe, and to their liking. So, they lusted and coveted after it, and they said to themselves, "Many of our brothers live here free and comfortable, for they will welcome us with open arms and the inhabitants within them are weak and have no power to defeat us, for they have paved a way for us to overtake their cities and dominate them. For we will be their gods, and they will worship us. Therefore, let us siege our paradise and wage war against them that have power. We shall call this place 'Babylon the Great,' and it will be glorious." For those that have an ear, let them hear what the Spirit of the Lord is saying to them who are of the world and the church.

For Armageddon is coming to America, and the judgment is nigh because when the Lord said "Repent," many did not and rejected His corrections. Therefore, the end is near. And will you be aware when it comes? Therefore, repent and turn away from your wicked ways, for the kingdom of heaven is at hand! For wise are they that come into the narrow gate bearing the salvation of the Lord. End time warning to America!

September 24, 2019

Woe Unto America:

America, why do you think not that many tragedies in your country have happened like in other countries? For I say unto you, you truly do not know the grace and mercy in time that God has bestowed upon you to repent and turn away from your evil ways. And the more time He gave you, instead of you getting better, you have gotten worse. Therefore, because you are the worst of all nations, you are also the last to reap the wrath of God. When He has called you, you denied Him. Therefore, He denies you. You were once His children. When was it that you have disowned Him as your Father and have chosen Satan to raise you? You have forgotten your Father and have chosen to stay away from His voice. Why is it that you did not know that He was trying to save you from what is to come? Therefore, you were once named America, "home of the free," but now here comes Armageddon, "home of the enslaved." Repent and return to your first love, who indeed is the great "I Am," King of kings and Lord of lords; worthy is the Lamb of God.

September 25, 2019

Unto you who are in the world, beware, for the separation of the church is at hand. For many are being tested in this season, and many are choosing darkness rather than light. But you who love the Lord your God, stand strong in truth and keep our Father's commandments in your hearts. Do not give up your inheritance, your birthright, and soul for any man nor evil spirit. And trust no one but trust ye in the Lord thy God. For as the kingdom of darkness rises, so does the kingdom of light, for we who are of light are more than conquerors. And we are not "only human." We are sons and daughters of the only one true and living God.

September 25, 2019

I am not here to post photos of scriptures for your amusement, nor for a career choice, nor for your likes or loves. But only so that you may see, hear, and know truth, coming into light from out of darkness so that you may repent, and do that which is right in the sight of the Lord who is your only one true and living God, who you have not known. For Christ calls for you, come unto the Lord your God who loves you dearly for the kingdom of heaven is at hand, blessed are they that come unto Christ who is our Lord and Savior.

September 26, 2019

Do not give up on the will of God, for you are stronger than you think. God would not put more on you than you could bear. And you are never alone, for Christ is with you, and if God is for you, who can be against you? Remember, my beloved family in Christ; you are more than a conqueror. You are a child of God in whom we have great power! And our victory has already been won in Jesus Christ!

September 26, 2019

The flesh is temporary, but the Spirit is eternal. Therefore, desire that which benefits the spirit rather than that which is of the flesh. For man shall not live by bread alone but by every word that proceedeth out of the mouth of God.

September 26, 2019

Our victory is beyond the thoughts and restrictions of this world! For it even defies the laws of physics! For worldly knowledge would never understand the truth of this, and it will always be a mystery and an impossibility unto them. But in our victory, there is life.

October 2, 2019

The Ten Commandments:

Those who are of the world see the Ten Commandments as judgment and condemnation upon themselves, but those that love the Lord see the commandments as the law of liberty to keep them away from that which is evil and as boundaries around their borders to save them from the deeds of destruction. For in the law of liberty, there is life because they are the divine will of God for our lives. You who are of the world understand, God created the Ten Commandments for you so that you may flee from evil and know the light so that you may walk out of darkness into His marvelous light not to condemn you, but so that you may have life. If you receive Christ Jesus, then you receive His will, and if you receive His will, then you will receive life. But if you deny Him, you deny His will, and if you deny His will, then you have accepted condemnation and death. Therefore, Christ says unto all saved and unsaved,

> If you love me, keep my commandments. …He that

> hath my commandments, and keepeth them, he it is that loveth me: and he that loveth me shall be loved of my father, and I will love him, and will manifest myself to him.
>
> John 14:15, 21 (KJV)

Therefore, see the commandments as life, not judgment, as a way of freedom, and not as restrictions and bondage.

For the commandments are not meant to bind you. For in the past and even now, many used the law unjustly to bind others as a way of control and manipulation which brings condemnation to the heart. But Christ came to rid you of the bondage of the law and to make it your freedom in Him. Therefore, it is called the law of liberty to put it within our hearts so that our flesh may not sin against the Lord our God. So, love the law and do not hate it, for them that hate it loveth darkness and they doeth great evil and wickedness.

October 2, 2019

The Earth Was Given to You:

Many of you ask, "Why does God let all these things happen in the world? He has the power to stop it or never let it happen, but why does He not?" But now I shall say unto you for your understanding so that you may know the truth, He has given man dominion over the entire earth, has He not? And He has given us free will to do whatever we choose with it, whether it be good or evil, because of the love He has for us. Therefore, He gave you the right to choose to do good or to do evil. And He has told us as our Father where evil would lead to. But I say unto you that He rather you choose good and good is Himself, for God is good. And everything that is good is with Him. Therefore, He indeed desires you to come unto Himself through Jesus Christ so that you may have life and life more abundantly. So why does God let these things happen? It is because you have chosen to do these things and let them happen, and because of what you have chosen, there comes a reaction. For the cause had an effect, for the choices man has made came with a consequence for each one because it was made without God. For there's an old saying, "With great power comes great responsibility," and if you do not treat that responsibility well, then destruction comes.

But do not worry. God loves His people. Therefore, Christ is coming back for them that loved Him to save them from the destruction of the choices that man has made. Therefore, repent, turn away from your evil ways, and receive truth, for the kingdom of heaven is at hand!

October 2, 2019

Thou shalt not masturbate, lest ye kill off the seed that God has given you to produce a living vessel. Thou shalt not kill!

October 2, 2019

Thou shall not look upon anyone to lust after them, lest ye commit adultery with them in thine heart. Thou shalt not commit adultery! Thou shalt not get an abortion, remember my beloved sister, thou shalt not kill.

> "Look, children are a gift of the Lord, and the fruit of the womb is a reward. As arrows in the hand of a mighty warrior, so are the children of one's youth. Happy is the man who has his quiver full of them; he shall not be ashamed when he speaks with the enemies at the gate."
>
> Psalm 127:3-5 (MEV)

Therefore, trust and have faith in the Lord thy God who is able to keep thee. For even when you are weak, He is made strong. Fight the good fight of faith and believe in Him, Oh, my beloved sister.

October 3, 2019

Do you not know that fornication is still committing adultery against God? For you're first God's before you are anyone else's.

October 3, 2019

For did you not know that the wages of all sin is death? Free yourself in repentance and come unto Jesus Christ, your Lord and Savior. And He will do the new work in you. For the old will be passed away and behold the new.

October 3, 2019

The devil uses the Word to cripple you, but Jesus Christ uses the Word to set you free from bondage. Know the devices of the enemy.

October 3, 2019

We are not meant to be slaves to sin but instead set free from it and stay in freedom by the law of liberty in Jesus Christ, our Lord and Savior.

October 5, 2019

Those who claim to be saved beware, lest you make yourself a liar. For do you not know that they that do what the world does and speak what the world speaks are of the world? For I say unto you, friendship with the world is enmity to God. Therefore, be a peculiar people set aside for God and God alone. For thou shall have no other gods before Him, and you shall love the Lord your God with all your heart, with all your mind, with all thine soul, and with all thine strength, loving Him more than anything. For what the world does is of darkness but what we do is of light. Those that love light will come and do what we do, but those who are of darkness resist the light and try to corrupt them who are of the light instead of walking into the light lest they be transformed into a new creature, coming out of darkness walking into God's marvelous light. Therefore repent, turning away from your evil ways lest you suffer the same plagues as the world. For the wrath of God is upon them, and great condemnation is what they feel in their hearts.

October 5, 2019

God is the Father and creator of all. He reigns over the just as well as the unjust, the saved as well as the unsaved to give everyone according to their works. Therefore, you who do not know the Father, He knows you. He wishes you to know Him if you let Him through Jesus Christ, who is our salvation and life. Therefore, come unto the Father who knows you and loves you dearly. Come, you who weep and are hurt, you who feel like no one understands you nor what you are going through, you who are troubled by the weight of the world and do not know how to get through it, you who seek for peace and cannot find it, and all of mankind. Come unto Jesus Christ, and the Father will wipe away every tear from your eyes and give you a whole new life with a promise.

If you are burdened with sin, He will wash it away and

make you new as white as snow. Just come unto Jesus Christ, your Lord and Savior, and repent turning away from your evil ways. For the kingdom of heaven is at hand. Blessed are they that come and receive the Father's will enduring unto the end, holding fast to that which is true, for they shall be with our Father in paradise. For He will be our God, and we will be His people. Every knee shall bow, and every tongue shall confess that Jesus Christ is Lord. Glory, glory, unto the Lamb of God who sits upon the throne, worthy is the Lord of all!

October 6, 2019

My brothers and sisters, do you not know that the offenses you're harboring keep you from receiving the truth? Woe unto you.

October 7, 2019

The world has told you that if you have fame, a great job with benefits, and much wealth, you have succeeded in life. But I say unto you, they who succeeded in life are those that come unto Jesus Christ to be saved, having the love of God to obey the commandments of the Lord and having great faith to accomplish all that He wants them to do. For I say unto you, they are the ones that not only will succeed in life but also have life, yay, eternal life indeed. For material things fade and will come to nothing and are meant for destruction, but that which is spiritual lasts forever. For wealth will not get you into the kingdom of heaven nor can you buy your way into it but it's given unto them that will receive it and take hold of it, holding on to it tightly, and never letting up on their grip, for what they have is life and precious indeed it is unto them that find it. For they who are of the world would never understand the truth of this, lest they be freed from the ways of the carnal mind and be born again into a whole new life (becoming saved).

For they would finally know the truth, and the truth would set them free from the darkness that draws them closer to the eternal fire where there is weeping and gnashing of teeth. For the lake of fire is still not yet full of the souls of humanity. Therefore repent, turning away from your evil ways. Do not let the pride of this life rob you of eternal life the Father wishes to give to you freely. If only you will lay hold of it and never let it go. For this is the inheritance of them that love their Father (God) and Jesus Christ, who is our Lord and Savior.

October 17, 2019

I am not meant to gain followers nor idol worshippers. I am meant by the will of my Father to save souls, being a fisher of men, as a servant of God! For the kingdom of heaven is at hand! May all come unto repentance!

October 30, 2019

Come Back into the Truth:

Oh, my dearest brothers and sisters, many of you have turned your backs on God, denied His will, and have given yourselves unto the evil ways and abominations of the world. You have separated yourselves from the truth and forgotten who you are and also have forgotten your Father unto whom was your first love. For you were set free from darkness, why did you go back into it? And unto you, my unsaved brothers and sisters, many of you have resisted the truth and do not desire to know your only one true and living God. For you were born in darkness, and in darkness you have stayed because you have come to love it and not the light that comes to set you all free from it. For you say within yourselves, "This is my life, and I am free to do whatever I want in it, for I come to love evil and abominable deeds, and it is pleasurable in my sight." You say that you are free, but I say unto you, indeed you are as blind sheep, and your ears are covered, trained, and conditioned to not hear nor listen to anything of truth but only to receive lies, deceit, and manipulation. For the world (Satan) pokes you with a stick, then shows and tells you to go this way and that way and follow this broad path, and you blindly follow it being deceived. For do you not know that wide is the gate and broad is the way that leads to eternal destruction?

My unsaved brothers and sisters, you who lacketh knowledge and understanding, you are not free but are slaves to a system that is conditioned to guide you into the lake of fire that burns with weeping and gnashing of teeth, for this is the reason why Jesus Christ, our Lord and Savior, has died for you so that you may have a way of escape. This is even the reason why He raised Himself from the dead on the third day after His death, so that you may have hope in Him and follow Him into the narrow gate which leads to eternal life. But woe unto you who walked in the narrow gate but then turned back around walking out of the narrow gate, straying from the path of righteousness and following the path of the broad, for destruction awaits for you because you knew the truth and turned back unto lies. Why, oh men and women of God, would you betray the Son of Man unto lies?

Oh, how the mighty have fallen. Therefore I say unto all of mankind saved and unsaved, evaluate yourself and repent quickly, turning away from your evil ways, lest you suffer the same fate as the world. For the kingdom of heaven is at hand, and in the coming of the Lord, His eyes will be filled with the great fiery anger of God's wrath upon the children of disobedience and to cleanse the world of its injustice and wickedness, bringing salvation unto His people!

November 4, 2019

If you truly love the Lord your God, you wouldn't have to ask yourself if you're going to heaven or hell, neither answer that question to any man. For you would already know, not in ignorance of one's ways but in truth.

November 8, 2019

The only thing that separates us from angels and demons is redemption through Jesus Christ, who is our salvation, for this is how we know that God loves us all.

November 14, 2019

You who are of the world, know that the light of Jesus Christ can heal your brokenness and pain, make you whole, and give you beauty for your ashes. Just come and repent throwing away your wickedness, running to purity and innocence, receive Christ, and believe in Him.

November 14, 2019

Come into the light of Christ, which reveals the truth of all things!

November 15, 2019

My beloved brothers and sisters, it was once told unto you that not everyone that will be in the kingdom of heaven would receive a crown, but only some. But I say unto you, that logic is false. Everyone who will enter into paradise will have the crown of life. For all sons and daughters of God are meant for royalty in Jesus Christ as He is the King of kings and Lord of lords.

November 15, 2019

The hope of darkness is eternal death. But the hope in light is eternal life!

November 18, 2019

Endure and Persevere, Beloved:

Because of the lack of understanding of many, the ones with understanding are burdened by the oppression of the ignorant. But be of good cheer you who believe in Jesus Christ and deal righteously in truth, and praise the Lord for wisdom and understanding with all patience and perseverance. For the salvation of the Lord is nigh. But woe unto them that deal foolishly and take pleasure in it for the love of money. For they have caused the oppression of God's people, and careth not. Neither do they see their wrongs nor incline their ears to hear their suffering. Therefore, the wrath of God is upon them, and their end is nigh lest they repent and turn from their wicked ways.

November 28, 2019

You Can't Buy Your Way into the Kingdom of Heaven:

Oh, my unsaved brothers and sisters, the devil has deceived many of you by making you think that just because you do some good deeds, you might be good enough to get into heaven. But I say unto you, you have been lied to. For you cannot get into paradise by good works alone, nor can one buy their way into gaining eternal life. But God indeed rains over the just as well as the unjust. Therefore, you shall reap what you sow. The good deeds that you do will be rewarded by God with earthly goods. But with the spiritual, it is not so because you have not believed in the name of the only begotten Son of God. For it is through Jesus Christ that one receives eternal life. Therefore, you may ask, "Can one still be thrown into the lake of fire even if they do good things and still do not believe in Jesus Christ?" And I will say unto you, "Yes, because since they did not want to receive eternal life, they will not gain eternal life. Therefore, they have chosen eternal death."

November 28, 2019

One must be baptized by water (cleansed) and the second by fire (purified by the Holy Spirit) with also the confession of the heart and mouth that Jesus Christ is Lord of all and that He died on the cross for our sins and rose again from the grave on the third day to become saved from eternal death and receive eternal life in Jesus Christ. Then they will start their journey by fasting (in solitude, with no distractions), praying, and reading the Word of God (the Bible). In this, they will seek, and then they shall find and will knock, and the door will be opened. For in this, they shall meet their maker, being in direct contact with God, whether it be on earth or in paradise.

November 28, 2019

Do not stop fasting with God in solitude until He commissions you, and neither put a time frame on how long. The Father will determine that. For, the deeper we get in fasting and praying, the closer we get to Him. For God said, "Seek me, and you shall find me; knock, and the door will be opened; seek my face and hear my voice." (This is spoken of in Jeremiah 29:13 and Luke 11:9-10) We must deny ourselves to be one with Christ!

November 28, 2019

When fasting, we must let go of everything, denying our flesh everything, to receive God in everything! A half-attention fast will not do, but He desires our all at the moment!

November 28, 2019

Message unto all believers in Christ Jesus, message unto all believers in Christ! Faith, prayer, and the Bible alone are not enough to reach the fullness of the Holy Spirit! We must also fast denying our flesh of all things daily! Put away the distractions sent from the devil! Fasting is essential to being one with the Holy Spirit and being commissioned by God! We must go deeper! It is time!

November 28, 2019

The awakening is drawing near! For what was shall happen again! Awaken, children of God!

December 24, 2019

Sometimes deaths are to judge, sometimes deaths are to save, and sometimes deaths are to reward. But only you know, oh Lord, according to one's life, what their portion will be in the afterlife.

December 26, 2019

For this is the reminder, Christ is returning soon to make all things new. Woe unto them that are not watchful and are not waiting patiently in the truth (not doing that which is good and right in His sight) for His coming. For in the time that He does, His light will shine upon them, exposing their wickedness and abominable deeds, and they will be greatly ashamed and reap the wrath of God with great judgment by fire. But blessed are they that are watchful, patiently awaiting the coming of the Lord while standing on the Word of Truth and holding fast onto all that is good, being untainted by the world until the very end. For in His coming, He will give them a whole new life.

And we will be with Him and He with us. We will be His people, and He, our God. For the old will pass away, and behold, all things will become new. For the end is near and is already upon us. Be ready, my brothers and sisters, never giving up on the Word of Truth with great faith and hope in our Lord Jesus Christ, for He is the salvation of all the saints (all of them that believe and love Him).

December 29, 2019

There is only one that is good, that is God!

YEAR 2020

January 14, 2020

Do you not know that liars and those that loveth to make a lie will not inherit the kingdom of heaven? Therefore, tell the truth, and your burdens will be released.

January 14, 2020

Tell the truth, for lies cause more pain and add problems. And dragging out a lie causes much confusion along with torment, but the truth will set you free.

January 15, 2020

Repent quickly, and turn away from your wicked ways. For the judgment of God's wrath upon America is near and destruction cometh! Repent, not out of fear but in the sincereness of heart!

January 16, 2020

For indeed, these days are like the days of Noah. When everyone follows the wickedness of their own evil heart to submit themselves unto every evil act of abomination against God. And when God's messengers come and say, "Repent, for the wrath of God is near and destruction cometh," everyone turns aside and continues in their folly. Therefore, continue having ears but not hearing and having eyes but not seeing. For when the Son of Man sits upon the cloud of heaven, they that believe, and trusteth in Him shall be lifted up. But as for the abominable, disbelievers of truth, disobedient, and ignorant, when the judgment comes upon you, you will know it not, and thine end will be established. For the world was once cleansed by water, but now it shall be cleansed by fire! Repent, for the kingdom of heaven is at hand!

January 22, 2020

My brothers and sisters, do not fear but love the Lord your God as He loves us all, wishing that no one should perish but that all may come unto repentance.

January 24, 2020

My unsaved brothers and sisters, please understand, before Christ came unto you, you were already condemned, and you were already in darkness, but He has come as a light to save you from condemnation from the lake of fire which burns because of your sin. Do you not understand? He is not your enemy but your only salvation into life and your freedom. For you only know darkness because you are self-condemned. But look, your hope is near unto you if you only just believe with your heart and confess with your mouth that "Jesus Christ is the Son of God and Lord of all, who died on the cross for your sins and rose again on the third day after

His death," and then you will be no more in condemnation of your own soul but instead in life because you believe.

For God loves you all, do not make yourself an enemy of Him. For He died, then became alive again for you so that in His name you may have life. For He is the only way into eternal life in paradise after this life. Please all of you, He cries out to you, saying, "Do not delay, come while the gate is still open, come! For the time is at hand when it shall be closed forevermore unto them that do not believe, therefore come into my rest and know truth!"

January 24, 2020

Satan made religion so that the truth may be hidden from you, finding it and believing it! But the truth will set you free!

January 28, 2020

Perfection unto vanity is vanity, and that which one labored will one day be as nothing and will soon fade away. But perfection unto love will last forever, and the inheritance therein lasts for eternity.

January 28, 2020

Life is not about speed and gain, but instead, about

growth (in character) and maturity in the truth of one's self. For without truth, one is stagnant in growth, and if one ceases to grow, then is not that person ignorant? For ignorance comes when one resists truth and refuses to believe it. For because of ignorance, many fall into the spirit of error (always making mistakes in word and deed) and settle with the theory that "nobody is perfect" and that true perfection is impossible to become. So instead of becoming who they are meant to be, they end up wishing for what they could have become. Therefore believe, for perfection in love (who is God) is essential to becoming who you are meant to be. And only in Christ can we be made perfect unto every good work, for it is He that useth us and not us ourselves!

January 29, 2020

For many of you have a very carnal and simple-minded perception of love and how to show it. For love and how to show love is not based on the pleasures of the flesh (lust, fornication, sexual immorality, materialistic benefits, selfish gain). For the pleasures of the flesh are not love but only inspired by lust and desire, which lead to covetousness, and covetousness leads to sin. Brotherly love is not selfish, nor is it just meant to be given unto whom you deem worthy of your kindness and giving. But brotherly love is meant to be given unto all freely with the readiness to always forgive. For this is the way of love,

> Love is patient and kind; love does not envy or boast; it is not arrogant or rude. It does not insist on its own way; it is not irritable or resentful; it does not rejoice at wrongdoing but rejoices with the truth. Love bears all things, believes all things, hopes all things, endures all things.
>
> 1 Corinthians 13:4-7 (ESV)

January 29, 2020

Mating was never meant for the sexual pleasure of fornication but only for the purposes of marital connection (bond of oneness) in the fullness of purity as a gift of God that manifests into the life of another vessel. For this was meant to be a blessing of God, but because of the abominations in sexual immorality of many, they have made it into a curse upon themselves. And instead of keeping marriage holy and pure, the world has used it for every evil and wicked act of filth and abomination against God to mock what He has meant to be a holy and sacred union. For one man and one woman are not just meant to become one with each other but also one in God, yielding their hearts and minds unto Him so that they may in one mind (the mind of Christ) agree on all things concerning the will of God.

January 31, 2020

The old will be passed away, and behold; all things shall be made new!

February 2, 2020

The church is not a building, but it is you, your vessel! Do you not know that your body is the temple of the Holy Spirit? Therefore, keep it holy and untainted by the world!

February 2020

My beloved brother, please understand and listen. I never said that we are justified by the law, nor am I justified by the law. For they that are justified by the law, condemns, judges to death, and kill in the name of the law unto the wicked and abominable. For I do none of these things that would show that I'm justified by the law. For what I do and speak through the Holy Spirit concerns edification (teaching and preaching the truth for the growing of them that believe in Christ's Word) and exhortation (bring correction unto the saved as well as the unsaved so that they repent turning away from their wicked ways). For what the Father does through me has everything to do with His mercy and grace for His people and warning them of the wrath to come if they do not take heed to the Word of God and to rightly understand (rightly divide) what God speaks through His Word. Therefore, how am I justifying God's law? For what God does through me is not justifying the law but only guiding people to the narrow gate and saying, "Walk therein," for wide is the gate, and broad is the way that leads to destruction. For I have condemned no one for the sake of the law but only preached truth unto them that may believe in Him. Blessed are them that believe in Him, and in believing in Him doing His will, because they believe.

February 16, 2020

Stop being so fearful, and begin to trust and have great faith, believing in the Lord our God! Wait on the Lord! For He is our salvation!

February 17, 2020

For who knows what we will become after we shed off the flesh of this mortal vessel from this world walking into paradise?

February 19, 2020

Blessed are they whose eyes are open and whose ears are not covered so that in seeing and in hearing they may learn, and in learning they may do, following the path of the narrow gate. For in that path leads to paradise!

February 19, 2020

Do not be stiff-necked as Pharaoh when Moses came unto him speaking the Word of the Lord, saying, "Repent, and turn away from your wicked ways lest the wrath of God comes upon you!" Pharaoh did not incline his ear to listen, nor was his heart convicted because of the evils in his deeds. For even though God knew that Pharaoh's heart was callous, God still even gave mercy upon Pharaoh in time. And throughout all that time, Pharaoh still didn't turn away from his wickedness and oppression upon God's people. Therefore, the time came when his end was established. For instead of choosing life, he chose death and was deceived by the devil, thinking that his own corruption was good. Therefore, learn from his mistakes and do not be like those that have given themselves wholeheartedly into the ways of the world, for their efforts will come to naught. So again, take heed, I say, "Repent, and turn away from your wicked ways, for the kingdom of heaven is at hand!"

February 20, 2020

If one only knew love, then they would have known the truth, but because they hate, they believe lies instead.

February 22, 2020

For why is it that the world is worried about survival when they should be focused on their souls instead? Is it not because Satan has deceived them into believing in his lies. For he has turned their heads unto vanity, blinding them from seeing the truth and hearing it. For because of this, fear troubles them daily. And in fear, they deal very wickedly and corruptly with great deceit sowing oppression and causing death upon God's people. For because of this, the wrath of God is coming, and their fear shall come upon them. Therefore I say unto you all repent, turning from your wicked ways and come unto Jesus Christ, who is our salvation and redemption from out of darkness (where there is death) and into light (where there is life). Come, my brothers and sisters, come quickly! Do not delay nor believe in the lies of Satan any longer! But this I say unto you, believe in the name of our Lord and your Lord, Jesus Christ, who is also God's Word!

February 22, 2020

This I can say, wherever my Father goes, I must follow, for He is my life. And I do believe we will see each other again someday, brother, but it may not be as quick or fast as you want it to be. Therefore, if you desire to be baptized, go to one of the local churches, and they will gladly help. Always remember this, never hold your salvation up for anyone, not even me, for even you must follow the path of where our Father takes you also. But remember, all of us who love the Lord our God will be led to the same place at the end of the journey. Therefore, maybe not now or maybe not later but soon enough we'll see each other again. Just stand strong and endure until the end, holding on tight to the truth, fighting the great fight of faith. And though I am not there with you, our eldest brother Christ and God our Father is always there to comfort you in times of sorrow, and even in the times of joy, God is always there with you. Just talk to Him just as you talk to me. He will listen, and He will speak. You just have to be sensitive enough to hear Him. For God is always speaking, we just have to listen.

February 23, 2020

Do not believe in religion, for there are many religions, and all of them are meant to deceive and confuse with great manipulation, for none of them are true. But yay, have hope because there is only one truth, and that is Jesus Christ. And in truth, there is an inheritance unto them that believe and endure in the truth until the end without falling back into lies. Therefore, believe in the truth! For in Him, there is life!

February 23, 2020

Do not put your faith in a beast nor believe in them lest you make them your idol and receive the mark of the beast. For many are falling into a reprobate mindset because they have resisted the truth and, in turn, resisted God.

February 24, 2020

For those of us who are in Christ Jesus, the walk that we walk is not about speed and haste but instead endurance and, with endurance, patience. Therefore, the question is, how much can you endure?

February 25, 2020

My beloved brothers and sisters, do not judge your neighbor if they want to get married or not, neither insult them. For either way, God will still be glorified. For if a person decides to stay celibate unto God as a lifelong commitment to Him, then they are indeed considered eunuchs for the kingdom of heaven. Therefore, whoever is able to walk that walk in the Lord, so let it be unto them. This is not a bad thing, but it is good, for they are one with Christ and Christ with them doing the work of the Lord. Now unto them that get married, one man and one woman only together must it be, so that the marriage may be blessed by God and not defiled and abominable resulting in being cursed instead. For the man and the woman will become one flesh, and if they remain together in God's will, not turning to the left or right but staying in the straight and narrow path, then they being one together will be one with Christ and Christ with them doing the work of the Lord. For even indeed, this is good in the sight of God. Either way, whether celibate in God or married in God, both are accepted and His divine will for your life as long as you remain in Him, staying in the narrow gate which leads to life.

February 26, 2020

It is God who uses me and not me myself. For I am nothing without Him, and every good and perfect work comes from Him. I speak not of my own power because I have none, but only the Holy Spirit who useth me. Therefore, give God all the glory, all honor, and all praise, for only He alone is worthy of it, only He alone is good, and only He alone is God.

February 29, 2020

The Agony and Suffering of Danyell's Heart from the Pain of the Trials and Tests of This Life:

I am hated by this world, and the people whom I was conceived by do not know me. For everyone hates me without a cause, and those who are supposed to be righteous in their faith condemn me. I do not know this world. What is my life, and why was I formed? Why do I feel cursed? Have I not loved, and did I not refuse anyone of myself? For I am hated by all, and no one knows me. Is this the end for me? I have no family, and the womb that I was brought forth out of knows me not. It does not respect me nor love me nor acknowledge the good that I do. My life is one to be perished and nonexistent. I realized that I have no family, and there's no one to love me the way I need to be loved.

I give, but everyone adds to my suffering. No one knows the pain that I endure (not just once in a while, but every day I endure great torment and suffering). Everyone just puts more and more on me and then adds judgment and scorning on top of that, right along with their expectations. When was it that the righteous in this world are found guilty and in the judgment seat and that the wicked are praised and looked up to?

I have no family; I have nothing. And the womb that I came out of curses and scorns me along with the world, adding to my torment. I do not know how much more my light can take of this life before it goes out; truly, I feel alone. Father, please help me to endure because I don't know if I'm doing anything right anymore, neither if I'm going in the right direction. My life feels like a waste and a failure. And I have nowhere else to turn nor go.

March 2, 2020

I do not do church, I rather be the church, and Christ is building me daily to become perfectly furnished unto every good work!

March 3, 2020

How is it that many of you have the spirit of Pharisee (religious) and know it not? Therefore I say this unto you, beware. Lest your righteousness is beyond the righteousness of the Pharisees, you will in no way enter the kingdom of heaven.

March 3, 2020

Did you not know that the Pharisees were of the world also?

March 4, 2020

Warning Unto the Churches and the Leaders of the Churches:

Those of us who are saved are also in the truth of God. Therefore, we are made to know more about what is good and bad in the sight of God than those who are in the world. So, I say unto you, who has made you believe, that one who knows truth, in spite of having knowledge of truth, can still deal wickedly and corruptly and will not have a greater judgment than them that did not know truth and does all kinds of abomination? For indeed you are deceived, those who know to do good and do it not and deal wickedly will receive a greater punishment on the day of judgment than them that do not know to do good but do evil not realizing that their work is indeed corrupt. Now, if one preaches the Word of Truth and teaches everyone to do good but the one speaking the Word of the Lord does not examine it for themselves to do good also, then has that person not become a hypocrite and self-righteous as the Pharisees were?

For they are of those that listen to the words of men and disregard the Word of God, abiding by the lies of the devil instead of the Word of Truth. For this reason, many in the body of Christ are not like-minded (Christ-minded) in the faith but instead are deceived by religion and tradition of men orchestrated by the devil to have that kind of mindset instead, turning them away from truth unto lies with manipulation and great confusion. For this is what is causing a separation in the assembly of the saints. For the ways of the world have crept into the church and have perverted and defiled it. For part of the body of Christ is holding on fast to the Word of Truth while the others are straying away from the path of righteousness, giving themselves unto the evils of this world. How is it, you who strayed so far from the truth can still say that "we worship God, and he is our Lord"? For indeed, your hearts and your ways testify against you, and you lie deceitfully.

You worship Him with your mouth, but your hearts are far from Him, for your fruit is rotten! And some of you who preach and teach are so far gone to where you preach a whole other gospel opposite of the truth. Some of you are preaching the kingdom of darkness and claiming it to be good and the will of God. Woe unto you who claim good to be evil and claim evil to be good, for this is an abomination and is against God and His people who truly love Him! For you have become worse than the Pharisees! Ye religious snakes and wolves in sheep's clothing, have you not read when Christ said in Matthew 5 saying,

> Whosoever therefore shall break one of these least commandments, and shall teach men so, he shall be called the least in the kingdom of heaven: but whosoever shall do and teach them, the same shall be called great in the kingdom of heaven. For I say unto you, That except your righteousness shall exceed the righteousness of the scribes and Pharisees, ye shall in no case enter into the kingdom of heaven.
>
> Matthew 5:19-20 (KJV)

Therefore, I say unto you all by the mercy of God, unto all of you who call upon the name of the Lord and deal wickedly and corruptly, repent and turn away from your wicked ways and let your minds be renewed in the Word of God with fasting and prayer lest you take the portion in the lake of fire with them who are of the world! Repent, for the kingdom of heaven is at hand, and the end is upon us! Come into the narrow gate, for many will only get into paradise by a string!

March 5, 2020

Ignorance towards the Word of God is worse than never knowing the truth at all!

March 7, 2020

Everything in America that the devil used this government from the beginning to make an upside-down, God is about to make right side up. But first comes the cleansing because when God gave them time and warned them to repent and turn away from their wicked ways, they did not and instead cursed and mocked God with their words and deeds. Therefore, the wrath of God has come and shall do what it was sent to do. For who shall survive it? This is only the beginning of great sorrows of this nation. And they that made this country the way that it is shall watch and say with great agony, "Oh, no, for this land in which we have trusted is coming down in flames." For Babylon the Great is coming to an end! Praise be to the Lamb of God who sits upon the throne, for His judgments are right and true! For God indeed is worthy to be praised! Therefore, all of you repent and turn away from your wicked ways, for the kingdom of heaven is at hand, and every tree that is not producing good fruit shall be cast out and thrown into the fire! For in this, you shall know that He is God and God alone!

March 9, 2020

Please understand, my beloved brothers and sisters in Christ Jesus who love the Lord their God, this Coronavirus was made from the wickedness of man in the will of God to be judgment upon themselves as the wrath of God. For we have nothing to fear, but they do because the wrath of God has come, and the end is here lest God has mercy upon them to be able to come unto Christ Jesus and repent, turning away from their wicked ways and receive salvation into eternal life.

March 18, 2020

Why is it that as I walk through the markets, I see everyone through fear giving themselves unto greed and selfishness? And with selfishness, hate unto their brothers and sisters who are sick and weak. For what has happened to love and kindness? What has happened to giving unto them that are in need? Why is it that your good fruit has gone bad and rotten? Why are you forsaking all that is good because of fear? For did you not know that God has not given us the spirit of fear? But instead unto you who love the Lord your God, He has given you love, power, and a sound mind to combat the spirit of fear. For perfect love casts out all fear.

Therefore, let God's light shine within you that man may see His good work through you, then glorify God unto all that see! For do you not know? We who are in Christ Jesus are the light of the world! Therefore, let love reign without partiality and wavering! And unto you who are unsaved, come unto Jesus Christ and repent, all of you! Turn away from your wicked ways and deeds. Do acts of love and not acts of hate; speak words of love and not words of hate. For everyone that is not bearing forth good fruit shall be cast out and thrown into the lake of fire!

Quickly come into the narrow gate before it is too late! For the rapture of the saints is near, and the kingdom of heaven is at hand! Blessed be unto the Lamb of God! For heaven is coming to earth! For even it quakes for its Savior! For even heaven and earth shall pass away and come back made new and eternal! For in the coming of the Lord, all things shall be made new! Blessed are them that truly believe in Him and do not give up on well-doing even in testing times! For Christ is our resurrection and life!

March 25, 2020

How is it that you think you can cast out the wrath of

God? Do you not see that this judgment is of Him? And because it was sent by Him, it will also leave when He sees fit for it to leave. What, would you also have tried to cast out the great flood that once covered the entire world in the time of Noah because of the judgment of the Lord? Would you also have tried to cast out the plagues on Egypt in the time of Moses because of the judgment of the Lord? Or even the judgment on Sodom and Gomorrah, would you have also tried to cast that out also? How is it that you think you can cast out God with God? Or who gave you the power to command Him? Therefore, I say unto you, repent because of your ignorance and understand the sign of the times. The judgments of the Lord come when a nation refuses to come unto Him and repent, turning away from their wicked ways and abominable deeds. What, does Jesus Christ not say in Matthew 10,

> Whoever will not receive you, nor hear your words, when you depart out of that house or city, shake off the dust of your feet. Truly I say to you, it will be more tolerable for the land of Sodom and Gomorrah on the Day of Judgment than for that town
>
> Matthew 10:14-15 (MEV)

Therefore, instead of trying to cast out the plagues, pray unto God that broken hearts may be healed and hardened hearts may soften and warm so that many more people may be delivered into eternal life being freed of fears of the final judgment to come, which is the judgment of the end. Because if many do not take heed to this plague to come unto Christ and turn away from their wickedness in repentance, then woe unto them that are stiff-necked. For greater plagues shall follow, for they will be worse than in the days of Moses and Sodom and Gomorrah. For the wrath of God is upon the children of disobedience around the world (concerning His will). Therefore, I say unto you all by the mercy of God in Christ Jesus, repent, turning away from your wicked ways! For the end is at hand!

April 2, 2020

God is about to change the design of the world you know today. For an earthquake that has never been seen before since the beginning of time is manifesting. A new era is coming, and what we know now will be like the history of old. And what has happened before shall happen again. Spiritual eyes will begin to open, and things unseen will be revealed. God shall work; who will allow it?

June 10, 2020

Why do you praise me when women give me their attention? Do you not know that the devil seeks to use these women to condemn my soul into the lake of fire that burns? Therefore, by the power of the Holy Spirit, I will not give him the satisfaction. For this is a very burdensome thing, for I have not yet found the woman that is good for my soul. So, therefore,

I put my faith in God, and my burden is released. He indeed is faithful unto them He has promised. And when God sends her, I will know that she is a gift from God, and we will be one in and with Him so that my joy in the Lord will be filled, giving thanks and worship unto Him unto eternity.

July 7, 2020

All the promises that God has promised His true people Israel are coming. And those that have oppressed and ruled over them with great hatred, jealousy, and greed shall watch and be amazed, and with amazement, great shame and guilt. God is raising His people back up from the ashes and putting them high. For they were made the lowest and a disgust as one to be dishonored by all nations because of their continuous abominations and wicked deeds in the sight of God. And because they did not stop from their sins, though they were very great and high in ages past, God has made them the lowest of lows in the sight of all men. But now, because of the fall of Judah's condition, many who oppress them with great iniquity have continuously mocked and blasphemed the name of the Lord our God. I say unto you, do not be deceived.

For God is not mocked, for whatever a man soweth that will he also reap. For God's name's sake, He is going to deliver His people from the bondage of their sins and lead them in a way that they have not known. Praise be unto the great "I Am," for the Lion of Judah is coming! Therefore, all of you, repent unto God quickly and turn away from your wicked ways, coming into the salvation of the Lord Jesus Christ so that you may be saved in the shadow of the Almighty from the wrath to come! For in this, you shall know that He is God and God alone, and besides Him, there is no other God! For He alone is the creator and God of all things!

July 17, 2020

We Are in the End:

Oh, inhabitants of the earth, the end is here, the end is here, and destruction upon destruction is proclaimed! Anoint yourselves with prayer and fasting with repentance unto God and turning away from all wickedness, perversion, and abominations running towards purity and truth that you may be found spotless in His sight. Be ye ready and watchful for the coming of the Lord, not out of fear but in the spirit of truth! And unto you who love the Lord our God, stand strong in the faith with patience, believing in our Lord Jesus Christ that all that was promised shall be fulfilled. But woe unto them that are still stiff-necked concerning the truth, for darkness comes.

Therefore, repent, oh inhabitants of the world, run with fear and trembling away from darkness and into the salvation of the Lord. And if you do good, will you not be accepted by the Father of lights? For do you not know that all of you were made by God and belong to God, and besides Him, there are no other gods before Him; He is God alone! The rest are lies and deceit orchestrated by Satan, the deceiver of all men and his legion of darkness! They are trying to deliver your souls straight unto the lake of fire that burns for eternity! Come, oh children of God, come into the light of truth, believe in Jesus Christ of whom you have not known and His words so that your souls may be saved!

August 11, 2020

The Parable of the Ripe Harvest:

How can a gardener sow a seed into soil if there isn't an opportunity to sow? How can one speak into someone's life if the person that the Word was given to was not able to listen? Therefore, there must be an open hole in the soil for there to be an opportunity for the gardener to sow a seed into the soil, and when the gardener does, he will cover it up.

But now, here is the test of the soil to see if it's compatible enough for the seed. For if the soil will not hold on to the seed and examine it for itself, then the seed will become rotten and wither away in the soil, and the soil will remain as it was before the gardener came to sow the seed, being closed without an opportunity to receive another seed until the soil has a hole and is ready to receive again. But if the soil did receive the seed that it has been given, the seed will begin to sprout, and then it would thirst for living water, for it is still in darkness. So, the gardener will come and give it living water, and the sprout will start to grow from out of the darkness of the soil to bear witness to the sun and receive its marvelous light, for it has received the living water which has given the seed life.

Now, the sprout has become a stem, and its roots are grounded. Therefore, if it continues being fed living water, it will remain in the sun, and its stem will continue growing stronger and begin to grow leaves as the light remains on it, turning into a beautiful plant. But if the plant stops receiving living water, the plant will begin to starve, and if the sun sees that the plant has no living water within it, it will burn the plant, and the plant will no longer be able to remain in the light of the sun, and because it was burned, it withered and died. So, then the gardener comes and sees that the plant is dead. For the gardener begins to weep and, while weeping, picks it up by the root and throws it away while saying sadly, "Why did you not continue drinking of my living water that always satisfies? For if you did, you would still have had life." For there was no more life in the plant, and it bore no more of the sun's light.

And if the plant is otherwise taken up by its root instead and put into a vase with different soil and it's removed from under the sun and not receiving its living water regularly, it will die, turn into ash, and back into the darkness of the soil no more bearing the light of the sun. Then the gardener will come, begin to weep, and, while weeping, pick it up by the root and throw it away while saying sadly, "Why did you not continue drinking of my living water that always satisfies? For if you did, you would still have had life." For there was no more life in the plant, and it bore no more of the sun's light.

But if the plant remains in its rightful soil, continuously receives living water, and has not been moved from the light of the sun, then the plant, after growing many leaves, becomes taller, and rising ever so closer to the sun, will then begin to bear forth fruit. For it continued receiving living water. And then many people came to look upon the beautiful and tall plant as it radiated with the glorious light of the sun upon it. And as the people circled around it, being amazed, tasted of its delicious fruit. For the people then went back home satisfied and were filled, for the plant was bearing forth good fruit.

Finally, then when the gardener came to the plant and saw that the plant was bearing forth good fruit, he was pleased with the plant's growth while he was away for a moment and then came back. He then said to the plant, "Oh, my good and faithful servant, I shall make all things new, enter into rest!" He then gently raised the plant up from the ground with its strong roots and placed the plant into a better soil in the sun with other plants that were placed in that soil also just as healthy, vibrant, and fruitful like it, and the plants became greater than they ever were before and lived an everlasting life. This thing happened to the plant because it did not stop producing good fruit.

To those that have an ear, let them hear and let them receive the seed that the Spirit of the Lord is imparting to the church and to the world. For the soil represents the person and the vessel (also known as the body) of the person, the gardener represents Christ, the sun represents the presence of God, the seed represents truth, the plant represents the soul and spirit of the person, the vase represents the change of direction turning away from the truth and light of God and into lies and darkness instead.

August 12, 2020

All of you who are upon the face of the earth, come unto Christ Jesus in repentance and turn away from your wicked ways! Desire to do good and no more delight yourselves in wickedness and abominations that your souls may be saved from the destruction and devastation to come! For the God of Enoch, Noah, Abraham, Isaac, and Jacob still yet lives! For He is the Beginning and the End, the First and the Last, the Alpha and the Omega! For the Great "I Am" has no end, and no one has born Him, nor was He created! For He is life and eternity incarnate, and death submits unto His will! For there is no other god besides Him, and He is God alone and the Father of all creation, even of the earth and the outer realms of the earth that we know not of, neither should we tamper with! Who are they that claim to be "gods" besides our Lord, and who are they that claim to be greater than our Savior and Redeemer, the King of kings and Lord of lords?

Let them set themselves against Him, watch and see as their end comes quickly in the flashing of an eye, and they become like a thing of nonexistence. For every knee shall bow, and every tongue shall confess that Jesus Christ is Lord! Therefore, all of you turn away from participating in lies, deceit, the love of vanity, jealousy, manipulation, oppression, and the causing of iniquity and suffering upon those who are around you! For all these things are influenced by Satan, and he entices the ignorance that is within you to not listen nor see the truth so that you may not be freed from the condemnation of your heart proceeding to your soul! Therefore, open your eyes, you who refuse to see and uncover your ears, you who refuse to hear and know the truth! Lest your ignorance inspired by wicked desire condemns your soul to the lake of fire that burns for eternity without an end!

For Satan wishes this upon you because he hates you, but God loves you and wishes that you repent and turn away from doing evil and know love! Therefore, come unto Jesus Christ quickly and believe in Him with your whole heart and confessing with your mouth that "Jesus Christ is Lord of all and that He is the Son of God that died on the cross for our sins so that we may have life and that He came back to life again on the third day after His death," so that you may be saved. Then renew your mind in the Bible, reading and meditating on His Word with prayer and fasting so that you may never be the same again but instead becoming a new creature in Christ Jesus, holy and acceptable in the sight of God. For God wants to give you eternal life. Will you receive it?

August 19, 2020

The evolution of mankind does not lie within the hands of technology but only in the hands of our Lord and Savior

Jesus Christ, who is indeed the Beginning and the End, the First and the Last, the Alpha and the Omega, the Lamb of God! Quickly, come unto Christ with repentance and turn away from your wicked ways, lest the very thing that you worship be the very thing that destroys you and curses you into an everlasting condemnation of torment with weeping and gnashing of teeth! For this is the warning to the world! Repent, for the end is here, and the image of the beast is trying to make itself manifest!

August 19, 2020

Evolution is nothing but the working of God's hand! Do not worship it, but worship God, who is the great "I Am," and believe in Jesus Christ also, for they are one! The Son is glorified in the Father, and the Father is glorified in the Son!

August 23, 2020

Why do you weep, oh, you who have lost a loved one? For death is not the end, but only the door to the beginning of a whole new life. Blessed are they that come unto Christ and believe in His Word wholeheartedly without forsaking the truth and remain in truth unto the return of our Lord. For indeed, I say unto you, eternal life is what they have inherited. And though some may have died in the physical, they will in no wise lose their inheritance in Christ Jesus. Because they believed in Him, death is nothing but a transportation to a new beginning with God our Father and Christ our Lord and Savior in peace and the fullness of gladness.

But unto the lawless, godless, and unbelievers of truth, death for them is the door to the beginning of never-ending death and existence of torment and suffering. And though they may be on their last breath, the death of the physical is only the beginning of their eternal sorrows. Therefore, beloved, for this reason, God so loved the world that He gave His only begotten Son, who is Jesus Christ. And whosoever believes in Him, living by His Word, shall not perish but have everlasting life. Therefore, I say unto you all who are in the world, come before it is too late, come this day, this hour, this second!

Come into the salvation of the Lord so that He may give you a whole new life! For this is to save you from the death coming upon the ungodly! Be in darkness no longer but come into the light of Christ so that you may be made new! For the kingdom of heaven is at hand! Blessed are they that receive it!

September 8th, 2020

For This is the Revelation of the Message of the Parable of the True King:

Thank God for everyone that is around you and for everyone that you come in contact with but do not make them in your life greater than they ought to be. Do not see them as gods and change the mindset and heart that God has meant for you to have. For I say this unto you, whoever forsakes the truth to believe in lies instead, will indeed perish. Many within this generation have the mindset of the world (Satan) and think of the things of the world, but I rather choose the mind of Christ, for in Him there is living water that always satisfies. To forsake living water is as to forsake life and to choose death. For whosoever forsakes the truth for lies and wholeheartedly holds on to lies instead of the truth might as well just claim that they committed suicide of their own soul. Therefore, for this reason, Christ said in Matthew,

"The Son of man goeth as it is written of him: but woe unto that man by whom the Son of man is betrayed! It had been good for that man if he had not been born" (Matthew 26:24, KJV).

> Think not that I am come to send peace on earth: I came not to send peace, but a sword. For I am come to set a man at variance against his father, and the daughter against her mother, and the daughter in law against her mother in law. And a man's foes shall be they of his own household. He that loveth father or mother more than me is not worthy of me: and he that loveth son or daughter more than me is not worthy of me.
>
> Matthew 10:34-37 (KJV)

September 9, 2020

Blessed is the one who loves the truth and listens to the truth when he speaks. For by the truth, they are enabled to see through the deception of the wicked and know him who uses the wicked behind the curtains for his own evil devices. Because they remain in the truth, their spiritual eyes are open, and nothing shall remain hidden from them. And eternal life is what they shall find because, in the truth, there is life and that more abundantly. But woe unto them that loveth lies and listen wholeheartedly to lies. For they have resisted, rejected, and condemned the truth. And when the truth comes to them, they know Him not.

Therefore, because they have ears but cannot hear and have eyes but cannot see, and because they love the path of Satan so much, their own ignorance will be the cause of their own downfall. Because when Christ called for them, they did not listen. When He was near them, they did not see Him. When He blessed them, they misused Him and took Him for granted. And when He had given them His mercy and grace, they did not thank Him, neither did they weep and repent of their evil works but instead continuously mocked, mistreated, trampled over, and brought more anguish and injustice upon the Son of God. Therefore, the wrath of God is upon them, and indeed, will they not say within their own ignorance and wicked hearts, "Why have all these bad things happened to me and my family? For I am a good person!"

September 15, 2020

For what is that you seek by following me? For you watch me, and then, you follow. What is it that you seek to obtain by these repetitive actions? I say unto you, the one that you seek is not I but only Christ who lives within me and uses me to fulfill His perfect will within this world. For it is not I that do these good works and neither I that speak these good words, for it is Christ who does these wonderful things through me. I am nothing but a vessel of the Holy Spirit. So, I say again, what is it that your soul seeks? Therefore, I say unto you, your soul does not seek me but only Jesus Christ that giveth living water that always satisfies unto them that thirst for it. For Jesus Christ is the way, the truth, and the life. For your soul desires for the salvation of the Lord so that it may be saved from the gates of hell coming into eternal life in paradise in which the Lord our God has prepared in the end for all of them that love Him.

Therefore, if you shalt believe in thine heart and confess with your mouth that "Jesus Christ is Lord of all and the Son of God who came and died on the cross for our sins so that we may have life and resurrected Himself from the dead so that we may continue to have hope in Him," then you shall be saved. After you do this, pray unto God to forgive you of all your sins and abominable deeds so that you may do them no more and continue in the Bible to know the truth. For the Lord, our God, has drawn you near unto Him being captivated by His light! Therefore today, you shall know the truth, and the truth shall set you free! Glory, honor, and praise be unto the Lamb of God! For indeed He is worthy above all to be praised!

September 15, 2020

It is better to do good and be loved by God than to do evil and wickedly on account of the expectations of man!

September 24, 2020

Ignorance produces anger, anger produces hate, and hate leads to death. For if one loves death, they will find themselves in eternal fire! Therefore, know love, and in love, there is understanding, and understanding leads to the truth. And if one abides in the truth, they will find life!

September 27, 2020

Who Are You?

At this time, there became a great calm in the atmosphere. Who are you?

To the one who is always near me, neither of whom I can't find a place to escape from: Are you the blessing sent from my Father, or are you another curse and distraction sent from Satan to try and take me away from God? Are you of my Father's light, or are you a part of the darkness of Satan in disguise as a light? Are you the angel sent from God to bear these burdens with me in this walk unto eternal life, or are you one of Satan's demons sent to try and take me off the path of righteousness that I may be destroyed into eternal fire? Are you my Sarah, or are you Jezebel? Are you my Ruth, or are you Delilah? Are you the soon-to-be love, or are you a momentary affection that leads to death and suffering?

For indeed, time will tell and expose what you are and where you have descended from. Therefore, if you are of Satan and sent from him, then your infatuation will wear off of me, and you will be led away by the lust and covetousness of others because of your own desires. But if you truly are sent from my Father in heaven, then you will continue to hold fast and pursue that which is true, despite the distractions Satan tries to throw at you, you will have the ability to see through his deception and desire it not and will continue to grow in love with that which is true. Therefore indeed, time will tell to see what you are, for I am patient in my Father's will by His mercy and grace. As for me, by the salvation of my Lord and Savior Jesus Christ, I will remain in the liberty of my Father's love.

For I am not meant to give my strength unto a woman but only that the chosen woman of my Father will come being drawn by my Father's light and abide with me in His glory. Together in the abode of Christ and being in Christ, in the Father that His will may be made manifest within us as one in the fullness of His glory and the fire of the Holy Spirit. Blessed are we in God if you are the promised gift. Please, oh Lord, help me to receive it and treat it well as You see fit. Make it to where I can neither decline this gift nor push it away.

It is as if her soul is trying to connect with mine, for I have never received something like this before neither know what to do in this position. All I can do is trust in You, oh Lord. Please guide me, Father, with Your wisdom, understanding, discernment, and truth. May Your divine appointment and angels be around about on guard, for my heart and soul remain in You, and may my wife's heart and soul be one with me in You also that we cannot be broken nor torn apart but only think alike with Your mind, oh Christ Jesus. For in You, we are secured and protected. For in You does my heart trust.

September 30, 2020

At first, God had me being the only great light within this place of darkness for a time, and then with His glorious light brought you into this place also, and then there was a great calm in the atmosphere which I have not felt in many years. For, who understands the meaning of this? Please help me and be with me, oh Lord, that I may operate in Your perfect love and perfect will in this new change that all things go as You see fit. Your will, not mine, keep my heart remaining in You.

For only in You does my heart fully trust, and it trusts no other. For who is this that worships my Father with me? For I pray that she is for You in the Spirit of truth. Nevertheless, if You trust her, oh Christ Jesus, then I will trust in You concerning her. For I will hold on to faith in You, oh Lord my God, my keeper, and defense that You have me and my soul in Your hand, for I trust in you. For if she is a deceiver, I know that You will reveal these things to me. But if she is the one You have promised, please do not hold back Your confirmations from me, oh Father, that my faith in You concerning this may increase with confidence and not remain in doubt and indecisiveness. Please hear this conflict within my spirit, oh Lord, for I can do nothing without You.

October 2, 2020

The Love of God for His People:

Oh, my beloved unsaved brothers and sisters, do you not see how much God loves you? Do you not feel His pain for you? God loved you so much that when He looked upon your suffering, anguish, and sorrows, knowing that your souls were all in jeopardy, came down from heaven and chosen a mortal and fragile body of flesh as a vessel so that even He Himself may even endure the betrayal of others, the false accusations of manipulative and deceitful liars, the abuse and jealousy of others full of hatred, the mocking's and demeaning "jokes" of others, the scorning's of self-righteous people who don't look at the wrongs within themselves but instead try to find wrongs in others always erring within their judgments, being even spit on and treated like trash and garbage. His own family didn't even understand Him and discounted Him a worthless and hopeless, a lost cause and good for nothing.

He was a lowly and humbled unto the end servant unto people in higher positions of authority who ignorantly hatefully used Him and put Him down while He served them as they always watched Him intently in their "superior" groups with wicked thoughts and demeaning talk about Him to see if they can find something against Him to condemn Him. For their tormenting tests and demeaning questions of knowledge were never-ending, and they wearied Him greatly as if hell were on earth and felt like it was eternity enduring their meaningless arguments and debates against Him. He bore the expectations of men who always want but never give.

He has dealt with the feelings of hunger and starvation, He has dealt with the thoughts of suicide and depression, He has wept unto God many nights because no one understood Him, but they all just came to Him to see what they could take from Him. He has dealt with the desires of the flesh and the desire of the things to be acquired of this life. He has even been tested with the affections and lustful temptations of this sinful and abominable flesh and suffered death even to the fear of it. And many more things than these has He endured but overcame them all and sinned not once, for our sakes. For do you not see and understand, God loved you so much to where all that you have been through, He suffered it all with you and then took it further by dying on the cross for our sins so that we may have life in and by Him with grace and mercy unto salvation. Then He raised Himself from the dead so that we could still have hope in His coming.

Therefore, He did not only just came to suffer our affliction with us but also gave us the gift of salvation into eternal life with Him and the gift of redemption (mercy and grace) and the sword (who is the Holy Spirit) so that He (though He left) and the kingdom of heaven may still fight with us against Satan and his kingdom (who with great hatred inspired by jealousy and pride, desires with deceit, lies, and manipulation for the purpose of trying to take away our eternal life with our Father and condemn us like himself into eternal damnation in the lake of fire that burns for eternity with weeping and gnashing of teeth). For God did all of this to show you how much He loves you.

Therefore, unto all of you who are unsaved, come unto Christ and believe in Him and His words so that you may be made new in His image receiving the gift of salvation along with the gift of the Holy Spirit so that you may be enabled to fight against the forces of darkness that have bound you for so long. For these are the magnificent gifts that the Father and our Lord and Savior Jesus Christ (who is God) have given us because He loves us and wishes not to see us be condemned. For condemnation ends here if you will just believe and receive Him! For He loves you all, therefore let His love overtake you that you may be made new in His glory! Praise and glory be unto the Lamb of God! For indeed He is worthy above all because He has overcome the world, and by Him so can we! For with man, this is impossible, but with Christ, all things are possible unto them that believe!

October 9, 2020

Oh, inhabitants of the earth, how long will you continue to falsely judge each other without knowledge and understanding? Judging only by what you see and hear with your own perception and not with what you know. Only believing lies from your own wicked thoughts and not the truth. And you gather up in a group with people who listen to Satan just like you so that you may condemn the righteous. You have excelled in Satan's ways and turned away the wisdom and correction of God. Therefore, you have made Satan your father because your delight is in him. And how is it that you think you will be able to survive the coming of the Lord?

Quickly all of you who love sowing oppression and iniquity unto thy neighbors, come unto Christ Jesus and repent, turning away from your wicked ways and choose the Word of God to be your way on how you should live and throw away the world's council lest the wrath of God remains upon you! For do you not know that a friend of the world is an enemy of God? Therefore repent quickly, for the kingdom of heaven is at hand, and every tree that is not bearing forth good fruit shall be cast out and thrown into the lake of fire that burns with weeping and gnashing of teeth! You would do right to take heed to the warnings of the Lord. For warning comes before destruction. And woe unto you who fall into the hands of an angry God.

October 12, 2020

Woe unto you who love speed and haste for gain! Do you not know because of your selfish desire, you sow oppression and iniquity unto thy neighbors, making their burdens harder than they can bear? Because of your selfish desire and greed for wealth and control, you oppress and condemn forever, increasing your sins. For Satan has deceived you well, making you think that your actions are just and good. For look, do you not see that the wrath of God is heavily upon you and your desire for wealth and vainglory has cursed you? In the time that was given unto you, you have had nothing to fear, and no one could overthrow your judgments nor reign. But woe unto you, for how did you not know that you were being set up for destruction, getting higher just so that you may fall and the fall will be great.

For you shall meet your maker, and in His judgment will you be condemned, and the lake of fire for eternity will be your portion, for you have sold your soul for materialistic gain that is meant for destruction. Therefore, because you love following vanity, unto eternal destruction you go. Woe unto the world because of the love of money! For within you is the seed of darkness and the way of death and torment! For you are cursed, and whoever admires your ways shall bear the same curse! Therefore, repent and turn away from your wicked ways washing yourself in the blood of Jesus Christ. And pray that God will grant you mercy and grace to be worthy of entering the new Jerusalem.

October 13, 2020

Let go of witchcraft, sorcery, idol worship, and unnatural passions of lust and sexual immorality! For do you not know that those things only bring death and cannot save your soul nor that of others? Therefore, let it all go and come unto Jesus Christ with repentance turning away from all that is dark and wicked! For only in Jesus Christ can one's soul be saved and redeemed from the lake of fire! Come into the light of Christ so that He may make you new! For the old things will pass away, and now comes the new! Come, beloved, He calls for you, and your redemption is near! Come, save yourself, through the blood of Jesus Christ!

October 13, 2020

Oh, inhabitants of the world! Quickly, repent and become saved and come inside the ark of the Lord (which is the Word of God) and remain in it with fasting and prayer, lest you suffer the wrath of God to come upon the world! For the rapture of the saints is near! Will you be inside the boat when the flood comes or outside with the ungodly?

October 13, 2020

Love those that make themselves your enemies. For you must not make yourself an enemy of them though they make themselves an enemy of you.

October 13, 2020

Indeed, the Word of God is within you and speaks through you. Hold on to that, beloved, continuously believing it. For if what you speak is by the Holy Spirit, then it should line up with the Word of God, and should you not also believe it for yourself? For indeed, you should. Whatever the Holy Spirit speaks through you, it is also for your hearing and growth in Christ Jesus also. You will know if what was spoken through you was from God if it lines up with the Word of Truth. If the Bible spoke it, then you have been used by the Holy Spirit whether to give revelation or to preach for the saving of the souls. If you remain in the love of God and the Word of Truth, God will speak through you always.

October 22, 2020

There are no longer going to be many nations, for now come two distinctive kingdoms! The kingdom of light and the kingdom of darkness! For things unseen will be revealed, and the spiritual world is intertwining with the physical! The time has come when you will know who is of the darkness and who is of the light! For the real world is beginning to expose itself! For you shall know the truth, and the truth will set you free! For who is it that is worthy of entering the holy city of our Lord and Savior, Jesus Christ? For the future is come! Blessed are they that believe in Jesus Christ! Glory be unto the Lamb of God who sits upon the throne! He comes for His people! Be ready, my brothers and sisters in Christ Jesus!

For the war above all wars is about to begin! For the only one and true power is coming in all His wondrous glory!

October 22, 2020

For heaven is coming down to earth! Even so, come, Lord Jesus, come.

October 23, 2020

Oh, you private parts, you are not to yield your functions unto unfruitful works to kill off life within the temple of the Holy Spirit! For your purpose is to hold life within for the appointed time to create holy living vessels for the Lord's good use in a holy union in the name of Jesus Christ, yield yourself to the command of the Holy Spirit, in the mighty name of Jesus Christ, in the mighty name of Jesus Christ, in the mighty name of Jesus Christ, be ye fruitful and multiply!

October 27, 2020

Woe unto them that judge quickly what a person speaks because of offense instead of discovering for their growth in Christ the meaning of what has been spoken! For they know not whom they judge, neither whom they condemn!

October 27, 2020

The Revelation of the Fire of the Holy Spirit:

Greetings, my beloved family in Christ Jesus. I felt in my spirit to bring revelation about the fire of the Holy Spirit. For the true believers in Christ Jesus, the fire of the Holy Spirit is good because it makes us stronger in our walk with Christ. But as for the ungodly, it is not the same case but instead the opposite. It will burn them because they have denied our Lord and Savior, Jesus Christ. And if one denies Christ, then they have denied God. So, therefore, they remain condemned unto eternal fire (the lake of fire) unless they come unto Christ and change their ways with repentance. For Paul, in 1 Corinthians 3:13, explains that we will all be tested by fire. For what is the fire? Fire is the tests and trials of life that we all are allowed to go through.

Therefore, for this reason, I have told you that fire for the true believer is a good thing that we in Christ become greater than we were before, excelling in the love of God, which is manifested by the fruit of the Spirit in deeds and speech from the heart. So, when John the Baptist said in Matthew, "He will baptize you with the Holy Spirit and with fire" (Matthew 3:11, MEV), after a believer has been tested by fire, if they are found worthy in the sight of God, fire will inflame them, not to harm them, but to give power over demonic forces. For the Holy Spirit is the sword (which is also the Word of God), and fire is the power to bring forth deliverance, healing, and miracles with faith. For what does the Word of God say about a true believer that has been through the fire? For Job said in Job 23:10 that he would come out as gold, better and fitting, holy and acceptable for the Lord's good use. For if one does not have the fire of the Holy Spirit within them, they are defenseless against the attacks of Satan. They'll be overcome, be thrown into the furnace, and be utterly burned by the flames because their hearts and minds were not wrought in the love of God.

Therefore, for this reason, the ungodly cannot make it through the fire because they are not in God, neither in the love of Christ. So, in the short term, fire destroys and exposes all things that are dark (evil) and unclean (wicked and abominable). And fire separates darkness from light. Fire is a cleanser and purifier for the true believer but death for the ungodly because they love their evil and do not desire to give it up for the will of God. Therefore, the ungodly will burn while the redeemed of the Lord shine forth as bright as the sun, for this is the revelation of the fire of the Holy Spirit. I pray that this helped your understanding of the truth and clears all confusion concerning this topic. May God bless you with more of His truth and bring you more wisdom and understanding for your growth in Christ Jesus so that you may rightly divide the Word of God and not from your own opinions and perceptions. May you all be blessed, my family in the Lord.

October 28, 2020

You cannot think in the mindset of an intellectual nor

in any other way of the world while reading in the Word of God lest you will not understand nor believe the truth when it is spoken, and you will take the Word of God out of context and distort the Word of truth with great confusion and be left with questions that do not profit anyone's salvation in Christ Jesus. For you do not need the mindset of the world; you need the mind of Christ! Then you will understand the truth, and the truth will set you free!

October 28, 2020

Those of us who are true believers of the Word of God do not read the Word of God based on "fact" but only by faith! For Satan gives you "fact" to take you away from the truth but only by faith in believing what the Word of God says will you then find the truth! For "fact" is blinded from the truth when the truth is already in front of it because of the spirit of error led by unbelief! For if you do not wholeheartedly believe in the Word of God, then you are not truly saved, and you will not truly understand the words that it speaks until you do.

October 28, 2020

"Fact" is still a lie because it is full of error! Believe in the truth and not in "the facts" lest you be led astray by vain deceit and manipulation orchestrated by Satan instead of remaining in the truth, who is Jesus Christ! Anyone who does not believe in His Word does not truly believe in Him and will not understand Him nor that of which He speaks. For unbelief breeds out error!

October 28, 2020

To love oneself in a pure and holy manner is to love the ways of the Lord with humility, humbleness, and servanthood and to keep thy temple (the body) untainted by sin and wickedness (also known as the world, who is also Satan). For the body is the temple of the Holy Spirit; this is the way of light. Now, if a person "loves" themselves in the ways of the world, then they are indeed conceited and self-righteous in heart, and if they don't stop, it leads to pride, and pride comes before a fall, and the fall is great. For that is the way of darkness.

November 3, 2020

Oh, my brothers and sisters, saved and unsaved, within this hour, many of you have your eyes set on earthly things that cannot profit your own souls. Many of you, even some of the greatest among you, are blinded and are deceived by Satan with fears and the anxieties of this life, and all of them are earthly and vain. It is to where out of fear and anxiety, you are abiding in the will of social media and not in the will of God. You are believing in vain dreams and visions and not listening to that of which God has shown you and told you personally. For us who are in Christ Jesus, our lives are not of this world; neither should we be concerned about anything of it because our lives are in Christ Jesus and the promised kingdom to come unto all of them that love Him, for we are not of this world though we have been placed in it for His purposes.

For all of these things that are happening within this life all around us should not be a surprise to us. For is it all not written already in the Word of God? For indeed, it is. And did Jesus Christ not explain in Matthew 24:6 that we should not be troubled, for all of these things must come to pass so that Christ our Lord and Savior may return? For indeed, He did. Therefore, set your minds on the things above and not the things beneath, lest you be tossed around back and forth, and side to side by the winds of change instead of holding fast onto the Word of Truth and believing what He says so that you would not be easily moved by vain deceit and manipulation orchestrated by Satan to blind you from what God is truly about to do in this season.

For there is about to be an outpouring of the fire of the Holy Spirit like never before upon the whole earth on those who are ready to receive it. For it will be to where so many people will be doing miracles, signs, and wonders by the glory of God to where no one can deny that Jesus Christ is the Son of God, who came in the flesh to die on the cross for our sins so that we may have life, and that He rose again from the dead on the third day after His death so that we may have hope in His coming. Even that also the great "I Am," the Father of all creation is the only one and true living God! The evidence of God will be undeniable! But woe unto you ungodly who will still be stiff-necked and in unbelief when these things come to pass before your eyes, for you are they that will make up excuses to disqualify the truth, claiming that it's witchcraft and other types of sorceries and incantations. Therefore again, I say unto you, "Woe!" For you will do this unto the forsaking of your own soul! Therefore, in this season, God is telling His people to remain in His Word with prayer and fasting, believing in the truth and all His words so that they may be made manifest within us! Blessed are they that truly believe in Jesus Christ! For the war of the kingdom of light and the kingdom of darkness is being made manifest upon the whole earth! Blessed are them that are ready for the fire! For the coming of the Lord is drawing near, and the kingdom of heaven is at hand! Repent and turn away from your wicked ways and be focused, men and women of God, for our salvation comes!

November 4, 2020

Give to Caesar what is Caesar's, and give to God what is God's! You belong to God, so focus on Him, not the world!

November 4, 2020

My beloved family in the Lord, this is the truth that many are blinded in these days from seeing. Do not be distracted by the things that are happening in this world. Christ already told us that all these things must happen and be fulfilled for the coming of the Lord. Therefore, instead of us being fearful, worrying, having anxiety, and being anxious, we should be praying unto God about all things, praying unto God for everyone, praying for direction and guidance in His divine will, repenting, and remaining in His Word with prayer and fasting in all patience and endurance not giving up hope in our Lord and Savior, Jesus Christ.

For we are not of this world, neither is it promised to us, but only the promised paradise with Him for everlasting unto everlasting to come, for this is the divine promise unto them that truly love Him and endure unto the end! All glory, all praise, and all honor be unto the Lamb of God who sits upon the throne! For He alone is worthy of it! Be of good courage, my brothers and sisters, for He has overcome the world! Therefore, I say unto you all, endure in Christ Jesus! For it will be all worth it in the end! For no one truly knows the glorious and magnificent plans that He has for His chosen ones in the Lamb's Book of Life in paradise! Therefore, let us endure that we may take our portion with our heavenly Father in the new Jerusalem! Home at last! Home at last! Oh, I truly say unto you, beloved, good God Almighty home at last! For our souls are what matter the most in this world, not the cares of this life. Be blessed.

November 14, 2020

Both fire and water are manifestations of God's magnificent power. But indeed, know and believe that God is not just limited to these. For with God, all things are possible, and nothing is impossible for Him, for He does things even beyond mankind's comprehension and the capacity of their knowledge. The thoughts of all the Lord's works are unfathomable. For much is still unknown, hidden, and a mystery unto mankind because we are limited by flesh and have not yet ascended into our immortal bodies that Jesus Christ, our Lord and Savior, has prepared for all of us that love Him. But even in our immortal vessels, we would still not be able to know the fullness of God's greatness. For the Great "I Am" is God, and He is awesome in power, and no one fully knows Him but Himself. For this reason, He called himself "I Am" because there is no end to His glory. Neither can His beginning be searched out. For He is the beginning and the end! But indeed, do know, God has no end, and His reign is everlasting unto everlasting!

November 17, 2020

My saved and unsaved brothers and sisters, you have heard an old saying, "Don't be so heavenly minded to where you're no earthly good." But I say unto you, you must be heavenly minded to be any earthly good for the Lord's good use. What? Did not Jesus Christ say in Matthew, "You are the salt of the earth. But if the salt loses its saltiness, how shall it be made salty? It is from then on good for nothing but to be thrown out and to be trampled underfoot by men" (Matthew 5:13, MEV)? Therefore, do not receive and yield yourself to any sayings like those, for they are of the antichrist spirit because it is saying that it is okay to be carnally-minded (worldly-minded, the mind of Satan) and deny the mind of Christ. For indeed, that was a deceitful lie from Satan himself.

To be heavenly-minded is to have the mind of Christ. For you may ask, "Then how does one become heavenly-minded?" And I would say to you, "By believing and meditating on the Word of God night and day and day and night and then you shall know the truth, and the truth will set you free!" Therefore, all of you who believe in Jesus Christ, give up the carnal mentality that leads to death and be of one accord receiving the Word of Truth, who is the living Word of God and walk in His counsel and wisdom, not the world's counsel! The world curses you, but the Word of God sets you free! For Jesus Christ came so that you may have life and that, more abundantly!

November 18, 2020

For indeed, my beloved brethren, this is a sad truth within this generation of "Christians." So many are preaching, teaching, and even hearing the Word of God but are not living the lifestyle of Jesus Christ (not walking in Jesus Christ's teachings nor keeping His commandments). For this reason, they have deceived their own selves believing that they are doing the Lord's will, for they will indeed at moments be used by the Holy Spirit for the sake of God's people but for their own salvation, they have not abided in the love of God. Woe unto those "Christians," for they have become hypocrites like the Pharisees. Listen to what they say but do not do what they do, for they do not practice what they preach. And if they continue in wickedness, evil, and pride, then they would begin to preach that evil is good and that good is evil, becoming worse than the Pharisees (antichrists and false prophets) deceiving others, even, if possible, some of the very elect.

Therefore, for this reason, fire has been poured out upon all flesh to test the hearts of the people and separate the wheat from the tares, the righteous from the wicked, those that truly love God from the ones that don't. May we who truly love the Lord our God stand holding firmly onto the Word of Truth abiding in the love of God as we set our hearts for the coming of the Lord, being watchful with prayer and supplication for others remaining in the Word of God. For if we abide and remain in Jesus Christ's words, then we are truly His disciples. For He said that if we love Him, we would keep His commandments. For if we love the Lord our God with all our heart, mind, soul, and strength, loving Him more than anything, and loving everyone as we love ourselves, then we indeed, by the grace and mercy of God, have fulfilled the whole commandment of God. For if we do not have the love of Christ above all things within us, we then have nothing and are nothing. But if we truly have His love within us, then it shows in all that we say, think, and do. For the love of God extends to all things.

For without love, we can do nothing, and only hate and evil would then be present. But with love, we can do all things through Christ, who strengthens us. For who is love? For God is love. Therefore, let us have God with us in all we do and speak. For it is He that does the good through us and not us ourselves. Therefore, give all glory, honor, and praise unto our Lord and Savior, Jesus Christ, and God our Father in heaven, for He alone is worthy of it all! Glory be unto the Lamb of God who sits upon the throne! For great are His works and majesty!

December 15, 2020

For many are deceived and ignorant to the truth about Christmas because of their desire, they lay aside the commandment of God to hold on to their own traditions. For how is it that they do not know that this holiday (like many other holidays) is a mockery and an abomination unto our Lord and Savior, Jesus Christ? For this work is the deceit of the antichrist spirit orchestrated by Satan to mislead and confuse. This worldly holiday does not worship nor glorifies God. This holiday worships idols, greed, entitlement, falsehood, fakeness, religiosity, lies, deceit, and manipulation so that those that lack knowledge may participate in the wickedness thereof. And the world loves it so. Do they not see the blasphemy against Christ in this holiday?

It lied about the day of His birth and uses His name to trap His people into participating in its abomination. My beloved brothers and sisters in Christ Jesus, do not participate in things just because you see everyone else doing them. But this I say unto you, be a peculiar people set aside for the Lord and the Lord only! For have you not read that friendship with the world is enmity to God? Whoever is a friend of the world is an enemy of God! One that is a friend of the world does what the world does and speaks what the world speaks and disregards the Word of Truth as if it never existed!

Therefore, beware, for reasons like these, the wrath of God has come and is still yet manifesting against the ungodly, and greater destruction and devastation is coming upon the children of men! And in the coming of the Lord, His wrath and fiery anger will be against those who continuously rejected His corrections and reproof (instructions of His goodness)! Therefore, let us all repent and turn away from our wicked ways so that in Christ Jesus (when He comes), we may be found watchful and cleansed without spot nor wrinkle. Let us become holy and acceptable for our Lord's good use working out our own salvation in the Lord with fear and trembling. Be blessed, my brothers and sisters.

December 15, 2020

My brothers and sisters saved and unsaved repent and turn away from doing evil unto each other, from speaking evil and wicked language against each other, and from devising evil and mischief against each other! For do you not know that a stranger is nothing but a brother and sister that you have not known? The only difference is that some are of darkness, and some are of light. Therefore, know the truth! Come unto Christ Jesus and become saved so that you may know the love of God to be enabled to love others in the fullness of truth and the pureness of heart!

Come quickly, for the kingdom of heaven is at hand, and the coming of the Lord is even standing at the door! Be ye ready and watchful in the Word of God with prayer beloved, for you know not the day nor the hour of when our Lord and Savior shall return to deliver His chosen from the wrath of the Lord that shall come upon the ungodly suddenly! For His coming is very near and is nearly upon us! Be ready, in the shadow of the Almighty! For in an instant, we shall be lifted up into the clouds of heaven awaiting to look upon the glory of our Lord and Savior, who is indeed the Lamb of God who had come to save the world from their sins! Worthy is the Lamb of God who was slain for the redemption of His people! For He above all is worthy to be praised, glorified, and honored! For He is our risen king! The Lord of lords and the King of kings! The Great "I Am" is His name!

December 16, 2020

Fast and pray, remaining within the Word of God without ceasing! Remain watchful and keep your oil filled by meditating in the Word of God night and day, and day and night! For these days are now as like the days of Noah! For those who will come into the ark of the Lord in the shadow of the

Almighty, let them come! But those that will remain in ignorance unto the wrath of God, then let them remain set up for the destruction that is about to befall upon the children of mankind! For as rain descended unto them in Noah's time, so shall it be like in this wicked and perverse generation!

But they that remain in the shadow of the Almighty and trust in the Lord their God shall be saved! This is the warning unto the inhabitants of the world! May we all humble ourselves in the presence of God that we may be found by our Savior in the appointed time! Blessed are they that are watchful for the coming of the Lord.

YEAR 2021

January 6, 2021

Religiosity for a person of the faith of Christ is one who has the form of Godliness but denies the power thereof. Who is the power of God? Is it not the Holy Spirit? And is not the Holy Spirit also the Word of God? Therefore, whoever comes unto Christ and rejects the Word of God and does not abide in the word of God rejects the power thereof, for they are of a religious spirit. They are those that become antichrists and false prophets, for Judas was the first of many and an example of what will happen to a people who denied the will of God and teach others to do likewise. For this is one who betrays the Son of Man by believing in lies instead of remaining in the truth. For did not Judas die a horrible death? Therefore, horrible deaths await those who betray the Son of Man. For Jesus Christ said in Mark 14,

> The Son of man indeed goeth, as it is written of him: but woe to that man by whom the Son of man is betrayed! good were it for that man if he had never been born.
>
> Mark 14:21 (KJV)

For this is a part of the wrath of God to come upon Christians who rejected the will of God. For they are the deaf, and they are the blind, because when He corrected them many times, they did not listen to the truth, nor did they see it when He presented it to them many times the right way. Therefore, they become laid up with the ungodly that are meant for shame and destruction.

January 21, 2021

My beloved brothers and sisters in Jesus Christ, when you get the chance, read Leviticus chapters eighteen, nineteen, and twenty fully. For these are the deeds of the ungodly of which we must be aware of in these days and stay away from them all in the fear of the Lord. For these deeds are great abominations in the sight of God in which many have already participated in, in which the wrath of God is marked upon them, lest God through His mercy and grace enables them to repent and turn away from their wicked ways. Stay always away from these things, for the wicked and ungodly are increasing greatly in their sins in these last and evil days.

But those who love the Lord their God and remain abiding in His Word with prayer and fasting, not forsaking the Word of Truth, shall be covered under the shadow of the Almighty. And as the world goes into deeper darkness, we shall go into greater light. And our Father in heaven shall take us away from the midst of the ungodly that we may be with Him in His arms. Therefore, let us not give up in well-doing, for in due season, we shall reap the rewards of our fruit. For one thing I have desired of the Lord, and that will I seek after that I may dwell in the house of the Lord all the days of my life and to inquire in His temple that I may behold the beauty of the Lord. Amen.

January 23, 2021

3 Guidelines As A True believer:

1.Relationship With God:

• Prayer and fasting in the Word of God with a pure heart.

(The first will enable you to do the second, and the first must be maintained while doing the second.)

2. Abiding in the love of God:

• Keeping His commandments

  • You keep His commandments by loving God with all your heart, mind, soul, and strength. Loving Him more than anything. And that will enable you by His grace and mercy to love your neighbor as yourself, and even those that make themselves your enemies by loving them with the fullness of forgiveness.

(Now, after abiding in the first and second, it will enable you to do the third in the pureness, humility, and humbleness of heart. The first and second must be maintained while doing the third.)

3. Feeding and tending to the sheep (all people) and lambs (children and newly born-again believers):

• Tending: —always *helping* and *giving* to the:

• Elderly	• Fatherless	• Poor and Hungry
• Widow	• Disabled	• Sick

- Giving unto all that ask without expecting anything in return.

- Feeding: Preaching & teaching the Word of God in the Spirit of truth.

For these are the commands of Christ Jesus our Lord and Savior for one being His true disciple (truly being saved), spoken from scriptures John 15 and John 21:15-17, Matthew 5:13, 44 and Matthew 17:21. Even by the words of Isaiah in Isaiah 58:5-12, and of course, the Ten Commandments in Exodus 20, written by God Himself, given unto Moses for the discipline and knowledge of the people. These three requirements must always be done in the balance of this order and maintained continuously in the Spirit of truth and pureness of heart! If not, it will be done in the spirit of error and wickedness of heart!

Warning unto the Church and the World:

If you claim to be saved but do not have a relationship with God, you are a liar and a deceiver. If you try to love without the relationship with God, your love is corrupt with partiality and only meant for your self-serving purposes. There is no true goodness in this; this is the work of manipulation. If you claim to be saved preaching and teaching but do not have the relationship with God nor the love of God within you, then you are speaking out of the spirit of error and confusion because you are still of the mindset of the world reading the Word of God to teach and not to receive the mind of Christ by meditating in the Word of God for yourself so that your mind may be renewed in Christ Jesus! For you can't receive the Word of God right if you're only reading it to be "biblically correct" or trying to "find a new sermon to teach." No, this will not work for your salvation nor that of others. Preaching and teaching must come naturally and not forced!

If you do not pray and fast in the Word of God for your own relationship with Him and do not have the love of God within you and you are preaching, teaching, and even prophesying, claiming to have done miracles, signs, and wonders, woe unto you, for you are nothing but another religious lukewarm Christian! For their righteousness is no greater than the scribes and the Pharisees! Woe unto them, for this is a dangerous level to be at. If they do not reposition themselves quickly, they will become even worse than the scribes and Pharisees, no longer remaining in the truth but instead turning to the lies, deceit, and manipulation of Satan, becoming antichrists and false prophets puffed up with pride! For God said in Revelation 3:16 (KJV), "So then because thou art lukewarm, and neither cold nor hot, I will spue thee out of my mouth." Christ even said in Matthew 5:20 (KJV), "For I say unto you, That except your righteousness shall exceed the righteousness of the scribes and Pharisees, ye shall in no case enter into the kingdom of heaven." These are the same people on the day of judgment that Christ has also spoken about in Matthew 7, saying,

> Not every one that saith unto me, Lord, Lord, shall enter into the kingdom of heaven; but he that doeth the

> will of my Father which is in heaven. Many will say to me in that day, Lord, Lord, have we not prophesied in thy name? and in thy name have cast out devils? and in thy name done many wonderful works? And then will I profess unto them, I never knew you: depart from me, ye that work iniquity. Therefore whosoever heareth these sayings of mine, and doeth them, I will liken him unto a wise man, which built his house upon a rock.
>
> Matthew 7:21-24 (KJV)

Now, do you understand and see that there is no room for religious practices, traditions of men, vainglory, and debates on genealogy in the will of God? For if it is not good for nor going to help your or someone else's salvation, should it not then be cast out of our site and thrown into the fire? For indeed it shall be, along with those that continue to do these things in the sight of God! For how is it that they do not know that they out of error are causing iniquity, obligation, and oppression upon God's people? For they are all indeed deceived, believing that they are doing God's will and are blinded by pride and selfish desire. For what they do are abominations in the sight of our Lord. Therefore, repent, I say, and turn away from your wicked ways. For God corrects those whom He loves hoping that by correction and warning, none should perish but that all come unto repentance and be saved!

Throw away your precepts, mythologies, analogies, and physiologies, psychologies, philosophies, and science of the worldly knowledge of men and receive the living Word of

Truth that gives living water that always satisfies, for Jesus Christ gives unto them that hunger and thirst for righteousness! Praise be unto the Lamb of God for the revelation of truth! Blessed are they that receive it to walk truly wholeheartedly in the ways of the Lord our God and turn not backward unto evil and wickedness! For you shall be forgiven of all the things you have done and shall be saved!

But woe unto the stiff-necked who curses the Word of Truth! For if you do not repent and turn away from your wicked ways, the wrath of God will remain upon you, and the judgment of the Lord shall you face! Woe unto that person who falls into the hands of an angry God! Indeed woe, for I would not wish their portion upon no man, no, not even them that maketh themselves the worst of mine enemies! You would do well to heed God's warnings working out your own salvation with fear and trembling! Therefore, for this reason, Peter, who was persuaded by the Holy Spirit, said,

> The Lord is not slow concerning His promise, as some count slowness. But He is patient with us, because He does not want any to perish, but all to come to repentance. … Therefore, beloved, since you are waiting for these things, be diligent that you may be found by Him in peace, spotless and blameless. …You therefore, beloved, since you know these things beforehand, beware lest you also fall from your own firm footing, being led away by the deception of the wicked. But grow in the grace and knowledge of our Lord and Savior Jesus Christ. To Him be glory, both now and forever. Amen.

2 Peter 3:9, 14, 17-18 (MEV)

February 8, 2021

Blessed are the children who desire their heavenly Father's will. For God will make it so that they will not fail Him, and with gratitude, they glorify Him. But woe unto the child that does not desire their heavenly Father's will. For do they not dishonor Him and them that dishonor their fathers, are they not disowned and thrown out into utter darkness? And does that child not have a fearful expectation of death? Therefore, beloved children, young and old, youthful and advanced in age, always desire the will of your heavenly Father to do them so that He may be pleased with your works.

February 18, 2021

What makes you think that because you were attacked, you are in darkness? Just because one faces spiritual warfare doesn't mean that they are in darkness. For all faces spiritual warfare, no matter if they are in light or in darkness. The only difference is that some are overcome by the warfare and end up worse than they were before, and the others overcome and conquer the spiritual warfare and become greater than they were before. Only those who remain in Christ Jesus will be able to overcome and conquer spiritual warfare because the Holy Spirit is their sword and with faith believing in the name of Jesus Christ brings great fire. Hmm, but it also doesn't hurt to wonder what was the purpose and reason for this coming to pass? For everything happens for a reason.

February 18, 2021

For even I have my battles with Satan that I face, but I know that God has me in His arms. For always He keeps me, protects me, and delivers me from going down into a horrible pit, and He will lift me up and set me upon a high rock to where the wicked one cannot touch me. For this is the same for all of God's children that love Him and His ways to do His will with a pure heart. All glory, honor, and praise belong unto the Great "I Am" and the Lamb of God who sits upon the throne. He is indeed a righteous and just God. For He sees all and knows all, even the true intentions within the heart of every creature and being. Nothing is hidden from God nor impossible for Him. For His judgments and justice are right and true. There is no error in Him, and all His ways are perfect.

Blessed are they that wholeheartedly trust in the Lord our God. There is no one nor nothing like Him, nor has there ever been, and nor will there ever be. For the Great "I Am" is the only one and true living God, and besides Him, there is no other. For He created all things and reigns over all! He is God and God alone for all eternity, and there is no end for Him! He is the beginning and the end! For great and mighty is our God, who is also the King of kings and the Lord of lords! For there is no end to the greatness of our God! Hallelujah to our Lord, Savior, and Redeemer! For He lives!

February 18, 2021

Becoming Born-Again:

The baptism of water is still essential for salvation in Jesus Christ, just as the baptism of the Holy Spirit is essential for salvation in Christ Jesus. For Jesus Christ said,

> Jesus answered, Verily, verily, I say unto thee, Except a man be born of water and of the Spirit, he cannot enter into the kingdom of God. That which is born of the flesh is flesh; and that which is born of the Spirit is spirit.
>
> John 3:5-6 (KJV)

To be born again of water is the baptism of water so that one may be cleansed of their old man's debts to sin (This is the first humbling state of submission unto the will of God). For your baptism of water confirms your confession of Jesus Christ by faith. Then to be born again of the Holy Spirit is to be purified by the fire for the Lord's good use, for we cannot fully be one with the Holy Spirit until we are cleansed and then purified.

For this reason, Jesus Christ also said in regard to fasting,

> And he spake also a parable unto them; No man putteth a piece of a new garment upon an old; if otherwise, then both the new maketh a rent, and the piece that was taken out of the new agreeth not with the old. And no man putteth new wine into old bottles; else the

> new wine will burst the bottles, and be spilled, and the bottles shall perish. But new wine must be put into new bottles; and both are preserved. No man also having drunk old wine straightway desireth new: for he saith, The old is better.
>
> Luke 5:36-39 (KJV)

Do you still not understand yet? Both of the baptisms, along with the confession of Christ from the heart coming forth from out of the mouth (as the blood is also a witness), are needed for God to prepare our vessels (also known as the old bottle/old garment) for the bonding (oneness) of the Holy Spirit (also known as the new wine/new garment). For we must be first made new to receive the new man. The Holy Spirit needs a freshly made new temple. For then, the old will be passed away, and now comes the new. But first, one must desire to be baptized, and whosoever does not desire nor willing to participate in both of these baptisms will not be able to make it into the kingdom of heaven. For their salvation requires them to be born again.

For if one receives the baptism of the Holy Spirit but not the baptism of water and they do not be baptized by water soon, they will not be able to remain in the will of God but instead turn back into darkness because the fire became too great for them and was overcame because they weren't cleansed from the debt of their sins by the baptism of water. And if one receives the baptism of water but not the baptism of the Holy Spirit (if they do not desire to be tested by the fire), then they will be left defenseless against the attacks of Satan and the demonic forces of darkness and be overcome. Therefore, either way, they will not make it and utterly perish unless God has mercy upon them to overcome, but taking that chance is risky and is playing with hellfire! For this reason, John said,

> For there are three that bear record in heaven, the Father, the Word, and the Holy Ghost: and these three are one. And there are three that bear witness in earth, the Spirit, and the water, and the blood: and these three agree in one. If we receive the witness of men, the witness of God is greater: for this is the witness of God which he hath testified of his Son.
>
> 1 John 5:7-9 (KJV)

Therefore, both baptisms are required for one's salvation, and God will make a way for His people to be able to be baptized by both so that we may be made new to be used by His glory and so that He may be glorified. For God, our Father, is faithful and just, He will not leave one unbaptized unless that person is not willing to become baptized. Again, I say unto you, that person will not make it unless he fixes his heart and will unto the Lord and become baptized.

> Then Peter said unto them, Repent, and be baptized every one of you in the name of Jesus Christ for the remission of sins, and ye shall receive the gift of the Holy Ghost. For the promise is unto you, and your children, and to all that are afar off, even as many as the Lord our God shall call.
>
> Acts 2:38-39 (KJV)

February 24, 2021

Don't let Satan deceive you any longer, making you think that you're not worthy enough to get baptized! The devil is and was a liar and a deceiver from the beginning and the father of all lies! This is the truth: you need to be baptized in order for you to be worthy of the change that God is about to do within you! For the water baptism is for the remission of your sins to do them no more being cleansed from the debt of them.

February 25, 2021

If you only knew the Father, you would not have spoken out of ignorance concerning His existence. For when you get to know the Father, you would have the knowledge and understanding of the truth. But until you come unto Christ with repentance, the lies of Satan are all you know and believe. You first must believe in Christ Jesus to receive Him, *for He is the truth*. If you come unto Christ, you will know the truth, and the truth will set you free! Just believe in Him, beloved.

February 25, 2021

God has already proven Himself to be real and the truth time and time again. Therefore, the true question is not "Is He real?" but only why do you continue to resist Him even though the answer is already right in front of you and has always been around? For He even provided the Word of God to help you understand. For that is even in your midst. But again, I say unto you, why are you resisting God, our Father who loves you dearly and wishes greatly for you to be set free from an existence of lies, lack of purpose, and death? Why are you resisting Him? For He desires to give you a whole new life that is laid up for eternity because He loves you, but why are you resisting Him?

February 25, 2021

Beloved, do you not know and have you not read that God has given you free will out of His love so that you can choose to receive Him or deny Him freely? Therefore, it is you that must come unto Him and not Him to you though He is already near you and around, but you choose to be blinded by ignorance and lack of knowledge concerning His existence. For when you decide to believe in Jesus Christ, then you will be able to know the truth and forsake all lies that Satan has deceived you to believe before. And why would you want to wait and see when He returns to then believe in Him? For do you not know that when He returns, He will come with great fierce and fiery anger to cast the judgment of His wrath upon them that are abominable, ungodly, and disbelievers of the truth. And what will you do when that day comes upon you, unaware as you look up at the sky and see great glory? For I know what you would do because the Word of God has already spoken it. Because you have denied the Son of God and have not believed in Him nor His words so that you may be saved, fear will overcome you, and you will weep bitterly and be greatly ashamed with guilt because you have already heard these words and seen the signs but have not believed.

And you will know that the end with no more time for redemption has come for you. Therefore, come quickly unto Christ Jesus, quickly, believe in Him and repent so that dreadful day will not come upon you the way that it will come upon the ones that desire to remain ignorant because of their own evil and wicked desires. He is telling you all this because He loves you and wishes to save you from this condemnation that shall befall upon the whole world, hoping that in knowing this, you will come unto Him with repentance, for He desires you to live and not perish. But will you let Him save you from your end? For even Satan knows that his end is coming, and he fears this day greatly wishing for you to be condemned just like him. But if you come unto Christ Jesus and believe in Him, you shall be saved and given eternal life and shall never die nor fear death ever again.

February 25, 2021

Well then, it seems you have already chosen your path. I just pray that God wakes you up from the dead soon before it is too late for your soul. I pray for you, beloved. You believe in a life that is vanity and will not last, for this will all soon fade away and be nothing as if it never existed. But where your soul is being led to in the afterlife, that is what will last forever. Woe unto you, I pray for your soul. I'm even praying for all of them that are agreeing to your ignorant words of foolishness and mockery against our Lord.

You all are in a very dark place within your souls, and only by God's mercy can you be saved now because by your ignorance and hardness of hearts; you have closed your eyes and have covered your ears so that you may not see and listen to believe in the Word of Truth. But blessed are you of whom are listening to the words that Christ has spoken through me and, by being convicted within your hearts by the Holy Spirit, are beginning to believe! Yay indeed blessed are you, for if you come unto Christ with repentance and become baptized in His name, you shall indeed be saved, and Jesus Christ will receive you with the fullness of forgiveness and His arms opened wide unto you because you have believed in Him! And He will take you from out of darkness and bring you into His marvelous light that you may become a new creature!

For the old thing will pass away, and behold, you will be made new! Come, my brothers, come, my sisters, let Christ our Lord redeem you away from the gates of the lake of fire and bring you into paradise! For your true Father calls for you so that you may be saved! Come, He says, "Come into eternal life with Me my children, For I will be your God, and you shall be My people for everlasting unto everlasting!" (This is spoken in Revelation 22:16-17 and Jeremiah 30:22.)

February 25, 2021

The only true and living God is not a religion as Satan has deceived many to believe. For the Great "I Am" is the only one true and living God, and there are no others besides Him, nor was there ever any before Him, nor after Him. He is always, was always, and will always be God alone. It was always Him. For religion today is nothing but lies and deceit with great manipulation and confusion made from the imagination of wicked men to detour many from believing in the truth and coming to Him. For there is only one truth, and that is Jesus Christ, who is the Son of God that came to earth in the flesh to die on the cross for our sins so that we may have life by mercy and grace to be drawn back unto the Father.

Then God raised Him again from the dead on the third day after His death so that we still may have hope in His second coming. For God sent Him out of His love for us so that whosoever believes in Jesus Christ shall not perish like the ungodly of this world but, instead, have everlasting life. For God is real, and His Word is truth. Believe and become saved. For it is by faith we believe and not by sight, for this is a test that must be passed in you! Doubt no more but believe, and then He will manifest Himself to you! *Believe!* For this is the fight that the world faces for their salvation, and many are not making it because they are believing instead in the deceit of Satan!

March 11, 2021

Revelation of the End 1:

God is about to take His faithful people and set them upon His holy mountain and establish them there in safe habitations and prosper them. And will tell them to wait steadfast on these hills, and then He will go and get the rest of His people in the world gathering His sheep all together on the mountain (of prosperity and favor). (The evidence of this is spoken in Isaiah 27, Isaiah 30:18-26, Isaiah 60:1-22, Ezekiel 11: 17-21, and Ezekiel 20:33-44.)

Then once it's all fulfilled, everyone would have already chosen their way. For darkness would have already filled the world (the sun nor the moon will no longer give its light) and manifest deep darkness inside of all the people of the world because of the children of disobedience (The children of Satan/ the kingdom of darkness). But the light of God shall remain upon His redeemed remnant as we wait patiently for our Lord and Savior, Jesus Christ, with joy and praise glorifying God and in waiting, abiding in the love of God. (The evidence of this is spoken in Matthew 18:11-14, Revelation 14:1-5.)

And then the Lord shall break forth open the clouds of heaven, and His redeemed remnant shall be lifted up, and the kingdom of darkness would be left to suffer the wrath of God. Then the Lord will lead His people unto the beloved city, and we shall stay there for one thousand years (evidence of this is spoken of in Revelation 19:11-21 and Revelation 20:1-6), and after that, Satan will try to deceive the other nations abroad and bring an army against us, but they shall not be able to even touch us. (The evidence of this is spoken in Revelation 20:7-10.)

For God, our Father, will fight for us, and we shall be preserved. Then the great final judgment of the end will be made manifest, and all things shall be made new. (The evidence of this is spoken in Revelation 20:11-13 and Revelation 21.)

March 12, 2021

The Apostle Paul in Acts 19:3 shows us that the water baptism is for the releasing of debt from sin *(Cleansed)*. The baptism of the Holy Spirit is for the reconstruction of oneself in Christ Jesus, taking out the old and putting in the new, and that is produced by the fire of the Holy Spirit *(Purified)*.

March 12, 2021

Let God purge you of all uncleanness, purifying you of all unrighteousness by the fire of the Holy Spirit for His good purpose! Let us submit and humble ourselves unto the command of the Holy Spirit and the working of God's hand! To God be the glory!

March 12, 2021

Repent, all of you, and turn away from your wicked ways to do that which is good in the sight of God so that you may be preserved by Jesus Christ! For the kingdom of heaven is at hand, and every tree that is not producing good fruit shall be cast out and thrown into the lake of fire that burns with weeping and gnashing of teeth!

March 14, 2021

Oh, my brothers in the Lord, take Adam as an example of a single man in wait for his soulmate (wife). See, though he had seen while he was working tending to the vegetation and the animals of the field and noticed that every animal, beast, and insect had a mate except for him. He, therefore, then being curious, began to then believe in faith that God had created a mate just for him also. But look and see, Adam did not then stop laboring in the will of the Lord and began to go try to find his mate himself neither did he began to wave up a banner stating "I am single and I am right over here" to be in hopes that any of the opposite sex notices, but only instead, he continued with faith focusing on the work and the will of God not seeking a wife but waiting for God to send him the right mate for God's glory when the time was right.

And as he continued and remained faithful in the will of God, then the appointed time came when God sent the woman made specifically for him to Adam and filled with the joy of the Lord was he because the Father had given him the desire of his heart. Therefore, see my beloved brothers in Christ Jesus. For God is not a man that He should lie and neither the son of man that He should repent. God is faithful unto them towards whom He has promised. Therefore, continue to have great faith in the Lord, remaining in the will of God, and wait with patience and trust in the Lord our God, and at the appointed time, He will give you the desires of your heart. Do not become anxious but wait upon the Lord and stay focused on the will of God!

March 21, 2021

No more complaining even when serving others in the will of God. Do not complain every time you continuously see a mistake from others but instead serve with humility, humbleness, and a pure heart. And when others come to you with a complaining spirit, be humble and remain quiet. For it is better to say nothing than to say anything at all. Be quiet and remain humbled in the servitude of the Lord with all love and forgiveness. Hold your peace and let the Lord fight your battles.

March 24, 2021

The Process of Godliness in Christ Jesus:

Faith brings love, love brings righteousness, righteousness brings holiness, holiness brings maturity, maturity brings growth, and growth brings forth good results. Therefore, it all begins with and by faith. For without faith, it is impossible to please God, and it is by faith that one comes unto Christ Jesus with repentance and receives salvation into eternal life.

March 28, 2021

Woe unto you who are of the world! For because you have denied Christ, darkness is coming upon the face of the whole earth, and you shall be in utter darkness. But unto them that truly love the Lord their God and have denied the world and the wickedness thereof shall show forth the light of Christ and shall be forever in God's marvelous light! For the kingdom of darkness and the kingdom of light shall be revealed! For the end is here! Therefore, come unto Christ, repent and deny your flesh so that you may be a part of the kingdom of light that shall be established for everlasting unto everlasting! Glory be unto the Lamb of God who is coming to save them of whom He have redeemed from the world! Blessed are they that truly love Him!

April 1, 2021

God is about to manifest Himself unto His chosen people, and we will be with Him and Him with us, and we will know Him in a deeper way than we have ever known Him before. But as for the ungodly and disbelievers of the truth, His manifestation unto them will not be until the time of His great wrath upon the whole world, which is His second coming.

April 5, 2021

Beloved, whoever abides in hate abides by the will of Satan unknowingly, and whoever abides by the will of Satan is controlled by him and becomes his slaves because they love his ways and not the ways of God; for they are deceived into thinking that the ways of Satan is the way to gain in this life. But little do they know, it is the way of death, and the cost is their own souls. For Jesus Christ said,

> For what shall it profit a man, if he shall gain the whole world, and lose his own soul? Or what shall a man give in exchange for his soul? Whosoever therefore shall be ashamed of me and of my words in this adulterous and sinful generation; of him also shall the Son of man be ashamed, when he cometh in the glory of his Father with the holy angels.

Mark 8:36-38 (KJV)

April 5, 2021

Justification by Faith vs. Justification by the Law:

People who are justified by the law (all laws created by

men, even for religious purposes) are those that believe that just because they do or act upon what is written in the law, they are truly "innocent" and "good" people. But they do not understand that it's not just on the outside of what a person does that other people can see that makes them truly guilty or innocent but only that of which is inside of the heart. In the heart is where the true judgment remains. For the intentions of a person is greater than the actions of them. For this is the reason why mercy and grace were brought forth by Jesus Christ so that many may be redeemed from the judgment (condemnation) of the law that only judges the outside appearance of a person but not that of which is truly going on within their heart as well. For God knew that ever since mankind ate from the tree of knowledge of good and evil, they had evil within their hearts and could not fulfill His commandments in the purest of heart (therefore they were condemned), so He sent the Word (the Son of God) wrapped in flesh into the world to change that. Therefore, this is the reason why Jesus Christ said, "Think not that I am come to destroy the law, or the prophets: I am not come to destroy, but to fulfil" (Matthew 5:17, KJV).

That is why by believing in Christ Jesus, we are justified by faith through mercy and grace. And with Christ, we become enabled to love in the purest of heart to fulfill the whole law (the commandments of God proceeding to the laws of the lands), being made blameless unto all people and perfect unto every good work. Therefore, it is by the love of God that we reap the salvation of the Lord into eternal life, and only by remaining in Christ Jesus is this possible. Do you understand? Jesus Christ was sent to change the condition of the hearts of mankind. And He has given *mercy* and *grace* to help us through the process (to forsake all sin) and *the Holy Spirit* to help us prevail against the kingdom of darkness in spiritual warfare. Therefore, we are not justified by the law but only by *faith*, and your faith will influence your works.

But they that are justified by the law are self-condemned, and in turn, they judge, condemn, and kill others based on the works of the law only and not in the truth. So, therefore, why are they that wholeheartedly trust in man's law self-condemned? It is because instead of putting their faith in Christ Jesus to save their souls, they put their faith in man's judgment. Therefore, they are condemned because they believed in their own law to save them and not in Jesus Christ. For they are cursed and shall surely die, but they that believe in Jesus Christ shall never die, and though a person that believeth in Him may die in the physical, they will yet still have life!

April 6, 2021

The Beloved City of Our Lord:

A time is coming and is nearly upon us (after the second coming of Christ) when all of God's creation will be in harmony once again as it was in the Garden of Eden, but greater will it be than it was before. No more will we eat and kill each other for food nor for gain! But instead, God will provide the vegetation naturally grown from the ground, and He will make it be as food for all creatures and His people. We will not have want of anything but only to please the Lord of all, the Great "I Am," the Father of all creation!

But woe unto them that remains of the world (Satan)! For they will never understand the meaning of this, and jealousy and hate will become them! The ungodly will stand watching us in awe with shame and guilt as we shine forth in the light of Christ while they remain confused and condemned in darkness! For the kingdom of darkness will ask us, "Where do you come from, and who are you?" And we will say, "For we are of the kingdom of light and are the children of God!" Blessed are they that are worthy of entering the beloved city of our Lord and Savior, Jesus Christ! For we will be His people, and He will be our God! For we are the redeemed of the Lord that was saved since the foundation of the world!

Blessed are they that truly believe and have faith in our Lord and Savior, Jesus Christ! For worthy is the Lamb of God who shall preserve all of us that put our trust in Him! For our Redeemer lives and shall reign over all upon the face of the earth. *For every knee shall bow, and every tongue shall confess that Jesus Christ is Lord of all creation!*

April 9, 2021

Revelation of the End 2:

The disappearing of the saints (second flight—to preserve the redeemed) and the rapture of the saints (third flight/final flight out—to save) are two different major and extremely important events in future time.

After God blesses and gives all His people the promises that they asked for, Jesus Christ, in Matthew 24:27-28, speaks about the disappearing of the saints (them that are ready and are purified). We will be *taken to the holy mountain* of our Lord Jesus Christ from out of darkness and into light, and we will be with Him, and He will be with us. No, the rapture has not happened yet at this moment. It's just the separation of them of light from them that are still in darkness. Many lukewarm Christians that are not in Christ Jesus nor truly believed in Christ Jesus will be left in darkness still with the ungodly. But blessed are they that was ready when the thief came on the second flight. *For that was the second flight.*

But as for the lukewarm Christians that are left will have to suffer much with endurance and patience for a time without mercy and grace without forsaking the truth, being in hope of our *Lord and Savior's second coming* so that they may be saved by the rapture of all the saints because darkness shall befall in the dwelling of them spiritually and physically because they were still left in the haven of darkness and was not ready when the thief came on the second flight. Therefore, many of them would have to suffer as the earlier saints did, as in the days of Peter and Paul, unless God gives such mercy and grace to repent and escape the tribulation of the ungodly. Matthew 24:29 explains that darkness shall cover the entire world. After that for a time, Matthew 24:30-31 shows that then the second coming of the Lord will happen and in that same moment (simultaneously/split second, one after the other—as like in the day that the angels of heaven came and got Lot out of Sodom and Gomorrah before great judgment and wrath hits hard upon the ungodly) the angels will gather all of God's people (them that truly believe and love Him) from everywhere (the four winds: on the mountain, and in the places where darkness lies, from within the graves, and in the heavens). This is the second coming of the Lord and the rapture (the third and last flight out for the salvation of all mankind!). For this reason, Christ said, "When these things happen, look up and lift up your heads, for your redemption is drawing near" (Luke 21:28, MEV). After this, the door for salvation will be closed for the rest of all mankind!

No more redemption! So, therefore, the last of mankind that is left after the rapture of all the saints is indeed the kingdom of darkness which is the last of the ungodly! Woe unto them in that number! For they are *marked* for the portion of the lake of fire with the beast, the false prophets, Satan, and the rest of the demons and fallen angels that follow him! In Ezekiel 28:25-26, it also explains this part of the revelation, and in Luke 12:37-38, Jesus Christ explains that He will come to take away His saints in more unknown moments in time's future.

So, then you would ask me, then when was the first flight out? Matthew 27:52-53 explains, right after Christ died on the cross and released redemption (mercy and grace) for all humanity (dead in the grave and living), Christ in the spirit went into Tartarus (hell) to save all the saints that believed in Him from out of hell because before Christ came and died on the cross for our sins those who was righteous in the faith from the beginning after Adam ate from the forbidden tree (all of the future of mankind) was condemned with the ungodly until the time of Christ's death in whom now they and us who believe in Christ Jesus are now saved unto eternal life. So, that means the first rapture was to resurrect the dead in Christ from the graves (all the saints from Adam to John the Baptist and when Christ died physically, His Spirit/soul was released into Tartarus and He saved them all, taking them from out of darkness and into His marvelous light and was freed from hell. Do not get this rapture confused with the rapture of the dead Prophesied about for in the end times, they are not the same. For the rapture of the dead of the end is the beginning part of the second rapture, which is the third and last flight out.) When Christ came, everything changed in the spiritual world and in the land of the living, and mercy and grace began to abound.

But after this *second flight* out that God is about to manifest in the season to come is fulfilled (Which is the separation of the godly taken away from the ungodly to preserve the redeemed of this generation spoken of in Ezekiel 20:33-44), grace and mercy for the wicked and abominable will no longer abound, whoever "claimed" to be saved but was left with the ungodly will have to endure much of a harder fight (this is so that they may repent and turn away from their wickedness being purified to be able to get onto the second rapture (the last and final flight out to save all the saints upon the face of the whole earth) from the great wrath of God (the second coming of the Lord) unto the ungodly (spoken about in Revelation 19:11-21 and Matthew 24:30-31) that will send them into everlasting hellfire.

So, therefore, there are three flights out from among the ungodly, but only two of those flights are raptures. One rapture is passed, one more rapture is left but blessed is that pure and humbled servant that is worthy of the second flight when it comes, for you will be with the rest of the eagles. For this reason, Christ said, “Therefore watch always and pray that you may be counted worthy to escape all these things that will happen and to stand before the Son of Man” (Luke 21:36, MEV). Therefore, wait upon the Lord and trust and believe in Christ Jesus, for He is our Redeemer and will save us.

Matthew 24:28 and Revelation 14:1-5 states that we will be with our Lord in a safe land (on Mount Zion as the 144,000 redeemed from the world and sealed in the truth) and the yoke will be easy, and the burden will be light unto the coming of the Lord (the last rapture for all saints that are living and dead in the grave that remained in Christ Jesus and having endured unto the end not receiving the mark of the beast nor his chip upon the earth from the time of Christ ascended into heaven unto the coming of the Lord, which is one whole generation) when we shall be lifted up unto heaven until the wrath has ended and Satan be put into the bottomless pit for one thousand years as Christ reign over the whole earth. In the beloved city, there will be no wall around our borders, but God, our Father, will be a wall of fire for us spoken of in Zechariah 2:4-5. And after the one thousand years is over, Satan will then be freed to send an army against the beloved city of our Lord, but Satan's efforts will come to naught and would not be able to step one foot in it. For God is our defense. And after Satan is defeated for all eternity, then comes the great and final judgment of all creation. Then all things will be made new. (The evidence of the last of this revelation is spoken in Revelation 19:11-21 and Revelation chapters 20-22.)

April 11, 2021

The verdict is in. The verdict is in! God is about to separate His redeemed from out of the dwelling of the ungodly. For this is to preserve His people from the wrath that is about to befall upon the unholy generation! Woe unto them that remain with the wicked and abominable in that time! For destruction, devastation, and deep darkness cometh! But the redeemed of the Lord shall remain secured in the pavilion of the Lord our God and radiate with the light of Christ! For we are marked on our foreheads by Christ Jesus as the children of God!

Thus saith the Lord God; When I shall have gathered the house of Israel from the people among whom they are scattered, and shall be sanctified in them in the sight of the heathen, then shall they dwell in their land that I have given to my servant Jacob. And they shall dwell safely therein, and shall build houses, and plant vineyards; yea, they shall dwell with confidence, when I have executed judgments upon all those that despise them round about them; and they shall know that I am the Lord their God.

Ezekiel 28:25-26 (KJV)

April 11, 2021

Woe unto you of the world! Because you have rejected and denied God, you have condemned the souls of your own children, lest God has mercy upon them to believe in the truth! For how did you not know that Jesus Christ was trying to save you all from the wrath to come upon the earth? Woe, for indeed, woe, I weep for your souls, beloved, because of what is ahead for you in the future!

April 11, 2021

They that are of the world will face the issues of the world, but we who are redeemed from the world are strangers and sojourners within it in wait for our true home that is not of this world. Therefore, we become separated from the world and think not of the things that they think, neither entangle ourselves with their affairs! For we know not this world but are of the one to come!

April 15, 2021

There Is Only One God and No Other:

Woe unto you who are of the world. Do you not know that you mock and insult the Lord our God by creating false gods and false idols and worshiping them? For the Great "I Am" is the only one and true living God, and there are no other gods before Him. How is it that you think you can replace His supremacy with images, statues, robots, and objects that you have concocted from your own wicked imaginations that you have crafted by your own hands or by that of which God has created Himself by the power of His own hand and the word of His own mouth? For do you not know, God is greater than all these things, creatures, and spirits that He has created all around you and in your midst? Do you not know that they are all submitted and subjected to Him and cannot do anything that He does not allow? For even the earth and all the outer realms of the earth and beyond of which we know not are all His master craftsmanship.

For He alone created and named them all, and no one created nor birthed Him. For He always was, is, and always will be God alone and no one can replace Him, let alone be or is worthy enough to do so! For you should be joyous and grateful unto Him because of the greatness of His majesty, because if God was no more everything that we know, everything that we see, and everything that we are would cease to exist! For there would not even be a reason to use the word "existence" any longer. Even that word itself would be extinct along with word and speech in general! For you truly do not know the greatness of God, and all knowledge we do know of our God is as little as a spec in the dust of the sand!

For no one, not even the angels of heaven, fully know Him but only He Himself! Therefore, it is not the wicked things that you imagine nor the crafted things and created beings that you should fear! But what you should fear is the God who created and made them all to be. For He can not only destroy them all if He desired but also can torment their flesh and souls before and even after death for eternity! Woe unto you ungodly; you would do well to repent working out your own salvation with fear and trembling! For even Satan fears Him and knows that the time of his everlasting torment is near. And the end is upon us; therefore, all of you upon the face of the earth come into the salvation of the Lord quickly before the narrow gate closes upon you with no more time for redemption, lest the wrath of God comes upon you suddenly! Woe unto them that falls into the hands of the fiery and fierce anger of the Lord of all creation! For when it comes to God, the death of the flesh is the least of your worries, for it is what comes next that you should be afraid of!

For this reason, God so loved the world that He gave His only begotten Son that whosoever believes in Him (Jesus Christ) should not perish but have everlasting life! For God does not desire you to suffer the death of the soul but desires to save you from it by you coming unto Christ with repentance turning away from your wicked ways, and you shall be saved! For when you truly believe in Christ Jesus to do His will, then He will save you from your sins! For with man, this is impossible, but with Christ Jesus, all things are possible unto them that believe! And with God, nothing is impossible! Therefore beloved, believe with faith unto salvation so that you may be saved from the day of destruction!

April 18, 2021

For the Holy Spirit lusts against the flesh for the sake of saving the soul that is within it, but the flesh lusts against the Holy Spirit for the sake of trying to condemn the soul that is led by the Holy Spirit. Therefore, let us not walk in the ways of the flesh, God forbid, lest our souls be condemned unto eternal death. But instead, let us walk in the ways of the Holy Spirit, for in Him there is life, yay, eternal life indeed. For it's not by power nor by might but only by the Holy Spirit we shall live! Therefore, glory be unto God for the redemption of His true people who walk not according to the flesh but only by His Holy Spirit! For the flesh operates by the ways (the will) of the world (Satan), but the Holy Spirit operates by the ways (the will) of the Lord our God!

April 18, 2021

Them who are of the world are condemned unto eternal death and unto death do they proclaim it upon themselves. But we who believe in Jesus Christ have received eternal life, and unto life do we proclaim it by faith upon ourselves!

April 21, 2021

Wake up, children of God, stop trying to please man, and start pleasing God with your whole life! For you cannot please God and man! Choose ye this day whom you will serve, the Lord our God or the world (Satan)! But as for me and my house, we will serve the Lord! Glory be unto the Lamb of God who sits upon the throne! Blessed be the Lord of all!

April 23, 2021

Servanthood vs. Man-Pleasers:

My beloved brothers and sisters, saved and unsaved, known and unknown. Please listen and understand the difference between serving everyone in the will of God and being a man-pleaser, for they are not the same. For serving everyone in the will of God is to humble yourself with humility without complaining, and with goodwill (pure heart and without partiality) to do what has been asked of you by man as service unto God by resisting no man *but* still yet uphold the standard and will of God (which is the love of God) in integrity as the temple of the Holy Spirit.

But.

As for the man pleasers, they out of fear of what would happen if they offend a person, forsake all goodness, innocence, and integrity so that they may save their own lives (influence, status, fame, power, control, money, vainglory, jobs, etc.). For man-pleasers are they that compromise with the ways of the world so that they may gain "favor" and "honor" (to be liked) by the world. Therefore, since they wanted to be loved by the world, indeed they are of it and do great evil, oppression, and abominations in the sight of God, adding on more guilt, confusion, and condemnation within their wicked hearts. For man-pleasers are those that will take hold of the mark of the beast with haste, and by taking it, they will forsake their own souls.

But.

Blessed by God are they that love the Lord our God, for they do not love their lives unto death but instead kept the faith and endured. Therefore, they shall be saved and receive eternal life with them that is written in the Lamb's Book of Life. But woe unto the man-pleasers, if they don't come unto the Lord with repentance turning away from their wicked ways before it is too late, the lake of fire with the ungodly, the beast, the false prophet, and Satan will be their portion!

April 25, 2021

Oh, how marvelous it is to sing a new song of melody from the heart unto the Lord? For, at the moment, it is like a river of life that never ends that uplifts even the weariest of souls. For you are in the presence of God, and everything and everyone else just fades away, and the spirit of peace overwhelms you with great and unspeakable joy.

April 25, 2021

True Worship:

True worship unto God is not within doing religious practices and traditions! True worship unto God is to abide in the love of God! A church building cannot save your soul from the day of destruction, neither the wrath of God, which is already here and is to come! Many of you (even some of the greatest) are deceived by Satan and false teachers, false preachers, false prophets, and false christs! For did you not already know, only by believing in Christ Jesus and abiding by His words can one truly be saved? Therefore, all of you, throw away religion and tradition, fakeness and performance, idol worship and conceitedness, vainglory and man-pleasing, pride and self-service, ignorance and wicked desire, judgment and gossip, arrogance and rudeness, manipulation and control, lies and deceit, ill will and schemes, jealousy and hate, lust and covetousness, compromise and perversion, witchcraft, abomination, and wrath. For these are the ways of the flesh and the world (Satan) and produce great darkness, and these such things should not be found within a true believer of Jesus Christ but instead purged away from out of us. For we do not operate in ways of the flesh but only by the Holy Spirit, for we must become dead to the ways of the flesh but only alive in the Holy Spirit.

Therefore, put into practice love and kindness, truth and conviction, mercy and forgiveness, faith and righteousness, goodness and purity, sound correction and compassion, justice and self-reflection, humbleness and humility, temperance and meekness, selflessness and understanding, giving and servanthood, and do it all unto God as service unto our Lord so that God may be pleased with your works and praise and glorify God. For these attributes are a part of the fruit of the Spirit. And the fruit of the Spirit is installed by God's mercy and grace within all that are willing to receive it. Therefore, praise and glorify our Lord for every good work and good speech. Do not glorify nor praise yourselves, for, without God, nothing good is possible! For with man perfection (love) is impossible, but with God nothing is impossible, and with Christ Jesus, all things are possible unto them that believe in Him!

April 25, 2021

God cares about your heart and soul more than your shouting and dancing. For when you are purged from all unrighteousness, then you would be enabled by Jesus Christ to praise and worship Him in the Holy Spirit and in truth with the pureness of heart and clean hands.

April 26, 2021

We who truly believe in Christ Jesus will be in the midst of darkness (on the earth), but we will not be in its presence (in their dwelling). We will be around them but not in their company.

April 27, 2021

The Wrath of God:

Many are facing the wrath of God within this hour. Many are dying horrible deaths by diseases, the slaughter of man, beast, animals, famine, and natural disasters. Others are becoming weak in their spirits and have forsaken the path of goodness and righteousness and instead turned to wickedness, evil, oppression, perversion, theft, abomination, hardened hearts, witchcraft, greed and the love of money, sorcery, sexual immorality, and idolatry worshiping false gods that do not exist nor are they God alone. For there is only one true and living God, and besides Him, there is no other. For He is the Great "I Am." For deep darkness has befallen into the hearts of the wicked, opening them up to demonic possession because they are following the ways of the world (Satan) and not the ways of God. For the workload, stress, and turmoil of the law enforcement and armed forces have and shall increase. For because of the deep darkness, they will be forced to do great evil and cause great deaths upon the wicked. Massacres from city to city running red with the blood of humanity shall it be (for this is the wrath of God upon this nation of whom forsaken Him for nothing). Very dark shall this nation become (unholy, foul, and a haven of demons, devils, and every unclean thing)—woe unto them with children in these days. But blessed by God are His redeemed remnant, for He shall save and deliver them from all these things and set them upon His holy mountain as great fire and destruction is down below. For everyone that puts their trust in God shall be saved and preserved. And they shall remain in the light of God. Indeed, blessed are they but woe unto them that are down below for it shall be darkened, very dark.

April 28, 2021

The Purge of the Fire of the Holy Spirit:

Within seasons of the years 2019-2021, through your tests, trials, suffering, and struggles, God was trying to produce in all of you fruit that's worthy and good and kill off of you the wickedness of the flesh, but many of you have not been submissive to the working of God's hand and have not been humbling yourselves to Him purging your vessels of all *unrighteousness.* How is it that you did not know that God was trying to purify you to escape the next wave of the wrath of God that is about to befall upon the world? For just as in the times of Moses, when the children of Israel withstood God by their ignorance and rebellion and walked in the wilderness for forty years when they could have already been in the promise that God was trying to give to them a long time ago but because they were not willing to go through the fulfillment of the purging of the fire of the Holy Spirit, the people of that time did not receive it, and as they have done so have you been with God also. And do you know what happened to them because of their constant complaining, continuous doubting and mockings of the Lord their God, and turning away from the ways of righteousness so that they may do greater evil, wickedness, perversion, and abomination in the sight of God?

I will tell you what happened to them. Because they didn't submit and humble themselves to the purging and cleaning of their own vessels so that God may take them to new and better habitations to save them from perishing, they, therefore, died there and did not make it, and only their descendants were able to receive it. Woe unto you who are of the world! Woe unto you who claim to be saved but do not want to submit and humble yourselves unto the will of God! For darkness, destruction, devastation, death, mourning, and desolation is coming for you and is nigh! Therefore, repent quickly, turning away from your wicked ways, and submit yourself unto the will of God, lest you suffer with the ungodly in the hell on earth that they will have to go through! Repent! For the time is a hand, and darkness shall cover the entire world!

April 28, 2021

The Word of God does not just come to speak blessings and peace, for He also comes to speak warnings and sound corrections so that you may listen and be saved from the day of destruction! This is also part of the love of God!

April 28, 2021

The Working of God's Hands Unto the One That Submits to the Baptism of Water and the Fire of the Holy Spirit:

My beloved brothers and sisters, after you are baptized by water, you will feel a weight of debts to sin fall off of you, and you will be lighter in your spirit. For you will have shown God that your confession of Christ Jesus is sincere in your heart because you submitted and humbled yourself to the requirement of being baptized by the baptism of water. This is the cleansing of vessels. The Holy Spirit will then purify it by fire (being purged from all unrighteousness) so that the Holy Spirit can use you for His glory. This is the baptism of the Holy Spirit.

Whosoever, therefore, accomplishes these two requirements fulfilling the baptism by Christ Jesus is freed in the Spirit and are dead to the ways of the flesh, and are instead alive in the Holy Spirit and that with fire (power) and are indeed new creatures. For the old man is passed away and now here is the new. For no demon in hell will be able to stop that one from fulfilling God's will because it is no longer the flesh that is in control, but only the Holy Spirit and the Holy Spirit is Jesus Christ! Therefore, it will be Christ who useth you and not you yourself! For He is the one that said, "For my yoke is easy, and my burden is light" (Matthew 11:30, KJV).

April 29, 2021

Unto you, that love the Lord your God and believe in Jesus Christ, be ye not troubled. For all these things must come to pass so that all may be fulfilled for the coming of our Lord and Savior, Jesus Christ! Therefore, be not afraid, anxious, nor have anxiety! But be of good courage, trust, and have faith with patience in Jesus Christ, knowing that He will keep your hearts and minds subjected to His divine will unto His coming! And with prayer and fasting, remain in His Word!

May our Lord and Savior, Jesus Christ, be with you always, even unto the ends of this world! Be blessed, my beloved brothers and sisters, in the salvation of our Lord and beloved Father of all! For our Redeemer lives, have great faith, and believe in Him! For He will not allow His righteous to be forsaken nor their seed begging for bread!

April 29, 2021

My Lord and Savior Jesus Christ said to me, "Come, Daniel, let's go." And I responded, saying, "Where are we going, my Lord?" He looked back at me and said, "To change the world."

April 30, 2021

God, my Father, let faith be in me and remain forevermore. Let fear scatter and be no more. For perfect love casts out all fears. And, Lord, you are my love that extends to all things. Therefore, thank You, Jesus, for my heart is in thine hands. In You does my heart safely trust and is comforted.

April 30, 2021

Oh, beloved mankind, look how far you have fallen! You have settled with the name humanity. You have forgotten your true purpose and, in turn, lost your identity. You know not what nor who you are. Come unto Jesus Christ with repentance believing in Him and His words, and abide in it. For He will redeem you, you will find your true identity and purpose in the Lord. If you submit unto Christ Jesus, you will know the truth, and the truth will set you free!

April 30, 2021

Who Are You, Mankind?

Oh, mankind, you have strayed so far from who you are and have forgotten your purpose. Satan has deceived you for so long that you don't even remember who you are. Do you not see the earth that God had put in our charge? Do you not see the state that it is in? It weeps and cries unto God because you have forgotten your purpose and your identity. Your ancestors in ancient times have forsaken the way of life and have chosen to destroy it instead, and you are doing the same and even worse than your fathers by polluting it with trash and foul sin. Do you not see all the creatures that God had put in our charge from the beginning? Do you not see the state that they are even in because you have forgotten your purpose and your identity? For how is it that from the beginning, we were meant to serve them in the love of God, but yet now we have bent them to our own will and have enslaved them? For they do not have homes anymore but instead feel like slaves in cages (yes, even in a house made by men). Do you not see that they are all going extinct one species at a time because you have forgotten your purpose and your identity? We were meant to be in harmony and in sync with nature and all the creatures thereof (For this is and was the fulfillment of the divine will of God), but when was it that we started destroying everything that God has created because of selfish desires, greed, and jealousy? Why have we allowed ourselves to listen to Satan's enticements for so long that we have forgotten who we are? Do you not know who we are?

We are God's children unto whom He has given dominion of the whole entire world and everything in it; He has given us the keys! He made us "gods" (Jesus Christ declared it in John 10:34-38)! For Psalm 82 says,

> "I have said, "You are gods, sons of the Most High, all of you, but you all shall die like men, and fall like a man, O princes."

Psalm 82:6-7 (MEV)

Please don't misunderstand the meaning and take offense to what I am conveying here, lest you miss the purpose (point) thereof! If we do not live in the way of our purpose, the earth and everything in it cannot either! When the head falls, so does the body, for the body cannot live without its head! And because the head (all of humanity equally) have forgotten their purpose (that the Great "I Am" our Father, the God of all has bestowed upon us all), their identities have followed and then turned to confusion, perversion, and lastly, abomination!

For lack of purpose leads to death! So, what was and is supposed to be our purpose again, you may ask? We were and are in charge of maintaining the creation that God our Father has created (the earth and everything in it), and from the beginning, unto now, we have failed because humanity has been trying to do it without God! For God is the only one and true living God, and there are no other gods besides Him, neither before Him! He is the God of all alone, and we must submit to His divine will to know our identity and to fulfill and remain in the purpose that He has for us rightly! For humanity is nothing but the purposeless condition of mankind! Therefore, come unto Christ with repentance believing in Him and His words, and He will make you into a new creature holy and acceptable in His sight who truly knows their identity and the purpose of God for their lives! Come beloved and know your true self in Christ Jesus!

But nevertheless, know that though humanity has failed, Jesus Christ will not. Our Lord is coming to make all things new. Blessed be the name of our Lord and Savior, Jesus Christ. For He is worthy above all to be praised, glorified, and honored. Until then, let us be used by Him to do better.

> So God created man in His own image; in the image of God He created him; male and female He created them. God blessed them and said to them, "Be fruitful and multiply, and replenish the earth and subdue it.

> Rule over the fish of the sea and over the birds of the air and over every living thing that moves on the earth." Then God said, "See, I have given you every plant yielding seed which is on the face of all the earth and every tree which has fruit yielding seed. It shall be food for you. To every beast of the earth and to every bird of the air and to everything that creeps on the earth which has the breath of life in it, I have given every green plant for food." And it was so. God saw everything that He had made, and indeed it was very good. So the evening and the morning were the sixth day.
>
> Genesis 1:27-31 (MEV)

May 1, 2021

Difference between the Goats and the Sheep:

The goats always tend to their own self-gain and only give to get back while the sheep humbly help and give to whoever they can, however they can, whenever they can, even to the point of sometimes sacrificing their own personal pleasures. For they give and expect nothing back in return neither hold unto an account to enslave their neighbors onto debts. The sheep's deeds are something to be admired. To those that have an ear, let them hear!

May 2, 2021

God's judgment upon lukewarm Christianity has come!

Many things are going to be exposed this season!

May 3, 2021

The True Believer vs. The Lukewarm Christian:

We have two types of believers in our midst: the true believer and the lukewarm believer. One of them is a deceiver sent from Satan to deceive. The lukewarm believer loves their sin and does not desire the will of God and misuse the spirit of grace and mercy so that they may continue to sin, always becoming offended when they are corrected and warned, and hating that which is good! *The true believer* desires to be freed from sin and desires to do the will of God with the pureness of heart! Blessed be the true believers, for because they desire to be free, they shall be free indeed! Why? Because *they believed* that Jesus Christ will deliver them! But as for the l*ukewarm believer,* if they do not repent from a true and pure heart unto God, they shall not be freed but instead, go into deeper darkness and become condemned, lest God has mercy upon them to be able to repent and become saved! Why? Because they truly *did not believe* in Jesus Christ, the only begotten Son of the living God but instead was only in the form of godliness! For if they did truly believe, they would have been thoroughly cleaned and purged by the fire of the Holy Spirit! But they have been fighting against the purification, and now they have become exposed with no more covering for their sins!

May 4, 2021

Warning Unto Churches All over the World:

Unto you church leaders and church people (American churches & churches all over the world), do you believe that God just cares about your church services? Do you truly believe that attending services in your temples and abiding by the practices within it is the reasonable service of worship that He requires? I say unto you, you have been blinded by Satan's lies. For these actions are not what God requires of you but are only practices and traditions of religious men. For this is what God truly requires of you, to keep His commandments by obeying His Word, loving Him with all your heart, soul, mind, and strength, *loving Him more than anything and anyone else.* And to love your neighbors who are also your brothers and sisters (of whom you have not known) as you love yourselves and as God loves you without partiality, for these are the true requirements of worship that God has commanded all of you to fulfill in His sight. The relationship of God & the love of God. For even the Apostle Paul said,

> I urge you therefore, brothers, by the mercies of God, that you present your bodies as a living sacrifice, holy, and acceptable to God, which is your reasonable service of worship. Do not be conformed to this world, but be transformed by the renewing of your mind, that you may prove what is the good and acceptable and perfect will of God.

Romans 12:1-2 (MEV)

But you have been so blinded and distracted by religious practices and traditions that you have forgotten about what God truly cares about, and that is the condition of your heart and soul. But only when you have established the love of God and the relationship of God within you, you would be able to come into the house of God and praise Him with the pureness of heart and in the Spirit of truth. "While it is said: 'Today, if you will hear His voice, do not harden your hearts as in the rebellion'" (Hebrews 3:15, MEV).

But if you do not heed to the correction of the Lord and continue in wickedness, abominations, oppression, and causing of iniquity upon God's people and come into God's house to mock and blaspheme His Word as hypocrites and like the Pharisees and scribes in the time of Christ, then now I shall declare to you the warning of the Lord concerning you, religious lukewarm Christians! For even God sent His true prophets to instruct you and warn concerning these things, but you have not listened to their corrections and judgments, but instead, you have taken their words lightly, condemned, spoken evil of them, turned them aside, and brought their spirits down.

Therefore, if you continue in the wickedness of your evil hearts, God's wrath will also be upon you and the church buildings of which you have called by His name, for they shall all be destroyed because you have not kept His Word nor the love of God within you, but you have all sought after your own agendas and personal gain.

> Thus says the Lord:
>
> Heaven is My throne, and earth is My footstool. Where then is the house that you could build for Me? And where is the place of My rest? For My hand made all those things, thus all those things have come to be, says the Lord. But to this man I will look, even to him who is poor and of a contrite spirit, and trembles at My word. He who kill a bull is as if he kills a man; he who sacrifices a lamb, as if he breaks a dog's neck; he who offers a grain offering, as if he offers swine's blood; he who burns incense, as if he blessed an idol. They have chosen their own ways, and their soul delights in their abominations; I also will choose their punishments and will bring their fears on them, because when I called, no one answered; when I spoke, they did not listen; but they did evil before My eyes and chose that in which I did not delight.
>
> Isaiah 66:1-4 (MEV)

Woe unto you, lukewarm Christians, for God's judgment upon you is coming! Therefore repent, all of you, turning away from your wicked ways, lest you be marked by the wrath of God with the world!

> Come to Me, all you who labor and are heavily burdened, and I will give you rest. Take My yoke upon you, and learn from Me. For I am meek and lowly in heart, and you will find rest for your souls. For My yoke is easy, and My burden is light.
>
> Matthew 11:28-30 (MEV)

May 4, 2021

Danyell's Prayer of Faith about Destiny:

Many of you are not going to like nor love my posts nor that of which I shall speak and do, but I did not come to be liked and loved! I was sent into the world so that I may do the Great "I Am" (who is my Father) will! So that He may be pleased with my work unto eternity! And I'm bringing home as much of my brothers and sisters as the Lord allows with me into paradise! Lord, let Your will be done, oh Father, not my will, but Your will! And let Your will be my will and my will Yours, so that You may use me to fulfill Your divine will within Your perfection in the pureness of heart and sound mind unto eternal life! Not by my own power, nor by my own might, but only by Your Holy Spirit in Jesus Christ's mighty name! I trust and believe in You, oh Lord, by faith, knowing that this shall be fulfilled in Your divine timing! For I can do nothing without You, Father! For You are my everything and everything good within me! For the glory of the Lord shall be revealed! All glory, all praise, and all honor be unto the Lamb of God who sits upon the throne! Thank You, Jesus Christ, my Lord, Savior, and Redeemer of all His people! For you alone, oh God, are worthy of it all! Blessed be the name of our Lord! Amen!

May 5, 2021

Understand God's Reproof:

Oh, my dearest beloved brothers and sisters, saved and unsaved, known and unknown, seen and unseen, please understand. God's corrections and warnings are meant to help you get into a place of true repentance. Though it may come with a strong hand, its purpose is to save. Though it may come with great fire and strictness, its purpose is to direct. Though it may come putting great fear within your heart, its purpose is to get you to run ever so quickly into the arms of your only salvation and life, Jesus Christ.

God's corrections and warnings are like barriers, barricades, the human capacity of oxygen concerning the depths of the darkest parts of the ocean down deep below, and the atmospheric heavens above the face of the earth. You may not understand why they are there, but you should not be offended by them, nor is it wise to be. But instead, know that they are there for a reason and should be taken heed to.

Wise and blessed are those children that do not try and force their way past the boundaries and tear them down. For if they did, they would have surely suffered much and (God forbid) perish. But instead, after noticing the boundaries, those children quickly turned around, running back with fear and trembling unto that of which the boundaries were meant to keep safe. For their lives and souls would remain preserved and saved in the arms of their beloved Father. Blessed are they that love and believe in the Lord our God. For in Jesus Christ they have life and that more abundantly, yay, eternal life indeed!

Unto them that have an ear, let them hear.

May 5, 2021

Many of you will have to die for the faith, but yet, in the end, you will be woken up into eternal life.

> You will be betrayed by parents and brothers and relatives and friends. And they will put some of you to death. You will be hated by all men for My name's sake, but not a hair of your head shall perish. In your endurance you will gain your souls.
>
> Luke 21:16-19 (MEV)

But there are some that are meant to remain in the life of the flesh to fulfill the will (servitude) of God with patience and endurance unto the coming of the Lord. For Christ said, "Truly I say to you, there are some standing here who shall not taste death before they see the Son of Man coming in His kingdom" (Matthew 16:28, MEV).

Both of us believers, the ones that must go for a little while and the ones that must stay for a little while unto the coming of the Lord, I pray that both of us be strong and courageous, having great faith in Jesus Christ our Lord and Savior unto eternal life in paradise. For the Lord is faithful unto them of whom He has promised. Endure in the goodness of the Lord and the power of the Holy Spirit until it is all over. For blessed and filled with the joy of the Lord shall we be because our names are written within the Lamb's Book of Life.

May 6, 2021

God's Compassion for His People:

The Word of the Lord came to me and said, "Daniel, I am the first and am with the last. Though I will separate the redeemed with you from the wicked to preserve them, I must still also go for a time to be in the thick darkness in hopes of saving the rest of My people. For though they have rejected Me and My ways, if they even in that time truly repent crying out unto Me with a pure and sincere heart, with faith, then I will be there to purify and save their souls and deliver them from the wrath of My coming. For I was numbered with the transgressor so that even the least of our brothers and sisters may be saved. For I am even the last. I did this to confirm to them how much I love them. For I desire mercy rather than sacrifice and to save that which was lost.

In the time appointed, I will call upon you, and you shall answer. You shall hear My voice clearly and know when I speak. Do not be afraid nor fear, for I will be with you, and you shall be with Me. For if I am for you, nothing nor anyone will be able to stand against you. I will make them all fear you. I am and will always be with you and never leave you nor forsake you. You are My chosen. Trust in Me, have faith, and believe in Me also. I will keep your feet from slipping; you are in My divine hands. I, even I will never let you go, My beloved son."

May 7, 2021

Observe how the caterpillar builds a cocoon, and after it is completed, that caterpillar dwells in it in solitude until the time needed to remain in it is completed. For the caterpillar is in the midst of a mini-morphosis, and no one can speed up the process, nor can the caterpillar come out of the cocoon prematurely. For it must take the time necessary to complete the transformation, and when the mini-morphosis is completed, it is then enabled to break free from out of the cocoon of the past and return to it no more.

For the caterpillar is now no more the same creature that it was before, neither of the same mindset of its old self. For though it was in darkness, it is now turned into a butterfly filled with glorious beauty which captivates the eyes of many in the light. For the old creature had passed and now here is the new, with no shadow of turning back. Therefore, just as it is for the caterpillar's process of transformation into a butterfly within a cocoon, it is the same for one in solitude seeking the Lord's face in fasting and prayer in the Word of God (the Bible). Unto them that have an ear let them hear and unto whom it is meant, let them receive it.

May 8, 2021

My beloved brothers and sisters in Christ Jesus, when God is about to do something great within our lives, at times, He first shows us the promises before the time of its manifestations. Therefore beloved, in the midst of the wait by faith, don't become anxious, worried, and filled with anxiety because of what you may see or have heard happening to the promises that were meant for you, for this is the testing of your faith. Do not be troubled nor quit believing in Christ Jesus in the midst of the process. For you will receive all the promises of God in its proper timing of which the Lord our God has appointed it to be for each and every one of them. Do not rush it because of anxiousness or anxiety, for this can mess up everything. For no one truly knows the appointed time for an event of a thing to occur but only God alone. Therefore, in the meantime, don't dwell on it (worrying and coveting) but instead let patience perfect its work within you, having unwavering faith in God knowing that all of His promises unto you shall be made manifest, remaining watchful in the Word with prayer in a grateful heart unto God. For God's timing is the best timing, and if one operates in His divine time, the promises will come in smoothly and be fulfilled in abundance with overwhelming joy along with an increase of faith in a higher level in Christ Jesus. Therefore, I pray unto God, beloved, that your faith shall not fail you but instead, increase unto even greater glory in Christ Jesus that His will may be fulfilled within you unto every good work without wavering in the faith unto the coming of the Lord. Fight the good fight of faith and remain in His love and mercy.

May 8, 2021

Do not become so busy to where you forget to feed your

soul and spirit with fasting and prayer in the Word of God so that you may be strengthened by Jesus Christ to do that which He speaks as good and abstain from that which He speaks as bad. For indeed, the Word of God is the way and the life and speaks no lie. For He is the truth, and God is good!

May 8, 2021

The promises that you desire the most are the very things that God will sometimes use to grow your faith through patience and endurance. And the greatest promise of them all is eternal life in paradise with our beloved creator and Lord of all. Therefore beloved, let patience perfect its work within you.

May 8, 2021

Do not let Satan use the cares of this life to rob you of your growth in Christ Jesus, neither let it make you forfeit the salvation of your soul! Have faith in Jesus Christ, believe in Him concerning all things with unwavering faith! First, seek the kingdom of God and all of His righteousness, and then He will give you the desires of your heart! Seek God in the pureness of heart, not for gain but only to build your relationship with Him and to do His will in the Spirit of truth unto the coming of the Lord in the love of God!

May 9, 2021

The Story of Jesus Christ and the Redemption 1:

There are three that reign over the heavens, the earth, and everything in them and outside of them and beyond them. For in heaven, the three bear record of everything that happens in the earth, with mankind, every spirit, every creature, and every being in it. The three are: the Father of all, the Word (who is the Son of God/ The Lamb of God), and the Holy Spirit (who is The Sword/ the Advocate/ the Comforter). And though they have separate responsibilities, they are only one, who is the Great "I Am," the creator and the only one true and living God of all creation, and there is no other god but Him alone! For anything else that claims or is claimed to be a god is a liar and a lie.

Now one day, the Word came down from heaven and impregnated itself into the womb of a virgin named Mary and birthed itself at the appointed time wrapped in the flesh as a human baby boy. From that day on, He was called Jesus. For Jesus Christ came into the world to die on the cross to save the living and the dead from our sins and rose from the grave becoming made alive again in His own body on the third day after His death on the cross so that we may also remain in hope and faith for His return to reign over the whole earth.

For this was the plan of God since the beginning of mankind. In the beginning, after God created the heavens, the earth, and everything living in the earth, He then made mankind, whose name was Adam. Adam was the first man on earth, and he represented us all. God made mankind the ruler and the keeper of the earth and of all the creation within it (not its destroyer), for God made mankind in His own image and likeness. He made us with purity, innocence, His goodness, and a mind to think (which is also free will and He did this because He loved us. Therefore, He desired us to desire His will freely. This was not a mistake, this was love as a Father to His children). He made mankind, all of His creation on earth, and the earth itself perfect. Even to where He admired His work repeatedly saying for each of His creations, "It is good."

(For God is diligent with His work, and all of it is and was done in the patience of His timing, for the timing of God is different from how He made the timing of the world. And there is no error in God, nor have, and nor will He ever create anything in error. Everything He creates is the way that it is meant to be. Everything by God is made perfect and beautiful in the way in which He intended it. *But listen well and take heed,* if one tries to change something that God has intended for His creation to do and to be and tried to make it do and be other things that it was not intended for, then, is not that creation corrupted, distorted, and perverse and is now an abomination that causes confusion? For indeed, the error is not with God but only with the deeds of mankind's choices. For God does not create mistakes. But we will get more on that subject some other time. So let us continue with the story.)

So, God was and is the Father of us all, so Adam obeyed

his Father as a good son and did all that our Father commanded him. Then God created the first woman that was made from the rib that came out of mankind, and woman was made to help mankind fulfill the will of God, helping each other selflessly for the will of God. For that is the purpose of woman, and she represented all the women. For woman was later named Eve, for she was the first woman and the mother of all mankind.

Now Adam and Eve did something that God warned them not to do. Because Satan entices woman, she then became deceived by Satan's lies and ate the forbidden fruit off of the tree of the knowledge of good and evil. And as she ate the forbidden fruit, woman being already deceived was used by Satan to entice mankind to eat the forbidden fruit also, and because mankind was weak, he became swayed into eating it also. And at that moment that mankind ate from that forbidden tree and disobeyed God, *everything* changed, destroying the natural order of the earth and every creature and creation in it from the way that God had made it to be. For sin and the evils of the flesh had entered into the hearts of mankind and in all flesh (every living creature). And at that moment, the gates of Tartarus busted wide open with great heat to draw in the souls of all humanity. For all the future souls of humanity righteous and wicked, good and evil, pure and defiled were condemned to hell with much torment and suffering. Mankind did not realize that because of his disobedience unto the will of God, he has condemned the souls of all future generations into hell. For this reason, mankind's heart and soul ached badly unto death many times within him, and in turn, so was the woman. But because God loved Adam and Eve, He forgave them, healed their hearts, and showed them mercy and care.

For God already knew from the beginning of time and Him creating the earth that this would happen. God wrote this story from the beginning to the end, and only He knows the end. Therefore, He allowed this misfortune of mankind. Why, you may ask? Well, don't you already know? God did it for His love's sake concerning mankind. And because God already knew the choices that we made and will make was and is going to be wicked and sinful, He already had a marvelous plan to save our souls from eternal death and free us from the sinful nature of the tree of knowledge of good and evil and deliver us into eternal life in which all things shall be made new.

And that plan was the man, Jesus Christ. Hallelujah, glory be unto God! For God sent Himself (the Word) into the world for the fight of our souls. He endured great torments and temptations, endured the evil acts from the wicked intentions of men, was bruised for our transgressions, beaten for our iniquity, and died on the cross for the redemption to free us from our sins, for He humbled Himself as a lamb unto death for slaughter. For this purpose, He has made it so that whosoever believes in the name of Jesus Christ, in Jesus Christ Himself, and in His words, to obey them, receiving the baptism of water and that also of the Holy Spirit with fire shall be saved from eternal death and be delivered unto eternal life.

For when Jesus Christ died on the cross (within the three days of death), He released His Spirit into the Tartarus (hell), bearing forth the glorious light of God and delivered from hell all the souls of His people from the beginning generations of Adam and Eve unto the days of John the Baptist and raptured them unto the heavens as they came up from the graves within His glorious light! For this was the rapture of the dead of all the generations before Christ. (The first rapture.) For the Lamb of God fought gloriously and was triumphant in victory against Satan and his army, and conquered death in His hands. For concerning this, the Apostle Paul said,

> But grace was given to each one of us according to the measure of the gift of Christ. Therefore He says: "When He ascended on high, He led captivity captive, and gave gifts to men." (In saying, "He ascended," what does it mean but that He also descended first into the lower parts of the earth? He who descended is also He who ascended far above all the heavens that He might fill all things.)
>
> Ephesians 4:7-9 (MEV)

Therefore after Christ then arose from the grave on the third day, He said His last parting words,

> And Jesus came and spake unto them, saying, All power is given unto me in heaven and in earth. Go ye therefore, and teach all nations, baptizing them in the name of the Father, and of the Son, and of the Holy Ghost:

> teaching them to observe all things whatsoever I have commanded you: and, lo, I am with you alway, even unto the end of the world. Amen.
>
> Matthew 28:18-20 (KJV)

"He who believes and is baptized will be saved. But he who does not believe will be condemned" (Mark 16:16, MEV).

Then He ascended unto glory to sit at the right hand of God as they watched Him in awe and praised God. And He remains there until the time of His return (second coming) to make all things new and put His enemies under His feet. For there are many gifts that God has left upon the earth after His ascension. They are:

The redemption—by believing in Christ Jesus from the heart and the confession of Him from their mouths with repentance to be freed from the condemnation of eternal death and receive the salvation of eternal life.

Mercy and grace—to help in our mistakes through the transition of becoming a new creature in the Holy Spirit and enables us to fulfill all righteousness in God's divine will for our lives. For favor and blessings dwell in this.

The baptism—this cannot be fulfilled within a person unless that person truly believes that Jesus Christ will save them from their sins and purge them from all unrighteousness.

• The baptism of water—for the releasing of debts to sin. (The cleansing.)

• The baptism of the Holy Spirit by fire—to end the committing of sin ripping it from off of your life so that you sin no more, only then submitting unto the love and fear of God in the fruit of the Spirit with fasting and prayer. Becoming holy and acceptable in the sight of God. For whoever the Son of Man sets free, he is free indeed. (The purification.)

The Gift of the Holy Spirit and That with Fire:

The Holy Spirit—the sword, which is the Word of God that can cut deep into even the hardest of hearts and shuts the mouths of men. For He is God living within us.

The fire—after one is found worthy in the sight of God being made holy and acceptable for His good use, the fire of the Holy Spirit will consume them with power from on high. They will be enabled to heal the sick, raise the dead, cast out demons bringing forth deliverance, bring sight to the blind, and make whole the crippled. For according to the measure of one's faith, nothing will be impossible for them. This is the power and glory of God! Remember, beloved, to always give God the glory unto all that bear witness, for it is Him that uses you and not you yourself. Therefore, neither praise nor glorify yourself. For it is done not by your own power, neither by your own might, but only by the Holy Spirit, glorify Him so that His people may be saved! For God is worthy to be praised, glorified, and honored above all flesh and spirit. *Glorify Him!*

For all of these gifts are acquired by only one thing. And that requirement is faith. Faith in Jesus Christ is all there is to it. But this I will also tell you, the greatest out of all these gifts is love. For love lasts forever. Blessed be the Lamb of God, who is our Lord, Savior, and Redeemer, Jesus Christ. For He is worthy above all to be praised, glorified, and honored. For our Redeemer lives, and He sits upon the throne, the Lord of All! He is our risen king!

May 9, 2021

Oh, woman, do you know and understand your purpose?

Oh, woman, if you only truly knew the reason why you were created, mankind would not have been in the state that they are in now. Oh, woman, if you only have loved the Lord your God who is the Great "I Am" with all your heart, soul, mind, and strength. Loving Him more than anything and believed in Jesus Christ and believed in His words to do His will, then you would have realized that your purpose of being a *helper* of mankind is more than just that of the physical but also of the spiritual. You have been given a gift from God from the beginning of when you were created to either build up the soul of a man or destroy it with ease. For do you not know, oh, woman, that God made you a doorkeeper for the soul of mankind. My brothers and sisters, have you ever thought that Satan attacked woman not just because she was physically the weaker vessel but mainly because woman in the spiritual realm bears a great gift to influence mankind?

For if her gift remained in the hands of God, she would be used to turn even the hardest, hardened man's heart soft and the cold-hearted man's heart warm and draw them back unto the Lord, even to where mankind would desire to fulfill the will of God. For God made woman to be able to get close to throw off the trash from mankind's heart and to expose his true nature, making him in the way that God made him to be.

But as for a woman that becomes deceived and gives her gift to Satan, instead of her helping to build the soul of mankind, she will be used to corrupt it and, in turn, destroy it without even realizing it. Instead of healing mankind, she would cause him more anguish, pain, and grief. For a woman without God can't fully do her intended purpose of God unless His mercy and grace are upon her to come unto the salvation of Jesus Christ, but other than that, she is used to rip out the heart of mankind from his chest and leave his soul for dead in the lake of fire that burns for eternity.

For only a man that puts his faith and trust in God alone will be able to survive and escape the snare of seduction. For witchcraft has no power over the *Son of God.* Woman, come unto Jesus Christ and know your true self in Him. God will forgive you, and He is the only one that can make you new. For with Jesus Christ is where your true purpose is found and maintained. You can find your true identity in Christ Jesus, our Lord, Savior, and Redeemer.

May 10, 2021

Being with God is not for what you can gain, but it is only about having that relationship with Him that grows unto eternity and to be enabled to help your neighbors all around you to understand the love of God as you do so that they may come and abide in His love also unto eternal life with Him forever. For this is the purpose of salvation, so that one may know God and in knowing Him, becoming miraculously changed by His all-consuming fire for His good purposes!

May 12, 2021

Spend time with God in prayer, and pray for wisdom and understanding, read His Word. Believe in Him, remaining in the Bible so that you may know Jesus Christ for yourself personally! Know His Word and do what is taught by Him! Come unto Christ and believe in Him, so that He may set you free, for whosoever the Son sets free, is free indeed!

May 13, 2021

I Am Waiting to Go Home:

From the beginning, since the day that my Father had brought me into this world. The world has hated me and has known me not, nor knew for what I was meant. I was credited as weak and was seen as nothing and a waste. I was a stranger, outcast, and loner to them. I was separated from the rest. And as they did not know me, I did not know them.

But You, oh Lord, my God, my Abba, You have made me know who I was from the beginning. Though at first, I didn't understand what I was and the purpose of my being, through time, You have revealed it more and more unto me. Thank You, oh Lord, for Your wisdom, understanding, the Spirit of truth, and the Holy Spirit. For You have hidden me from the world until the proper timing of You making me known.

And now, little by little, You are revealing Your light through me upon the world. For I was born into this world but am not of it. But I am of my eldest brother's kingdom to come. For the world knows not my eldest brother, Jesus Christ, as it does not know me. For my eldest brother, Jesus Christ is the Lamb of God and the only begotten Son of God, and whosoever believes in Jesus Christ are sons and daughters of God also and are my brothers and sisters.

Therefore, who am I? My heavenly Father has made me know from the beginning, for I am a son of the Great "I Am" (who is God alone), a child of the light that has been here since the foundation of the earth. What am I? I am a king wrapped in the glory of God in waiting for His home. What is my purpose of being? I was brought into this world to be used by my Lord to bring my brothers and sisters from out of the darkness of the world and bring them into His marvelous light. For it is Christ, who is my eldest brother, who uses me and not me myself. For the good works are all

His and not mine. For without Him, I would be and am nothing but, with Christ Jesus, we are together in everything that our Father may be glorified in every good work. For the Son is glorified in the Father and the Father in the Son. Worthy is the Lamb of God who sits upon the throne.

For I am a stranger and sojourner within this world. Though I settle in one place, it is only for a moment, and when I move and settle in another place, and many of my brothers and sisters join in my dwelling, we will only be there for a second. For when our eldest brother comes, He will gather us and take us to a whole new land and establish us there for a time, and when it is over, He will lead us unto our everlasting home. For I am not of this world and love it not but only of the world to come. For my eldest brother will lead us into a whole new life. Blessed be the Word of God! For though heaven and earth shall pass away, God's Word will never perish but is everlasting unto everlasting! For He is worthy above all to be praised, glorified, honored, and adored, for He is the salvation and redemption of His people. For He is the King of kings and Lord of lords, the Great "I Am" is His name! Alleluia unto the God of all! For His love is without an end!

May 14, 2021

One keeps the Word of God not just by speaking it but by believing it and living it. Only through faith in Jesus Christ is this possible. For all things are possible unto them that believe in Jesus Christ and His words to fulfill them.

May 15, 2021

The Battle of the Mind:

Now, my beloved brothers and sisters of the faith who have received the baptism of water and the Holy Spirit, having been thoroughly cleansed and then purified for the Lord's good use and become dead to (freed from) all sin and alive in Christ by the grace and mercy that Christ Jesus has bestowed upon you. Remember to be aware of also Satan, your adversary. For though you have been freed from desiring the ways of the flesh, he will still try to tempt you to resurrect that which is dead from within you. Therefore, I say unto you, beloved, stand fast on the Word of God, casting down imaginations and every high thing that exalts itself against the knowledge of God, bringing every thought into captivity to the obedience of Christ. Be patient with endurance overcoming temptations, beloved, resisting the devil, and he will flee from you. And then, after you have been tested, you shall receive the crown of life.

For with Christ Jesus, all things are possible unto them that believe in Him. Pray unto the Father that He may give you mercy to not be led into temptation but instead to be delivered from evil, believing in Christ Jesus knowing that God will not allow you to be tempted above what you can overcome through Him. But indeed, know that if you do give in to sin, feel conviction but do not fall into condemnation. For the Lord our God is faithful to forgive and is patient towards our growth in His perfection. But this I do say unto you and take heed very well, God's mercy and grace are not given so that you may continue to sin but is only to help you in your growth to get closer to God in relationship with Him that propels you into being fully established in the Lamb's Book of Life for eternity with God.

The purpose of mercy and grace is for the salvation of eternal life for our souls and that of others so that we may be with our Father in paradise forevermore. Therefore, woe unto them that take advantage of God's mercy and grace and feel no need of repentance and also feel no need to purge themselves from all wickedness, perversion, abominations (the ways of the flesh) to receive righteousness, holiness, purity, and the goodness of the Lord (the fruit of the Spirit). For they are setting themselves up to be marked for His wrath and to be cast down into eternal hellfire. Therefore, my beloved family in Christ Jesus, know that God has already given us the victory through Jesus Christ. So, fight the good fight of faith. For Paul said,

> For though we walk in the flesh, we do not war according to the flesh. For the weapons of our warfare are not carnal, but mighty through God to the pulling down of strongholds, casting down imaginations and every high thing that exalts itself against the knowledge of God, bringing every thought into captivity to the obedience of Christ, and being ready to punish all disobedience

when your obedience is complete.

2 Corinthians 10:3-6 (MEV)

May 15, 2021

Stop crucifying Christ afresh and let Him transform you into a new creature, holy and acceptable in His sight for His good purpose. Let God make you new, and remain with patience and endurance in His goodness unto the coming of the Lord. Fight the good fight of faith! Resist the devil, and he shall flee from you.

Deny your flesh daily! Stop giving in to the enticement and deception of Satan. Humble yourselves and yield your vessels unto the working of God's hand with fasting and prayer! Christ desires to set you free from sin and give you a whole new life. Therefore, stop fighting the cleansing and purification. For God shall work, but who will allow Him?

May 15, 2021

Grace and mercy are not here for one to abuse and misuse for the sake of wickedness, perversion, and abominable desire, but it's only here to help save from sin and maintain one's salvation unto the coming of the Lord! Woe unto them that see grace and mercy as a common thing! It is not for one to continue sinning but to help save us from sinning ever again. Therefore, Repent unto God with a true and sincere heart because of your transgressions, turning away from your wicked ways believing that Christ Jesus can and will free you from your sins. For the kingdom of heaven is at hand, and every tree that is not bearing forth good fruit shall be cast out and thrown into the lake of fire!

May 16, 2021

The Perverse and Adulterous Generation Has No Sign Except to Repent:

No sign shall be given unto this generation except the sign of Jonah! Repent, for destruction and devastation has been proclaimed! Come unto Christ turning away from your wicked ways, and pray that you are counted worthy by God to survive all these things! For the inhabitants of the earth have forsaken God and His ways. Therefore, the wrath of God has come upon this adulterous, perverse, and abominable generation! Repent!

May 16, 2021

Repent, all of you, repent, I say, turning away from your wicked ways! So that you may be preserved in the shadow of the Almighty from the wrath to come! For I tell you, the day of destruction and devastation is near and who shall survive it? For it has already begun in Israel, for this is only the beginning! For the wrath of God has come! Come unto Christ Jesus, all of you, so that you may be saved from what is about to happen from nation to nation around the world! Repent! For do you not understand, we are in the end times! Come unto Christ while there is time left! For the kingdom of heaven is at hand! May all come unto repentance!

May 16, 2021

Submit Unto the Will of God:

It's not about what we want to say and do, but it's about what God is saying and doing, whether positive or negative, God's Word is truth, and it reigns over all! Who can say "no" when God has said "yes" and who can say "yes" when God has said "no"? For God's wrath is judging the nations with fierce and fiery anger! For it will do what it was sent out to do! Repent, for the coming of the Lord is at hand!

May 16, 2021

Many of you still do not know who God (the Great "I Am") is nor understand Him, but you will! Woe unto this generation because of blind eyes and deaf ears concerning the truth! Christ came to save them, but they would not let Him! Repent for darkness comes!

May 16, 2021

Remain in the light of Jesus Christ, for in it there is life. For He is the way, the truth, and the life. Blessed are they that put their trust in Him! Be patient and endure, my beloved brothers and sisters. For our salvation and redemption is coming! For who is this Redeemer and Savior? It is the King of glory! Who is this King of glory? The Lord strong and mighty, mighty in battle! The Word of God, He is the King of glory! Open up ye everlasting doors, so that the King of glory shall come in!

May 16, 2021

All these things shall come to pass so that you may come unto Christ with true repentance for the salvation of your soul before the coming of the Lord. Therefore, repent to do good and stay away from evil works so that God may grant you grace and mercy to preserve you from all these things. Blessed by God are they that do. God wants to save your soul because He loves you but will you let Him? Believe in Jesus Christ, get baptized, then remain in His Word, believe in His Word, and do what He tells you so that you may be saved.

May 17, 2021

Satan, I have the victory over you in Jesus Christ! And my God has put you under my feet to trample on in the mighty name of Jesus Christ! Begone from me and my brothers and sisters in Christ Jesus and soon to come unto Christ brothers and sisters from out of the world, Satan! In the mighty name of Jesus Christ! Satan, you are an offense to me! You are an offense to my beloved brothers and sisters of the faith! You are an offense to the angels of heaven! You are an offense to my eldest brother Jesus Christ, who is the Alpha and the Omega! You are an offense to the Holy Spirit! And you are an offense to my Father in heaven, the Great "I Am"!

Begone from us, Satan, and run with great fear; all of heaven is against you! For the hour of our Lord is near, and by the power of His Holy Spirit with great fire, we are going to rock you and your kingdom of darkness into the deepest part of Tartarus and that without remedy! The lord of all has come to set the captives free with power from on high! For blessed be the Lamb of God, who has redeemed His saints! We have the victory in Christ Jesus! Blessed be the Word of God, who is the Great "I Am"!

May 18, 2021

The Snare of Money, Beware:

My beloved brothers and sisters, let no man deceive you. Do not serve the Lord to get money but only serve the Father to please Him and so that His people may be saved, baptized, and delivered, being freed from the sinful nature of the flesh and receiving Christ Jesus and the Holy Spirit to be alive within us, making us new creatures, of one mind (the mind of Christ), holy and acceptable in the sight of God! Therefore, the old man must die (sin, lust, wickedness, the ways of the flesh, and the worldly mindset within you) to receive the new man (Holy Spirit) as sons and daughters of God in the love of God in Christ Jesus.

Therefore remember, beloved, you cannot serve God and money! For love for money is the root and influencer of all wickedness and evil! For money deceives one that loves it to blaspheme the Word of God and deceive many to do great evil in the sight of God and (God forbid) take away those that believe in God from the love of God (the mind of Christ) unto a business mindset (Satan's mindset) which causes oppression and iniquity upon God's people, instead of showing mercy, grace, forgiveness, and charity (not unto others in partiality for self-gain nor vainglory) to show forth the love of God unto all people all around them of whom are their brothers and sisters that they have not known (also known as neighbors).

For do you not see the deception of Satan? The love of money does not bear forth the fruit of the Spirit within you but only the ways of the flesh. For these are the ways of the flesh from the words of the Apostle Paul being persuaded by the Holy Spirit saying,

> Now the works of the flesh are revealed, which are these: adultery, sexual immorality, impurity, lewdness, idolatry, sorcery, hatred, strife, jealousy, rage, selfishness,

> dissensions, heresies, envy, murders, drunkenness, carousing, and the like. I warn you, as I previously warned you, that those who do such things shall not inherit the kingdom of God.
>
> Galatians 5:19-21 (MEV)

For all these things can be and are inspired because of the influence and bewitchment of the love of money within the hearts of humanity!

> But the fruit of the Spirit is love, joy, peace, patience, gentleness, goodness, faith, meekness, and self-control; against such there is no law. Those who are Christ's have crucified the flesh with its passions and lusts. If we live in the Spirit, let us also walk in the Spirit. Let us not be conceited, provoking one another and envying one another.
>
> Galatians 5:22-26 (MEV)

Therefore, do not desire to be around worldly rich people nor think of them so highly because of their wealth, becoming partial in the way you love and treat others all around you, basing them off their own status and not the character of one's own heart. For even James said by the Holy Spirit,

> But you have despised the poor. Do not rich men oppress you and drag you before the judgment seats? Do they not blaspheme that worthy name by which you are called? If you fulfill the royal law according to the Scrip-

> ture, "You shall love your neighbor as yourself," you are doing well. But if you show partiality, you are committing sin and are convicted by the law as sinners.
>
> James 2:6-9 (MEV)

Therefore, I say unto you, do not let Satan bewitch and influence you by them because of their riches to think like them and do the wickedness and abominations that they do. For their riches are cursed laying them up for the wrath of God because their riches are built and made in the ways of deceit, not the truth; manipulation, not love; oppression, not kindness; and iniquity, not servanthood! For when they give, it's only to get back laying on interest carrying hidden agendas (this is not true charity, nor is it in the work of a pure and true heart but only of selfish gain because of vain desires). For do they not know that their greed for more is the cause of people working with heavy burdens that they cannot fulfill, becoming poor, in poverty, and in lack of necessity to live and keep their families? For because of their greed, they keep back the wages that are for the workers, and in turn, they work them to death, nor can those workers live on what they are given!

For the rich oppressors notice but careth not, neither feel their own shame with guilt because they are deceived by Satan to believe that their ways are "good" and have done "nothing wrong," feeling justified in pride and blame the poor for the problems of lack instead! And they judge the poor unjustly with hypocrisy, lies, deceit, and manipulation to justify the means being led by hidden agendas, for Satan uses greed with entitlement to be their influencer! For indeed, woe unto businessmen and businesswomen who oppress and cause iniquity for selfish gain and do works for vainglorious ambitions! For they will not make it into the kingdom of heaven, and hard will it be for them to receive the salvation of the Lord and be redeemed.

> Then Jesus said to His disciples, "Truly, I say to you that it will be hard for a rich man to enter the kingdom of heaven. And again I say to you, it is easier for a camel to go through the eye of a needle than for a rich man to enter the kingdom of God."
>
> Matthew 19:23-24 (MEV)

For they would have to lose all that they have gained, holding no one unto debts with all forgiveness. Then come unto Christ Jesus with repentance from a pure and true heart with confession from the mouth of the testimony of the Son of God, believing it within their heart. Become baptized by water in the name of the Father, the Son, and the Holy Spirit, believing in Jesus Christ and His Word (the Bible) to do what He taught from it abiding in the love of God with praying and fasting remaining in the relationship with God. If they do these things in a true and pure heart unto God all the days of their life, they shall be saved. For very rare is this for an ungodly rich person, but with Christ Jesus, nothing is impossible unto them that believe in Him. For according to one's own faith, shall they be saved! Therefore, oh ye rich man and woman, become low in the flesh so that you may be made high in the Spirit by Jesus Christ. I pray that even you may be saved. Amen!

For when you do, there will be great rejoicing in the kingdom of heaven unto God concerning the salvation of your soul! For God your Father even loves you, see, for even the angels of heaven and all the saints of the Lord will rejoice because of your redemption by Jesus Christ! Therefore, beloved, believe in our Lord concerning your soul, believe! Pick up your cross daily and come, follow Christ our Lord and Savior! And do not dare let Satan turn your head back around to doing evil, for this is for the fight of your own salvation, the life of your own soul! I pray indeed for your soul, beloved, that you may be able to endure these temptations and not be led into the acts of them but instead overcome them in the love of God! Believe in Jesus Christ, and you shall be saved! You shall know the truth, and the truth shall set you free! And whosoever the Son sets free, is free indeed! Do you believe this, beloved? Indeed, I say, believe!

May 18, 2021

Beware of your spirit when it comes to money, do not let Satan use it to influence you, but instead, always let the Holy Spirit influence you! For money is just a resource, not life! And it will soon come to nothing and be destroyed and never seen again! For Jesus Christ is the only life, and He lasts forever! Therefore, put your trust in God, not money!

May 18, 2021

Do not let love of money deceive you into forsaking the salvation of your own soul, but instead, come unto Christ Jesus with repentance and focus your heart onto the will of God so that when you do receive the gift of wealth, you will not only use it for yourself but also to advance the kingdom of God and the Lord's divine will! For this is the reason why wealth is given, to do the will of God concerning the purpose you were called more than you were able to before! For to whom much is given, much is required! Let the Holy Spirit guide you concerning all things in the Spirit of truth and pureness of heart with all wisdom and discernment to fulfill God's plan for your life! This is not possible without the relationship of God and love of God! For without God, nothing is possible! Pray, fast, and remain in His Word to fulfill what Christ teaches you and shows you to do! Let Him guide you and trust in His council, not man's!

For God uses the foolish things of this world to confound the wise! For the wisdom of the world knows nothing compared to the wisdom of God! For this reason, the wisdom of God is foolish to those that are of the world because they believe in the world (Satan) and not the Word of God. Therefore, the Apostle Paul explains,

> Now we have received not the spirit of the world, but the Spirit which is of God, so that we might know the things that are freely given to us by God. These things also we proclaim, not in the words which man's wisdom teaches, but which the Holy Spirit teaches, comparing spiritual things with spiritual. But the natural man does

> not receive the things of the Spirit of God, for they are foolishness to him; nor can he know them, because they are spiritually discerned. …For "who has known the mind of the Lord that he may instruct Him?" But we have the mind of Christ.
>
> 1 Corinthians 2:12-14, 16 (MEV)

For only the Great "I Am" is all-knowing and the only teacher! For this reason, even Elijah said,

> Elijah came to all the people and said, "How long will you stay between two opinions? If the Lord is God, follow Him, but if Baal, then follow him. And the people did not say a word.
>
> 1 Kings 18:21 (MEV)

Therefore, put your trust in God, not money, lest you be deceived by Satan's influence!

May 18, 2021

The wisdom of the world (Satan) teaches you how to forsake your own soul, but the wisdom of God shows you the way of life, yes, eternal life indeed. Blessed are they that love the wisdom of God and hates the wisdom of the world, for they follow in the straight and narrow path which leads towards eternal life!

May 18, 2021

Do you not know, the way you treat others is the way you are treating God? Love one another, pleasing God in all your works to be loved by your heavenly Father, not man. If you love Him, keep His commandments.

May 19, 2021

God Forgives Those That Truly Love Him:

Now, my beloved family in Christ Jesus, know that if you do end up in the act of sin because of the temptation of Satan, do not condemn yourself! But quickly, go and repent with a sincere and true heart with haste unto your heavenly Father, and He is faithful to forgive, but do not sin again. For we were bought with a price, therefore remain in the freedom of the Lord! For He loves us so much that He died on the cross so that we may be free from sin and rose again from the dead so that we may remain in Him. Therefore, since we love Him, also let us die to the ways and lusts of the flesh (stop sinning/deny our flesh daily), and remain alive in the newness (Holy Spirit) of Jesus Christ in all His righteousness! Let us not turn backward (God forbid), but instead, brush ourselves off and continue forward, going from glory to glory in Christ Jesus! Remain in Him and sin no more, for He has freed you, beloved. Remain in His freedom unto the coming of the Lord! Do not give up nor give in but fight the good fight of faith, believing in our Redeemer! For He will keep us from falling unto the end! For our risen king lives! For Apostle Paul explains,

> There is therefore now no condemnation for those who are in Christ Jesus, who walk not according to the flesh, but according to the Spirit. …For those who live according to the flesh set their minds on the things of the flesh, but those who live according to the Spirit, the things of the Spirit. To be carnally minded is death, but to be spiritually minded is life and peace, for the carnal mind is hostile toward God, for it is not subject to the law of God, nor indeed can it be, and those who are in the flesh cannot please God. …For if you live according to the flesh, you will die, but if through the Spirit you put to death the deeds of the body, you will live. For as many as are led by the Spirit of God, these are the sons of God.
>
> Romans 8:1, 5-8, 13-14 (MEV)

Therefore, believe in Him!

May 20, 2021

Renew Your Mind, Beloved:

My brothers and sisters in Christ Jesus, when you see that your mind is thinking of things that it should ought not, go then, therefore, to a secret place for yourself privately. Pray unto God, your heavenly Father, concerning these things with repentance of your thoughts and then meditate on the teachings of Jesus Christ to do them. For your mind must be renewed by the Word of God within the Bible. Remain in His Word and commit to doing His will, and then, your thoughts will be established in the mind of Christ. For God's thoughts are Christ's thoughts, and Christ's thoughts will become ours so that we may please our heavenly Father in all that we say and do. For indeed, whoever receives the mind of Christ receives God and is one with Christ in every good work.

May 20, 2021

Give All Worries and Care Unto God:

My beloved family in Christ Jesus, within this world, Satan tries to burden us with many worries, cares, and anxieties. Therefore, I say unto you, do not care about the materialistic things of this world (they are vain) neither worry about situations that you cannot control (for worrying is vanity and a vexation of the Spirit), for we are not meant to be in control of the situations and materialistic things all around us. (Because nothing within this world truly belongs to us in this life. For self-entitlement and the pride of life brings troubles and evil thereof.) Therefore, instead of worrying, go into your room, close the door, and lock it, making sure that no one is in there with you. Then get on your knees and close your eyes, and with faith, pray unto your heavenly Father concerning your problems. Cry, weep, and mourn before Him if you must and release all those cares unto Him, believing in the

Lord that He is in control, that He will keep you (no matter what it looks like), and that He will provide. For indeed, the Great "I Am" is God, and He is in control (not mankind but only God).

For man does not use God, but only God uses man. Everything happens for a reason, and God knows what He is doing concerning those reasons. For it is God who said, "For I know the plans that I have for you, says the Lord, plans for peace and not for evil, to give you a future and a hope" (Jeremiah 29:11, MEV). And all things work together for the good of them that love the Lord! Therefore, trust in the Lord with your whole heart, mind, soul, and strength in all things leaning not unto your own understanding, waiting upon the Lord and remaining in His Word (the Bible) so that your heart be comforted and to receive the counsel of the Lord. And in the midst of the wait, continue to humble yourselves with love, charity, and servanthood in all purity, goodness, meekness, and humility, being selfless as service unto God, not man, though you are helping them in the will of God in His love.

May 20, 2021

Give without an End:

Oh, beloved children of the Lord. Know that your treasures in heaven are eternal, but the treasures on earth are temporary and vain. Therefore, always give so that your treasures in heaven may be great and so that our Father in heaven may be pleased with your works. Even the Apostle Paul confirms this, saying,

> Yes, you yourselves know that these hands have provided for my necessities and for those who were with me. In all things I have shown you how, working like this, you must help the weak, remembering the words of the Lord Jesus, how He said, "It is more blessed to give than to receive."
>
> Acts 20:34-35 (MEV)

For the soul is eternal, but the flesh is temporal so, therefore, give unto those that ask of you, withholding nothing in the time that you have on earth. For what you see in the physical is not the same as in the spiritual. For one can be the richest person on earth but yet the poorest in the spiritual, and one can be the poorest person on earth but yet one of the richest in the kingdom of heaven. One also can be the most famous person on earth with everyone knowing their name therein, but in the kingdom of heaven, they are nothing, let alone their name ever being mentioned in glory, and one can be an outcast and hated by the whole world and their names spoken of with disgust and disrespect but yet in the kingdom of heaven they will sit as kings in paradise.

Therefore, beloved, love one another as you love yourselves without partiality and without favoring one over the other. What you do for one also do for the other in goodwill and the pureness of heart without hidden agendas. For those who are of the world (Satan in the kingdom of darkness) will be ashamed and their souls condemned to eternal fire, but those who are of the kingdom of God in Christ Jesus shall rejoice and receive eternal life in paradise with our God and Redeemer!

May 20, 2021

Do not be deceived; Satan cannot give eternal life but only try to manipulate and deceive for the sake of trying to make you forsake your own soul and, in turn, forfeit eternal life with our heavenly Father. For Christ came to save (redeem, restore, preserve, and fulfill), but Satan came to condemn (kill, steal, and destroy)!

May 20, 2021

My brothers and sisters, saved and unsaved, please understand and listen well. Whosoever wholeheartedly rejects Christ's will rejects Christ, and whoever rejects Christ forfeits salvation and remains condemned. Whoever remains condemned after knowing the revelation of truth goes deeper into darkness, and whoever goes deeper into darkness loves Satan. Whoever loves Satan after all these things happen to them is against Christ (for, at this moment, because they denied Christ's will [which is love], in turn, deny Christ [without even realizing it blindly], becomes condemned, and in condemnation [being deceived by Satan], they forsake love [who is God] and embrace hate (Satan), and when one embraces hate, they come against the work and will [love] of Christ).

For whoever comes against Christ, they are against God (love itself). And finally, whosoever is against God, their hearts have become fully darkened and have become children of Satan (they are abominations in the sight of God). Whosoever becomes a child of Satan, God will destroy them all from off the face of the earth and send them into the lake of fire that burns with weeping and gnashing of teeth for eternity with Satan and his fallen angels. (This must happen because these people are no longer human beings [mankind]. For they have denied and forsaken who they are completely and have become unnatural beasts [666], for they are the children of darkness, and Satan is their father because they do his will with all their hearts. They have become darkness incarnate, for legion has consumed them. They are no longer mankind nor God's children.)

If God did not take them away from our midst (God forbid), there would not have been a remnant of the saints spoken of to be raptured in the coming of the Lord, but all mankind would have been corrupted and be destroyed, it would have been worse than the great flood! But, for this reason, thank God for sending Jesus Christ our Lord and Savior, who saw fit to have mercy upon all generations of mankind so that all who believed in Jesus Christ (the Son of the living God) may receive redemption of the sonship of God and be saved from the wrath of God at the coming of the Lord! For without Christ Jesus, no one on the earth from the time it was created till the second coming of the Lord would have been saved.

Think of it like this, if God truly hated mankind, He would have fully destroyed us all in the great flood that covered the whole earth, but instead, He had mercy because of His love and preserved a remnant of His saints throughout all the rest of the generations of the future in the loins of Noah and His children and kept them throughout all that happened in the flood. For this is another (among many unending) examples of how much God has shown He loves us and how faithful He is unto them that love Him. For as God was faithful to preserve Noah in the great flood, so will He preserve all of them that believe in Jesus Christ having great faith to be saved in the rapture in the midst of the time of His great wrath at His second coming!

For God is not a respecter of persons, nor does He favor one of His saints over the rest of His faithful saints but loves us all as one body. For God will keep all of us that truly love Him, for we are the church without spot nor wrinkle who have been thoroughly cleansed and purified by the working of His hands to manifest His glory unto His coming, and He has not let one of us go that love Him, for we are the redeemed of the Lord and have been chosen since the beginning of time and the foundation of the earth! Blessed be the name of our Lord and Savior, Jesus Christ! For in ancient times, the whole earth was once cleansed by water, but now before the time of the great and final judgment day, it shall be cleansed by fire and only the redeemed saints that loved Him since the beginning of time from all generations throughout the time of this world shall be preserved even when this earth is no more. Then after that, all the sheep and goats (all the saints of God, the good and the bad) will be gathered together for the great and final judgment of our Lord Jesus Christ to send each one to their destination with which portion God judges! For then, after that comes to pass, the new Jerusalem in paradise that was promised and prepared all throughout the ages of the earth unto all the saints that truly loved Him shall be made manifest, and we will forever be His people, and He will be forever our God!

For this is the official end of the book of mankind, and the beginning of the new book with great mystery and wonder of a whole new life in eternity of paradise with our God and King, the Word of God! For indeed, blessed are all of us whose names are written in the Lamb's Book of Life. For even that book has already been written, but the revelation of that book is not meant for the eyes of mankind to bear witness to (for that life is not meant for flesh) but only new creatures whose vessels are converted in the spiritual into glorified bodies made Holy and indeed acceptable in the sight of God. For who knows what we would become (appearance)?

There may not be a name known for what we will become (a thing in which I believe only God knows until the time purposed that He desires to reveal it). We only know that we will be like (not become angels but only "as like") the angels of heaven no longer having a gender but taking on a muscular nature as sons of God being transformed into new creatures. We will even judge the angels of heaven, and all things will be given unto us as an inheritance as we are joint-heirs with Christ Jesus of the new Jerusalem in paradise. For the sons of God are of royalty in the glory of the Lord. (As Jesus Christ explained in Matthew 22:30, and also explained by the Apostle Paul in 1 Corinthians 6:2-3, Philippians 3:20-21, and Romans 8:17.) For indeed, blessed are they that are worthy of entering the new Jerusalem in paradise, for they are set up for eternity. Blessed be the Lamb of God who sits upon the throne, for He shall make all things new, even to make all things subjected unto Himself! Holy, holy, is the Lamb of God, the Lord God Almighty, the salvation of His saints.

> Look, I am coming soon! My reward is with Me to give to each one according to his work. I am the Alpha and the Omega, the Beginning and the End, the First and the Last." Blessed are those who do His commandments, that they may have the right to the tree of life, and may enter through the gates into the city. Outside are dogs and sorcerers and the sexually immoral and murderers and idolaters and everyone who loves and practices a lie.

Revelation 22:12-15 (MEV)

May 21, 2021

Whoever says, "Heaven is a boring place filled with boring people" is a liar and spoken by Satan (the father of lies) to deceive and is deceived. For they know nothing and speak out of lack of knowledge. Therefore beware, many perish for lack of knowledge because light has come into the world, and many loved darkness rather than light—woe unto them in that number. But as for paradise, it will be filled with glory and wonder and is laid up for all of them that love the light. Who is this light? Do you not know Him? For it is Jesus Christ, the light of the world. Blessed are they that walk in His marvelous light and remain therein, for they shall be called the children of light, which are the sons of God.

May 22, 2021

The True Israelites:

For many of you ask, who is truly Israel? I say unto you, is it not everyone that truly believes in Jesus Christ and His words and abides in it to obey His commandments, remaining in the love of God and with prayer and fasting, remaining in the relationship with God our Father? What? For did not the Holy Spirit use the Apostle Paul concerning Christ's teachings to say,

> And He came and preached peace to you who were far away and peace to those who were near. For through Him we both have access by one Spirit to the Father. Now, therefore, you are no longer strangers and foreigners, but are fellow citizens with the saints and members of the household of God, having been built upon the foundation of the apostles and prophets, Jesus Christ Himself being the chief cornerstone.

Ephesians 2:17-20 (MEV)

And even did not John the Baptist say to the ones that were currently the Jews and Israel from birthright,

> And do not think to say within yourselves, "We have Abraham as our father," for I say to you that God is able from these stones to raise up children for Abraham. Even now the axe is put to the tree roots. Therefore, every tree which does not bear good fruit is cut down and thrown into the fire.
>
> Matthew 3:9-10 (MEV)

And did not even Jesus Christ, our Lord and Savior, say,

> For whoever does the will of My Father who is in heaven is My brother, and sister, and mother.
>
> Matthew 12:50 (MEV)

Therefore, I say unto you, whosoever truly believes in Jesus Christ and abides in the love of God and remains in the relationship with God (no matter of race, lineage, color, nor appearance) are the true Israelites and are made the true descendants of Abraham, along with all the promises God has made concerning him and his seeds. Therefore race, lineage, color, and appearance doesn't matter anymore as it was in the Old Testament. For meditating and arguing about these things is vain and a waste of time, do you not see? For God has even made all races of mankind now one. For there is no more pure breeds, but all are watered down. Therefore, now it is not about race nor countries but only the kingdom of light and the kingdom of darkness. They that are of light are in the sonship of God and are the true descendants of Abraham and are called the true Israelites in the sight of God! Therefore, do not be deceived; God has not forsaken Israel! Unto them that have an ear, let them hear to what the Spirit of the Lord is saying to the church.

May 24, 2021

The Blindfold of Satan Called Religion, Do Not Be Deceived:

Oh, ye who lead the flock of God, who told you to have spiritual birthdays and appreciation services for yourself? For I tell you indeed, it is not God. See, now you deceive God's people to blindly worship and glorify you because of "your" accomplishments instead of glorifying and worshiping God for those accomplishments instead. For see, now you have become an idol and are puffed up with pride and loveth vainglory. Who has deceived you into thinking that vainglory and idolatry are the way of honoring one another? Woe unto you, for you are deceived by Satan's influence in religious practices and traditions of men. Wake up you who call yourselves pastors, prophets, apostles, with all other titles who glorify yourselves and not glorify God by your works, deeds, and speech (with all your being). For you do not abide in the love of God nor serve Him but only yourselves, if you did love Him, you would have loved your neighbor as yourselves without partiality, as how God has loved you, and you would have obeyed the Word of God instead of listening to the wicked counsel of religious leaders led by Satan to deceive the body of Christ.

For if you would have remained in the Word of God to receive good counsel for yourselves, believing in the Word of Truth, then you would know that Christ said,

> But do not be called 'Rabbi,' for you have one Teacher, the Christ, and you are all brothers. And call no man on earth your father, for you have one Father, who is in heaven. Nor be called teachers, for you have one Teacher, the Christ.
>
> Matthew 23:8-10 (MEV)

And that Paul said, "For who makes you differ from another? And what do you have that you did not receive? Now if you received it, why do you boast as if you had not received it?" (1 Corinthians 4:7, MEV).

See, now you are blinded by pride and have become hypocrites contrary to the Word of God and have now become confused, corrupting and blaspheming the gospel of truth to fit your logic by what you have learned by the world. For see, now you are a false prophet and do not have the mind of Christ but instead the mind of the world (Satan) teaching others that what's good is bad and that what's bad is good. Woe unto you, I say, woe. Quickly, let go of religious practices, traditions of religious people, and forget men's counsel and remain in fasting and prayer unto God to deliver you from the religious mindset so that you may receive the mind of Christ and remain in the Word of Truth to understand it rightly dividing what it speaks. Clear your mind, beloved, of all that you have learned from men and renew your mind by the Word of God for yourself.

Slow down and receive the wisdom of God and not the wisdom of the world so that you may do what Jesus Christ speaks and not what blind religious people speaks lest you remain blinded and deaf by religion not receiving the truth because you rather believe in man than believing in Christ Jesus, who is the Word of God. Repent and renew your mind in the truth, lest you blindly fall into the pit. I pray for your soul, beloved. Therefore, Christ said,

> Whoever hears these sayings of Mine and does them, I will liken him to a wise man who built his house on a rock. And the rain descended, the floods came, and the winds blew and beat on that house. And it did not fall, for it was founded a rock. And every one who hears these sayings of Mine and does not do them will be likened to a foolish man who built his house on the sand. And the rain descended, the floods came, and the winds blew and beat on that house. And it fell. And its fall was great.
>
> Matthew 7:24-27 (MEV)

Believe in the Word of God, not the words of religious men who are secretly of the world, and know it not because they are blinded by the blindfold of religion orchestrated by

Satan believing in building a vain church building (that shall be destroyed) to deceive them that are truly Christ's disciples instead of believing in the truth which comes to bring life to our mortal bodies (the true church building) so that we may be freed from sin. "Then Jesus said to those Jews who believed Him, 'If you remain in My word, then you are truly My disciples. You shall know the truth, and the truth shall set you free'" (John 8:31-32, MEV).

May 24, 2021

The Snare of Religion, Come Out of It!

Therefore, my true brothers and sisters in Christ Jesus who love the Lord their God. Beware of religious people who love control and compromise with the ways of the world and whose fruit is rotten and do not bear the fruit of the Holy Spirit within them and are blinded by idolatry and are easily influenced by the teachings of the world and not by the Word of God. For if they do not bear the mind of Christ as you do, but instead, the mind of the world, not receiving nor believing in the truth when they are corrected, but instead, distort the Word of Truth, then I say unto you, why are you still in their assembly? For they are blinded of the world by religion and are the blind leading the blind, but you are not blind nor deaf to the truth and can see and hear when He speaks, for you are of Christ and led by the Holy Spirit, not the world.

For Jesus Christ said in John 10,

> I am the good shepherd. The good shepherd lays down his life for the sheep. But he who is a hired hand, and not a shepherd, who does not own the sheep, sees the wolf coming, and leaves the sheep, and runs away. So the wolf catches the sheep and scatters them. The hired hand runs away because he is a hired hand and does not care about the sheep. "I am the good shepherd. I know My sheep and am known by My own. Even as the Father knows Me, so I know the Father. And I lay down My life for the Sheep.
>
> John 10:11-15 (MEV)

You are not like them nor of them; therefore, come out from among them and do not let them deceive you by using the Word of God unjustly and with deceit and manipulation of Satan by saying scripture from the words of Apostle Paul, "Let us not forsake the assembling of ourselves together, as is the manner of some, but let us exhort one another, especially as you see the Day approaching" (Hebrews 10:25, MEV). For I say unto you, surely they do not know that they are blaspheming the Word of God to keep you bound and in chains unto their "church building." For I say unto you, the same Apostle Paul that said that also is the same Paul that also said,

> Let no one deceive you with empty words, for because of these things the wrath of God is coming upon the sons of disobedience. Therefore do not be partakers with them. …And do not have fellowship with the un-

> fruitful works of darkness; instead, expose them. For it is shameful even to speak of those things which are done by them in secret. But all things are exposed when they are revealed by the light, for everything that becomes visible is light.
>
> Ephesians 5:6-7, 11-13 (MEV)

Therefore, do not be deceived; if they were the true assembly of the brethren of Jesus Christ, they would have had the love of God within them to do His will and not the ways of the world, being led by worldly desires and vainglorious ambitions filled with the love of money. Therefore, free yourself from their midst, for they practice oppression of the Holy Spirit and know it not. Therefore, come out from among them, lest you begin to think the way that they think and (God forbid) forsake the way of truth and, by wicked influence, beginning to do the evil and abominations that they do.

> What agreement has the temple of God have with idols? For you are the temple of the living God. As God has said: "I will live in them and walk in them. I will be their God, and they shall be My people." Therefore, "Come out from among them and be separate, says the Lord. Do not touch what is unclean, and I will receive you."
>
> 2 Corinthians 6:16-17 (MEV)

Therefore, run out quickly and remain in the Word of God, receiving His counsel to do His will with prayer and supplication unto God for all things until He leads you unto true believers of Jesus Christ that truly love Him and remains in His Word also. So that you may be among those who have the mind of Christ also, for you will know them by their fruit.

> For you were formerly darkness, but now you are light in the Lord. Walk as children of light—for the fruit of the Spirit is in all goodness and righteousness and truth—proving what is pleasing to the Lord.
>
> Ephesians 5:8-10 (MEV)

"I will be a Father to you, and you shall be My sons and daughters, says the Lord Almighty" (2 Corinthians 6:18, MEV).

May 24, 2021

Come into the Narrow Gate:

A time is coming when all flesh shall know the Word of God! A man will no longer need to tell his neighbor to know the Word of God, for He will be dwelling in our midst and shall reign over all the whole earth and everything in it! Therefore repent, for the coming of the Lord is at hand and the kingdom of heaven is nigh! He shall judge the nations, and all shall bear witness to the glory of God! For every knee shall bow, and every tongue shall confess that Jesus Christ is Lord of all creation! But beware, do not be deceived; if anyone comes and does miracles, wonders, and signs in your midst and claims to be Christ, believe him not, neither follow him!

For he is a false christ. And if false prophets come and claim that they found Christ, do not be influenced by them nor pay them any mind. For Jesus Christ will return at a time that no one knows and will come with the great and fiery wrath of God against the ungodly and unbelievers of the truth (also known as the children of disobedience) and bring forth justice and great judgment to the nations, and they all shall be ashamed with great fear because they know that their end has come! For they have wholeheartedly rejected Him and His corrections.

Therefore, He has rejected them with no more time for redemption! Because they did not believe in the Son of God, they shall be cast out into the flames of fire with weeping and gnashing of teeth! Come unto Christ Jesus with repentance while the narrow gate is still open! For the time is coming when it shall be shut for all eternity! Come beloved and receive the salvation of the Lord while there is still time left! For He is the only way that leads into eternal life!

May 25, 2021

Do not follow and submit yourselves unto blind religious leaders who do not have the mind of Christ and do not bear the fruit of the Holy Spirit. For instead of doing and teaching the will of God, they distort the Word of God in confusion to fit their own ideologies and theology. Flee from these deceivers, for they are not submitted unto God but only of their own vain and selfish desires blinded by Satan. Do not let these false prophets continue to deceive you!

> Now I urge you, brothers, to closely watch those who cause divisions and offenses, contrary to the teaching which you have learned, and avoid them. For such people do not serve our Lord Jesus Christ, but their own appetites, and through smooth talk and flattery they deceive the hearts of the unsuspecting.
>
> Romans 16:17-18 (MEV)

May 25, 2021

Know the Word for Yourself:

Better is it for one to become baptized and remain in the Word of God (the Bible) with prayer and fasting in solitude (no distractions) so that they may learn from Christ Himself to do His will in the perfection of the fruit of the Holy Spirit (receiving the mind of Christ) than it is for one who sits in the congregation of blind fools that are forever learning but are never growing in the Holy Spirit (religion)! Know the Word for yourself and pray for wisdom and understanding! And the Great "I Am," who is the revealer of secrets, will give it to you personally by His Word! For this is how you build a relationship with God!

May 25, 2021

Follow after Christ, not after men! "Peter and the other apostles answered, 'We must obey God rather than men'" (Acts 5:29, MEV).

May 25, 2021

Do not worship me. I am just one of your fellow brothers; glorify God.

My beloved family in Christ Jesus, do not believe in me but instead believe in Jesus Christ and His Word to do them. Do not believe me, lest (God forbid) you become idol worshipers and followers, making then all that I am doing in your midst vain. Beware of yourselves and take heed, for I am not God nor our Lord and Savior, Jesus Christ. Christ is He that lives within me by the Holy Spirit, and He does all the good works and good speech through me and not me myself. For look, without God and His love, I am nothing and can do nothing, let alone breathe and move. See, I am weak, but He is strong. I have no power, but He is power. Through Him, I have life and my being. For all good works, wonders, and power comes from and are done by God, not man. For I was not meant to receive idol worshipers nor followers, but only brothers and sisters who follow Christ Jesus with me in the faith. For I was sent to show you the light and that in seeing the light and hearing Him, you may believe in Him and follow Him. Therefore, glorify God, not man! For the light is Jesus Christ our Lord and Savior, who is also our eldest brother in

God our Father. Therefore, let us follow and trust with great faith in Christ Jesus with all that we are remaining in His love as brothers and sisters awaiting the coming of the Lord our God! *Glorify God, not man!*

May 25, 2021

I have only one Teacher, that is, Jesus Christ. I have only one Father, that is God, and we are all brothers and sisters! Whosoever is of this mindset and truly means it within their hearts are truly Christ's disciples and are called children of God. For they that are of this mindset remain in the Word of God to do what He speaks and truly loves God believing in Christ Jesus and His words!

May 25, 2021

Come and Know the True Life:

My beloved unsaved brothers and sisters, if you truly believe in Jesus Christ, then desire to read His words, and if you read His words, believe in them, and if you believe in His words, then obey His teachings to do them. This shows that you not only believe that He is real but also that you believe that His words are true and that He is the only way, the only truth, and the only life.

Let go of the ways of the world, beloved, for it cannot satisfy nor save your own soul. For Jesus Christ died mainly for you so that by Him you may be freed from sinning and the condemnation of it so that your soul may be saved and He became alive again so that you may be made new in His goodness remaining in the hope of His return by faith. Therefore, come unto Christ Jesus (confessing with your mouth and believing with your heart that Jesus Christ is Lord of all, the only begotten Son of the living God and that God raised Him up on the third day after His death and you shall be saved) and then, with repentance, turning away from your wicked ways become baptized in water by a believer in the name of the Father, the Son (the Word), and the Holy Spirit so that you may be cleansed from the debt of sin. Then, the Holy Spirit will come upon you to make you new by His all-consuming fire (purified)! Then remain in the Bible to learn from God. Come and receive the true life! For only Christ can make you perfect and give you your true identity! Let go of death and receive life, beloved! Let go of darkness and come into the light! Let Christ Jesus make you new in the way God meant for you to be!

May 26, 2021

Wake up and Repent, Flee from Evil and Do Good in the Sight of God:

How is it, oh, body of Christ, that there are still divisions among you? And the divisions have become worse in these days than it was in the time of the Apostle Paul. For even Paul said,

> For first of all, when ye come together in the church, I hear that there be divisions among you; and I partly believe it. For there must be also heresies among you, that they which are approved may be made manifest among you.
>
> 1 Corinthians 11:18-19 (KJV)

Many of you have not been operating in the love of God and, in turn, do not bear the mind of Christ. So, you have distorted the Word of God, perceiving it the way you want to understand it because of your wicked desires and agendas (intentions). Instead, you ought to have believed in the Word of God and abided in the truth by doing that of which it speaks to do, so that you may walk in the will of God, being made perfect by Christ Jesus unto every good work. For if you would have truly believed in the Word of God, you would all have been in agreement concerning all things with one mind, the mind of Christ, because the love of God would have born the fruit of the Holy Spirit, and the fruit of the Holy Spirit would have been evident concerning you that you truly have the love of God within you. But no, I do not see any good fruit within all of you but only thorns and thistles. You operate in partiality, pride, vainglorious ambitions, greed, selfishness, control, and the love of money. For this reason, the Apostle Paul said,

> I have fed you with milk and not with solid food. For to this day you were not able to endure it. Nor are you able now, for you are still worldly. Since there is envy,

> strife, and divisions among you, are you not worldly and behaving as mere men? For while one says, "I am of Paul," and another, "I am of Apollos," are you not worldly? Who then is Paul, and who is Apollos, but ministers by whom you believed, even as the Lord gave to each one? I have planted, Apollos watered, but God gave the increase. So then neither is he who plants nor he who waters anything, but God who gives the increase.
>
> 1 Corinthians 3:2-7 (MEV)

Do you see? This is not good fruit but only the works of the flesh. Therefore, the love of God is not found in you, and your intentions for serving God are corrupt. Because of this, they all turned away from the mind of Christ, having their own ideologies and theologies in the spirit of confusion. Then denominations (divisions) were created because of pride in the hearts of wicked men trying to make a name for themselves desiring control and power of authority to influence. They have made denominations such as Baptist, Lutheran, All Orthodox types, Catholic, Methodist, Pentecostal, Evangelicalism, Presbyterian, Jehovah's witnesses, and more such things as these, but none of them agree to abide fully within the Word of Truth because of their own wicked desires. Even though all religions may come together as a one-world religion, joining hand with hand, they are nothing but blind shepherds leading blind sheep and do not abide in the Word of Truth but instead pervert it to feel comfortable in their own wicked folly. Woe unto them in this number, I say, woe! For the wrath of God is strong upon them because they turn God's people astray from the path of righteousness. For this reason, King Solomon said, "Though hand join in hand, the wicked shall not be unpunished: but the seed of the righteous shall be delivered" (Proverbs 11:21, KJV).

Whosoever forsakes Christ to believe in lies instead is not of Him nor belongs to Christ but only of the world (Satan) to manipulate, cause confusion, and deceive! Whosoever operates in the works of the flesh instead of the fruit of the Holy Spirit does not serve God but only abides in the way of religion (Satan) to serve themselves. For many leaders of God's people does not even say "God's house, God's people, God's children, God's plan, God has built this house" anymore, but instead, because of pride, they have become self-entitled, saying, "My church, my members, my children, my ministry, I built this church." For indeed, they do not lie concerning this because the Spirit of God is not found in them, and they are the buildings of idols! For if it was led by the Holy Spirit, there would have been good change found in the hearts of them that dwell therein, but because it is ran by the vain desires of wicked leaders, the hearts of the people grow cold and become worse than they were before. For they idolize men instead of desiring the will of God! The hearts of the people show the heart of the one that they truly follow!

If one is not following after Christ, they are following after man, and if that man's heart of whom they follow is not wholeheartedly following after Christ but instead in works of the flesh, then the people are wicked too! For you will know the heart of a leader that "claims" to be in Christ by the hearts of the people that follow him side by side! And you will know a true disciple of Christ Jesus by their fruit! If there is no fruit, they are not true disciples of Christ Jesus! Wake up and know the truth, throw away your denominations and religions and receive the mind of Christ in the truth!

Do not claim to be Christian, Christianity in today's age has become the symbol of those that have denied the words of the truth and are false prophets and idols walking in the vanity of their own minds deceived by Satan's influence of lies puffed up with pride thinking highly of themselves and put people under their feet being of an antichrist spirit because of the ignorance within themselves not desiring to obey the Word of God. No, no one who truly believes in the Word of God is a Christian (though we suffer as one) but only are called by Jesus Christ, His true disciples (for we abide by His will not by the will of religious practices and traditions of men that does not help anyone's growth in the Holy Spirit, for they become idol worshipers) and we have received the sonship through Christ our Lord as the children of God and are all brothers and sisters with humbleness and humility in Christ Jesus! For even Jude said,

> But, beloved, remember the words that were previously spoken by the apostles of our Lord Jesus Christ. They said to you, "In the last days there will be scoffers who will walk after their own ungodly desires." These are the men who cause divisions, sensual, devoid of the Spirit. But you, beloved, build yourselves up in your most holy

May 26, 2021

Watch Your Spirits in the Midst of Correction and Warning:

Remember, faith without works is dead; therefore, beloved, let's work out our own salvation with fear and trembling. Let exhortation and edification continue in brotherly love to help one another grow in the love of God with all mercy and grace. And, beloved, let us be careful of how we treat one another when God sends corrections remaining in His love so that instead of becoming offended by what has been spoken, we listen, repent unto God, and work on correcting what needs to be fixed within ourselves. May God bless you all, my beloved family in the Lord.

May 26, 2021

Pride Kills the Soul:

The difference between King David and King Solomon was that King David always humbled and submitted himself unto God when correction came, and because of that, he grew forever with the Lord and became the apple of God's own eye. But this was not the same for King Solomon. King Solomon, seeing the greatness of "his" wisdom and all that it produced within his midst and for all the people around him, he allowed pride to enter into his heart, and his pride turned him foolish, and when God's correction and reproof came to him, he paid it no mind. Neither did he repent nor remained thankful unto God for wisdom and understanding. Therefore, because of pride, his foot slipped, and though he was made very great in those times, the fall of his soul was even greater unto the forsaking of it. For the fear of the Lord was not found in King Solomon as it was with his father to remain humbled with humility before God. King Solomon could not receive correction because of his own pride. Therefore, he became condemned. Let them that have eyes and ears, let us all hear and see what the Holy Spirit is saying to the church and the world.

May 26, 2021

Correction is better than compromise and an understanding heart rather than an ignorant spirit.

May 27, 2021

Danyell's Testimony

If it had not been for the Lord who was on my side, where would I be? I would have died coming out of the womb of my mother, yes indeed, I would not have even been able to reach the third trimester of my mother's pregnancy from within her womb. I would have been overcome by the demons that were trying to destroy me in my youth, yes, indeed if it was not for God and Jesus Christ my Lord and Savior for delivering me, I would have been torn asunder, and my name would not have even been mentioned in the land of the living. If it had not been for my God, the Great "I Am," the strength of my life, my protection, and my defense, I would have been overcome by depression and would have committed suicide a long time ago because I would not have been able to withstand the battles that came with life.

Yes, indeed, it was and is all Jesus Christ, in the midst of my weaknesses! Yes, indeed, it was God my Father, who was and is my defense! Yes, even, yes indeed, it was the Holy Spirit that was and has been my comforter and my sword! For the Great "I Am" is even my judge and jury! For I am weak, but He is strong! Yes, I am lowly, but He is my vindication! Yes, I am young and inexperienced, but He is my eternity incarnate and the source of all wisdom, all knowledge, and understanding! Yes, I have no power and am nothing, but He is my vengeance and authority!

Yes, my God alone has done it all; worship Him, all in the earth and the heavens above! Glorify Him because of His wondrous works! He is an awesome God, and no one can disannul His judgments! For what He makes crooked, no one can make straight, and what he makes straight, no one can make crooked! Bless the Lord, oh, ye creation, for He above all is worthy to be praised! Glory be the Lamb of God who sits upon the throne! Blessed be the name of our Lord Jesus Christ!

May 27, 2021

The more we believe in Christ Jesus, the greater the faith, and greater faith allows God to do greater works through us by the Holy Spirit. It is all about faith, for indeed, blessed are they that believe in Jesus Christ and His words.

May 27, 2021

Are you ready to come unto Christ Jesus yet? Surrender unto Him, beloved, stop running from the true life. All else is a false existence of lies that will not last, and they will all be destroyed, never to be seen nor heard ever again as a thing of nonexistence. But look, God and His Word will last forever. For in His Word there is life, and His Word is the life indeed! Stop running from Him; He is not a religion, but He is real and is alive. He calls for you to come out of death and receive life. All is vain if it's not done in Christ Jesus.

Come, receive the true life. Come, beloved, for you cannot hide it; in your heart, you know He is real. He wants to save you, but will you let Him? He is calling you! How long will you continue to have Him on hold? Answer it quickly, lest His phone disconnects and be no longer in service! And you become unable to get in touch with Him!

May 27, 2021

What has darkness to gain for your soul?

Beloved, what has darkness to gain for your soul over the light? I tell you, it is better to go through much hell in the light rather than much hell in darkness. For in the light, there is a promise of eternal life unto them that remain in Christ Jesus unto the end. For in the light, there is victory. Come, beloved, believe in Jesus Christ, and receive salvation and freedom from darkness. For there is an eternal inheritance in the light, but in darkness, the fight is vain and leads to nothing but one's own eternal damnation.

May 27, 2021

The Prodigal Children of God:

Prodigal children of God, come back unto God your Father who misses you dearly. All our heavenly Father is trying to do is save you from an eternal end, come back unto Christ, and He will make you new. Repent turning away from your wicked ways, and He will forgive you of all your sins. Believe in Jesus Christ and His words to do good, and you shall be redeemed! Believe, beloved, He is the only way, the only truth, and the only life. Without Jesus Christ, there is nothing but death, darkness, great sorrows, and torments. But look, your redemption is near. Come back into the light of Christ that you may be made new and led into paradise.

May 27, 2021

Come out of darkness and enter into light! Jesus Christ is calling you out, beloved! Believe in Him!

May 27, 2021

The Purification of Mount Zion:

God is purging and purifying His holy mountain so that, in the time appointed, His chosen people shall inherit it. For in this, the ungodly in darkness will see the glory of the Lord radiating upon that holy city. In that time, the wicked shall see the inheritance of those that love the Lord their God and shall be greatly ashamed in distress. The Lord, our God, declared it, saying,

> And I will bring forth a seed out of Jacob, and out of Judah an inheritor of my mountains: and mine elect shall inherit it, and my servants shall dwell there. …But ye are they that forsake the Lord, that forget my holy mountain, that prepare a table for that troop, and that furnish the drink offering unto that number. Therefore will I number you to the sword, and ye shall all bow down to the slaughter: because when I called, ye did not answer; when I spake, ye did not hear; but did evil before mine eyes, and did choose that wherein I delighted not. Therefore thus saith the Lord God, Behold, my servants shall eat, but ye shall be hungry: behold, my

> servants shall drink, but ye shall be thirsty: behold, my servants shall rejoice, but ye shall be ashamed: behold, my servants shall sing for joy of heart, but ye shall cry for sorrow of heart, and shall howl for vexation of spirit. And ye shall leave your name for a curse unto my chosen: for the Lord God shall slay thee, and call his servants by another name.
>
> Isaiah 65:9, 11-15 (KJV)

And it is manifesting now as the land of Israel is burning in flames of fire because of the great wrath upon wicked people (God speaks concerning them in Isaiah 65:1-7, KJV).

> For the rod of the wicked shall not rest upon the lot of the righteous; lest the righteous put forth their hands unto iniquity. Do good, O Lord, unto those that be good, and to them that are upright in their hearts. As for such as turn aside unto their crooked ways, the Lord shall lead them forth with the workers of iniquity: but peace shall be upon Israel.
>
> Psalm 125:3-5 (KJV)

May 27, 2021

God is purifying His holy mountain so that, in the time appointed, His true people may inherit it. For while the wicked suffer, the redeemed of the Lord shall be preserved and prosper in safe habitations.

May 28, 2021

Are You Tired Yet:

Oh, my beloved unbelieving brothers and sisters, religious and condemned, how long will our eldest brother and Lord and Savior, Jesus Christ, keep open the narrow gate concerning your salvation? How long will you abide in unbelief concerning Christ and His Word? How long will you remain contrary to the Word of Truth because of your own wicked desires? How long will you remain in the broad gate of darkness in which Christ our Lord is trying to save you from? How long will you remain indecisive of the two paths laid before you? How long will you abide between two opinions? Will it be the Word or science? Will it be God or man? Will it be God or money? Will it be light, or will it be darkness? Choose ye this day of whom you will serve, God in Christ or Satan unto the lake of fire?

For you cannot choose both, for the grey area is still the broad gate unto the lake of fire. Please, beloved, I cry out, even weeping for your soul, choose ye the narrow gate which leads to eternal life, for we will finally be with God our Father and Christ Jesus our beloved eldest brother and Lord, Savior, and Redeemer. For when Christ Jesus released salvation by His own death, the narrow gate became open for you so that you may be redeemed through Christ Jesus. Yes, our Lord died and became alive again for you; God loves you so much. Come, beloved, believe in Jesus Christ and receive the Word of Truth to abide in it and not the world any longer. Are you not yet tired of being in the midst of death, torment, and destruction? Are you not yet tired of doing things on your own strength? Are you not yet tired of being a slave to sin and condemnation?

Are you not yet tired of being in the midst of lies and hatred filled with manipulation and confusion? Are you not yet tired of not knowing and understanding what love truly is? Are you not tired of lack of identity and purpose? Are you not tired of being in the dark? For, beloved, all these things dwell within the broad gate with great sorrows, and all those that remained therein have no rest for their own souls and are burning with great fire. Come out of that oven, beloved, for it is set on the way of eternal damnation! But, look, the way of escape is near; it calls for you so that your soul may be freed, receive rest, and be restored! For your escape lies in the way of the narrow gate! Who is this way, you may ask? It is Jesus Christ, the way, the truth, and the life, and there is no other way that one can come unto the Father. It is only through Christ, our Redeemer!

Therefore, beloved, truly believe in Jesus Christ and His Word so that you may enter into freedom and life, yes, eternal life indeed! For Jesus Christ is the narrow gate, and they that remain in Him and His Word shall know true peace and find rest, they shall know the truth, and the truth will set them free from darkness and radiate within them and upon them His marvelous light. They will know darkness no longer and will walk into eternal life in paradise with all our family in Christ Jesus that love Him. Yes! For we will all abide with our creator, the Father of all, and our Redeemer, Jesus Christ, in paradise forever! We will see and feel no more pain, no more suffering, no more torment, and no more death! For all things will be made new!

Blessed be all those whose names are written in the Lamb's Book of Life, for they remained in the narrow gate and did not walk out of it! Glory be unto the Lamb of God who sits upon the throne and will reign forevermore! Come, beloved, come into the true life! Believe in Jesus Christ and let Him take the lead! Come quickly, for God will not remain patient concerning the ungodly always. For a time is coming when the doors of the narrow gate will be shut and all those who are not within it are destined for damnation within the broad gate and the way thereof is unto eternal death that never ends in the lake of fire that burns with weeping and gnashing of teeth! Therefore, beloved brothers and sisters come into the narrow gate while there is but a little time left! Come, for the hour of when the true nature of all things shall be exposed is drawing near!

May 29, 2021

The Unsaved in the World but Are Not of It:

Oh, my unsaved brothers and sisters who are in the world but are not of it. You have felt different and have been treated differently from everyone else ever since the day you were born. You have always had the desire to love and wanted to be loved, but the world (Satan) had taken you for granted, saw you as weak, and have continuously beaten and wounded your heart and soul. It was so much abuse to where you didn't see anywhere else to turn and escape to but to sin, wickedness, witchcraft, perversion, and abomination because you thought that it would help ease your pain. But instead, it caused your heart to grow cold and have been burdened with guilt and condemnation. Those who are religious have condemned and prejudged you with lack of understanding and knowledge because all they looked at was your sins and not what was within your heart.

For though you are dirty and have much filth, those are only the prerequisites of your wounds and pain that you have within your heart, and you had felt you had nowhere else to turn, that no one could save you from this darkness, that you are all alone, that no one understands you, that no one weeps with you concerning your sorrows. But beloved, do you not know that God has seen all these things, that He has felt your pain from the beginning to now and has endured them with you? Do you not know that you never belonged to the world (Satan) but are a child of God? For this reason, you are hated by the world (Satan), and even those who birthed you into this life couldn't understand you and were used by this world (Satan) to hurt you. For the world (Satan) has hated you because it first hated your true Father (God, the Great "I Am") and Jesus Christ (our eldest brother and Lord and Savior). For this reason, Jesus Christ died on the cross for your sins, to save you from them, and the condemnation and guilt thereof so that you may be redeemed from the lake of fire and receive salvation unto glory.

God made Him alive again on the third day after His death so that you may still have hope in His coming (return to the earth). But beloved, you have not known your true Father and eldest brother Jesus Christ. For if you did, you would not have fallen so deep into darkness. But look, your salvation is here, and light has come into the midst of darkness to save you because Jesus Christ and God our Father have loved you. You were an outcast of the world (Satan) because you belong to God. Jesus Christ is not a religion, He is the way, the truth, and the life, and no one can come unto the Father but through Christ Jesus, our Redeemer. Now, therefore, beloved, all God wants you to do now is just accept Jesus Christ as your Lord and Savior.

> That if you confess with your mouth Jesus is Lord, and believe in your heart that God has raised Him from the dead, you will be saved, for with the heart one believes unto righteousness, and with the mouth confession is made unto salvation. For the Scripture says, "Whoever believes in Him will not be ashamed."
>
> Romans 10:9-11 (MEV)

It doesn't matter who you are, and it doesn't matter what you have done in the past. After you have accepted Jesus Christ, believing in Him, you have received the fullness of the sonship of God and are now a child of God, and the salvation of your soul is now laid up for eternal life with Christ Jesus and everyone else that loves Him also for the promise of paradise in the end. Now you must go and be baptized by water for the washing away of debts to sin by a church of Christ, and then God will bring upon you the comforter, which is the Holy Spirit, and He will make you a whole new person. Then, after all these things from this point on, remain always in the Bible so that you may know God and Jesus Christ receiving the Spirit of truth and your mind renewed so that you may meditate on the teachings of Jesus Christ and walk in that way of life, for He is the only true life. Be blessed, my beloved brother and sister, from now on and forever. Continue in the will of Christ Jesus unto His coming, beloved. I pray for you, come unto Christ Jesus, and know that you are loved by God.

May 29, 2021

If you are hated by the world, it is because you do not belong to the world; you belong to Jesus Christ. Stop trying to be like the world and come unto Jesus Christ, beloved, and He will make you like Himself. For the world hates you because it first hated Jesus Christ, and the world hates Him because He loves you!

May 30, 2021

Do not be deceived; know the Bible for yourself and remain in the teachings of Jesus Christ so that you may receive the mind of Christ and obey His teachings by doing them.

Forsake all other influences and doctrines contrary to the Word of God, yes indeed, do not even entertain them, lest you be deceived. For many churches have become worldly with religiosity and have become vain, setting their minds on earthly things instead of truly believing in the Word of God. For if they did, they would have had the mind of Christ to walk in His ways and not the blindfold of religion remaining in lukewarm Christianity. Beware, for many are deceived by the world, but you remain as a true disciple of Jesus Christ, and that is only possible if He is your only Teacher.

May 30, 2021

Believe in Jesus Christ Concerning All Things, Believe in Him:

Unto my saved brothers and sisters in Christ Jesus, Jesus Christ will heal your broken heart and take away bitterness and unforgiveness from you so that you may be able to love again. Jesus Christ will keep you from falling. Jesus Christ is your provider. Jesus Christ is your strength. Jesus Christ is your salvation. Jesus Christ is your Redeemer. Jesus Christ is your deliverer. Jesus Christ is your light. Jesus Christ is the Word of God. Jesus Christ's Word is truth. Jesus Christ is the Lord of all! Jesus Christ is the truth. Jesus Christ is the way. Jesus Christ is your keeper. Jesus Christ is the life, and by Him, you live forever. Jesus Christ is the Beginning and the End. Jesus Christ is your healer, and He will make you whole. Jesus Christ has freed you from sinning and freed you from the condemnation of all past sin. Jesus Christ is your protection, shield, and covering from all that Satan may throw at you. In Jesus Christ, there is life. In Jesus Christ, there is restoration. Jesus Christ's Word (the Bible) is the food and water for your soul and for the renewing of your mind. Yes, Jesus Christ is the only food indeed.

Do you believe that He is and can do all these things beloved? Indeed, don't be afraid to believe in Him. Let go and believe.

May 31, 2021

The Greatest Promise:

My whole entire life is filled with the wonderful works of the Lord. Therefore, I shall give Him the sacrifice of praise and worship Him by humbling myself unto His good and divine will. Yes, I shall glorify the name of my God. For the Great "I Am" is good and all of His deeds are perfect and glorious in majesty. Oh, my Lord, how much so I desire to look upon the magnificent beauty of my heavenly Father and to dwell in His holy temple. For in my Father's house, there are many mansions, and they are filled with His marvelous light. For there will be no need for a sun because He is the light and no need for a moon for there is no night, neither would we sleep nor would we desire to sleep who dwell on high. For we have slept enough, and we are awakened and alive.

Therefore, I patiently wait with endurance upon the Lord my God to fulfill His promises that I may receive the greatest promise that my heart and soul longs for out of them all, and that promise is to be with God my Father and my eldest brother for all eternity. To be finally home, that is my greatest and longed-for desire, to be in the presence of my creator and Savior all day long. Oh, how great will my heart and soul rejoice in my Redeemer when that day comes. For truly, it will be so great that I cannot even fathom it. Oh, to rejoice in the midst of my King. To even think about it makes my heart faint with overwhelming joy.

June 1, 2021

Be Far from Pride and be Freed from Self-Entitlement:

One who desires to overcome pride must give more than they receive so that they may remain lowly and humbled with humility in heart. Therefore, within your wealth, provide for others to have much so that you may have little so that you may remain as a lowly servant unto the Lord in heart and deed with a pure conscience. If you see someone in need, if you have that need to give, then give it without thinking about it. Whoever asks, give unto them without partiality and unto an evil person resist them not that partiality may not be found within you but only the love of God. What you do unto one, do the same unto the other. Do good and hate evil so that you may please your heavenly Father.

I assure you, if a whole nation from the oldest person unto the youngest person and from the youngest person unto the oldest person in one mind (agreement) to serve God in this manner, the Lord our God would not allow one person among them to be poor. For they will want for nothing but only to do the will of God in Jesus Christ. Satan has no power against the love of God. Whosoever is offended by this bears wickedness and must repent unto God in prayer asking the Father to create within them a clean and pure heart (being purified) so that they may worship (do the will of) God and put His love within them so that they may always be able to forgive and let go of past hurts.

June 1, 2021

Do you not know that Satan wants you to care about the life of the flesh so much that you forget about eternal life with God our Father? And in turn, try to get you to (God forbid) forfeit your salvation! Therefore I say unto you, let the love of God reign over your lives and give without an end unto one another without partiality and worry! Be freed from pride and self-entitlement and receive a greater inheritance in our Lord and Savior, Jesus Christ. Build up your treasures in heaven that are set up for eternity, not on earth that shall last only for a moment. For wherever your treasure is, there will your heart be also. Therefore, think on the things above and not on the things beneath. Keep your hearts in the hands of God, forsaking not the path of righteousness.

June 1, 2021

All of you, repent and be baptized in the name of the Father, the Son, and the Holy Spirit! Turn away from your wicked ways and do them no more! Flee from oppressing your neighbors and the causing of iniquity upon them with heavy burdens that they cannot carry! Flee from hate, greed, love of money, covetousness of what others have, sexual immorality, abominations, witchcraft, and jealousy! For, oh, ye ungodly and unbelievers of the truth, do you not know that the wrath of God is heavily upon you and how is it that you say, "Why is my life a living hell"? Because you are continuously rejecting, mocking, and blaspheming Jesus Christ without knowledge of the truth you have been condemning your own souls. And how is it that you say, "God hates us"? God does not hate you; that is the whole reason why He sent Jesus Christ to save you; you just need to believe in Him, beloved! How long will you continue to believe in Satan's lies and manipulation? Believe in Jesus Christ, not science (Satan)!

Listen to the Bible's counsel (the truth), not the world (Satan's counsel and lies)! For Jesus Christ came to save you from the world, beloved! Come quickly, believe in Jesus Christ, and repent turning away from your wicked ways, and He will free you from the world! For the kingdom of heaven is at hand, and every tree that is not bearing forth good fruit shall be cast out and thrown into the lake of fire that burns with weeping and gnashing of teeth! May all come unto Christ Jesus with repentance! For it is even by God's mercy that many of you have not already been consumed because

He is giving you time to come unto Him and repent receiving the salvation of the Lord! God wants you to be free from darkness and come into His marvelous light! Come, beloved, repent and believe!

June 1, 2021

Do Not Believe in Science, Believe in Jesus Christ:

Oh, ungodly generation, why do you love to create vain arguments and debates based on opinions and the opinions of the world (Satan) that you all ignorantly believe to be "facts" so much that you do not listen to the truth? You are intelligent in knowledge of lies, and you see it as intelligence because the world has taught it to you from your youth, and that's all you know. And you have taught your children likewise the ways of darkness that lead to death. But you know nothing of the truth that came to save everyone! Science is the knowledge of lack of knowledge! They that believe in it knows nothing but vanity upon vanity and are cursed! Look and listen well! It doesn't matter what your opinion is nor what you have been trained to know (all worldly knowledge cannot save your soul but only believing in the truth can).

For this is urgent and for the sake of your own soul! Repent and come unto Christ Jesus, believing in Him and get baptized so that you may be saved receiving eternal life! But if you do not believe and you remain ignorant unto the coming of the Lord, then you have chosen for yourselves eternity in the lake of fire and don't blame it on God when it comes upon you suddenly! Remember, you chose that for yourself after all the time and chances God had given you to believe! Woe unto you of the world! For darkness comes! Repent beloved and believe so that you may be saved! For God wishes hell upon no one but only that all come unto repentance and be saved!

June 1, 2021

Jesus Christ is Real and Alive:

Jesus Christ is *not* a fairytale, religion, nor myth! *He is the only way, the only truth, and the only life!* All that repent, believe in Him, and are baptized in the name of the Father, the Son, and the Holy Spirit shall not perish but receive everlasting life! But woe unto you who will not believe, for your fears shall come upon you! Those who believe are not condemned, but those who do not believe are condemned already! Therefore beloved, believe so that you may be saved!

June 1, 2021

Praise and glorify God, my beloved brothers and sisters in Christ Jesus. For He has kept us a mighty long way and will keep us unto the very end even in paradise.

June 1, 2021

Therefore, beloved, be ready and watchful, for the whole earth shall be covered in deep darkness, but the redeemed of the Lord shall radiate within the light of Christ.

June 2, 2021

Blessed are the faithful in Jesus Christ, for their salvation is near. Therefore, remain steadfast and unmovable, beloved, for your Redeemer has already overcome the world, and He lives! Hope and trust in the Lord; He never fails! Remember, beloved, His faithful works of old concerning you and the rest of His people that love Him!

See, the Lord is good, a well-proven help, and all His works are for the good of those that love and trust Him. For yes, indeed, even I was young, now I am older, and surely I say, "I have never seen the righteous forsaken nor their seed begging for bread"! Let patience be your best friend and have endurance close to your side. Wait on the Lord, beloved!

June 3, 2021

Avoid False Christs:

Now, beloved, remember to avoid those who come in the name of the Lord and saying, "I am the Christ." Do not let your ear be swayed by them, neither follow them, nor be in their midst. Because of pride, they have turned to confusion, and Satan has manipulated them greatly being deceived. And therefore, by being deceived, these false christs are deceiving many by lies and manipulation, and the people who believe in them become idol worshipers, forsaking the truth because they have not known the Word of God. Therefore, beloved, *know the Word, and do not be deceived.* For many false christs are arising because the full exposure of the antichrist is near. All of these things must happen so that the coming of the Lord may be fulfilled. Trust and believe in Jesus Christ, beloved, and fear not but have faith in our Savior and His promises.

June 4, 2021

The Children of Disobedience:

I warn you, therefore, beloved brothers and sisters, saved and unsaved, known and unknown, seen and unseen, whosoever does not desire the will of God to obey the truth is marked for the wrath of God and are set up for destruction! They are counted as ungodly in the sight of God, the children of disobedience! For they are them that hate warning and correction and try to find fault and then point the finger to judge, scorn, create arguments, and manipulate with deceit so that they may feel comfortable in their own sin, being self-condemned! For I assure you, if they do not repent unto God, they will not remain in the mercy of God for long!

Therefore I say, beloved, repent and quickly turn away from your wicked ways so that you may be saved from the wrath to come upon the ungodly receiving the salvation of the Lord along with the baptism of water and the Holy Spirit! For the hour of God's wrath has come, and the ungodly will face great suffering in the time to come and that which is near. For the wrath of God has already begun! Oh, I weep for this generation of lost souls. *There are many.* For the Apostle Paul even said,

> But to those who are contentious and do not obey the truth, but obey unrighteousness, indignation, and wrath, will be tribulation and anguish, upon every soul of man who does evil, to the Jew first, and then to the Gentile. But glory, honor, and peace will be to every man who does good work—to the Jew first, and then to the Gentile, for there is no partiality with God.
>
> Romans 2:8-11 (MEV)

June 4, 2021

Do Good, Hate Evil:

Do not forsake the truth; forsake lies! Do not forsake love; forsake hate! Do not forsake goodness and innocence (purity); forsake evil and wickedness! Do not forsake righteousness and holiness; forsake perversion and abomination! Do not forsake integrity; forsake sexual immorality! Do not forsake the Holy Spirit; forsake witchcraft! Do not forsake charity and sharing; forsake selfishness and entitlement! Do not forsake humbleness and humility; forsake pride and conceitedness! Do not forsake mercy and compassion; forsake judgment and scorning! Do not forsake correction and warning; forsake compromise and complacency! Do not forsake forgiveness and understanding; forsake bitterness, wrath, and ignorance!

June 5, 2021

Be Saved from Babylon the Great:

America has allowed freedom of religion (idolatry), not freedom of the gospel of Jesus Christ in the Spirit of truth! If it was so, they would not have taught science and mythology in schools, but instead, the Word of God! It even has deceived the nations abroad to practice the abominations that it practices and to abide in the love of money. And indeed, they are forced to worship money because America has trained its inhabitants to depend on and seek after it. Therefore, repent, turning away from your wicked ways, America, lest the wrath of God destroys you swiftly because of your witchcraft, sorcery, abomination, perversion, and sexual immorality.

For because of your oppression and iniquity upon God's people and your rejection of submitting to the gospel of the truth, your transgressions have ascended unto heaven, and God has remembered your sins, and the mark of His Wrath is upon you and are laid up for destruction and devastation on every side. Oh, ye saints who are still blinded by religion which keeps you away from receiving the full revelation of the knowledge of Jesus Christ, wake up and become free from lukewarm Christianity! And come out from among them, lest you receive of the plagues that shall befall upon Babylon the Great! Wake up inhabitants thereof, and become freed from their practices and evil through the salvation of Jesus Christ in the Holy Spirit so that you may be saved from the condemnation that shall befall upon you, beloved! Believe in Jesus Christ, the Lord and Savior of all! For He is the only way that leads to life.

June 6, 2021

A True Servant of The Lord:

Let not your hearts grow heavy and faint at the departure of a man or woman of God (God forbid), but instead, let it increase your faith in God, knowing that their spirit has ascended into heaven and is established in the glory of the Lord! They are not dead, though their spirits are gone from the flesh. It is not the end for them but the beginning for them being laid up for paradise; we will see them again soon in eternal life! Blessed be the Lamb of God who sits upon the throne, for He is worthy to be praised above all, amen! Now, pick yourselves back up and remain focused on the will of God, continuing in the goodness of Christ Jesus unto His coming! Though all flesh fades away, the Word and the Holy Spirit remain. Abide in Him!

June 7, 2021

Oh Lord, my God, by You I was sent into this world, and by You I shall depart out of it for your good purposes. So is the same for all of them who are born of the Holy Spirit.

June 8, 2021

The Story of Jesus Christ and the Redemption 2:

In the beginning was the Word of God, and The Word was with God and is God. God's name is the Great "I Am." He created the heavens and the earth and everything in them. For all creation was made by Him, and there were no other gods; He is, was, and will be and forever God alone. And then He created mankind from the dust and clay from the ground, and God breathed life within us so that we became living beings (therefore God lives within all His creatures and every living thing, For He is life and our breath is His), as Adam being the first man of all humanity, as we came from Him. God made woman from the rib of Adam, who was called Eve. For God made one woman for one man, and one man for one woman, and their union was not meant to be given unto no others nor with any other being or creatures, lest it becomes unnatural, perversive from God's intended purpose for them, and abominable because it goes against who we truly are, which is sons and daughters of God as He is our heavenly Father of all creation. He made all creatures a male for a female and a female for a male of its own species. Whosoever mixes those species does not know that they are doing evil and are creating abominations and are causing confusion, which causes arguments and debates from the way things are truly meant to be.

Now let me continue. Please bear with me for a moment, because Adam and Eve then ate from the forbidden fruit of the forbidden tree that God told them not to eat, evil of the flesh entered all creatures and human beings because God had given the earth to mankind and if we fall so does everything else on and in the earth, even the earth itself was never the same again. So now, because the evils of the flesh entered mankind, all of them starting from Adam and Eve unto all future generations became condemned to where after they died in the flesh, their souls were automatically sent unto eternal hell. For Solomon by the Spirit of the Lord knew this by saying,

> Whatever your hands find to do, do with your strength; for there is no work or planning or knowledge or wisdom in Sheol, the place where you are going.
>
> Ecclesiastes 9:10 (MEV)

For this was the reason why God warned them beforehand, saying,

> And the Lord God commanded the man, saying, "Of every tree of the garden you may freely eat, but of the tree of the knowledge of good and evil you shall not eat, for in the day that you eat from it you will surely die."
>
> Genesis 2:16-17 (MEV)

For all living creatures and beings were immortal and vegan before Adam and Eve ate from the forbidden tree. And then everything changed; all creatures and mankind began desiring to kill each other, eat each other, and became selfish towards one another, being self-condemned unto eternal death. Therefore, God our father made a promise to Adam and Eve that He would come and restore mankind from their sinful nature.

Therefore, at the time appointed, the Word of God one day came down from heaven into the earth, wrapped Himself in flesh, and called Himself as a human being, Jesus Christ. For this reason, Jesus Christ died on the cross to save us from our sinful nature, and at that very moment, Christ our Lord and Savior went into hell and saved the people that believed in Him from out of it, and they were lifted up from the grave and ascended unto the heavens. For this reason The word of God explains in Matthew saying,

> "The graves also were opened, and many bodies of the saints who had died were raised, and coming out of the graves after His resurrection, They went into the Holy City and appeared to many."

Matthew 27:52-53 (MEV)

For on the third day after Christ's death, God resurrected Him from the dead being made alive again so that we may have hope in His second coming, and after, He gave instructions unto every one that believed in Him and His words while He lived on earth to obey them, He ascended unto heaven and has been sitting at the right hand of God until the time of His return to cast great judgment upon everyone who did not believe in Him and did not believe in His words to obey them.

For they are the ungodly and unbelievers of the truth, who do and speak great evil unto their brothers and sisters (everyone and those around them) and careth not. For they do great evil in the sight of God, and they hate love. But whosoever believes in Jesus Christ and abides, ever enduring with patience in His goodness unto the end, shall not perish but have everlasting life in the end. For Jesus Christ came to make all things new, and whosoever truly believes in Him shall abide in that newness, for Christ Jesus is the only way that leads to eternal life in paradise forever. But whosoever does not believe in Jesus Christ remains in the condemnation of the forbidden fruit and is set up for destruction and devastation on the earth in darkness, proceeding to eternal hellfire for eternity after their death on the earth.

God and Jesus Christ is not a myth, fairy tale, nor religion, as many are deceived to think. This story of mankind is the history of mankind that God is fixing now and has already fixed in all of them that truly believe in Jesus Christ. For there are many Christians who truly don't believe in Jesus Christ because they don't believe in His words (the Bible) to obey it. Therefore, they are stuck in religion and not the truth that came to set us free from the ways of the world (Satan). Therefore, they are "lukewarm Christians" (fake/ religious), but we who truly love God are His true disciples and are the sons and daughters of God and are redeemed from the world and are not of it but only of Jesus Christ. For we abide in His love and remain in His freedom. Again I say, Jesus Christ is not a myth; He is alive, and He is the only way, the only truth, and the only life, and no one can come unto God but only through Jesus Christ. For Christ died then lived again for you so that by Him you may be saved from the ways of the world and be far from the wrath to come upon the ungodly, being saved from darkness and remaining in His marvelous light.

June 8, 2021

Homosexuals in an Unholy Union (Marriage):

Now my sister, if you both desire to be saved, you must come unto Christ Jesus with true repentance. For if you believe with your heart and confess with your mouth that "Jesus Christ is Lord of all and that God had raised Him from the dead on the third day after His death," then you shall be saved.

After you have received Christ into your heart, this is the instruction for you and your sister so that your salvation in Christ Jesus is approved:

For you have made an unholy union between you and your sister, for the sake of your salvation you both must divorce each other and then become baptized in water baptism in the name of the Father, the Son, and the Holy Spirit. So that the Holy Spirit may come upon you and make you new. For you will be forgiven of past sins and be purified from sinning ever again. The old person you were before the Holy Spirit comes upon you will be passed away, and you will be made new in Jesus Christ our Lord, Savior, and Redeemer, being made alive in the Holy Spirit and dead to the ways of the flesh. I'm not saying this to judge you, but only by the Holy Spirit showing you the way of escape from out of darkness and into the marvelous light of Christ. For God, our Father, loves you both and wishes you to come unto repentance turning away from all evil and perversion so that you may become saved from the day of destruction and from eternal death of condemnation in the lake of fire that burns for eternity and receive salvation and redemption into eternal life. Come, beloved, into the salvation of the Lord, and He will make you the way you are meant to be, and you both shall have a whole new life living for the divine will of God.

June 9, 2021

Do Not Seek a Mate. Focus on God:

There are many beautiful women, but not many are virtuous. There are many handsome men, but not many are faithful. Therefore, if their hearts do not desire God, why are you considering them? And if your heart is not seeking after God, then why are you trusting it? For in today's generation, the timing of the days are passing away quickly, and wicked people are becoming darker within their spirit and deeds. For this is to expose the darkness because the fire of the Holy Spirit has come to test the hearts and intentions of the people, and they will either stray from the light and go into deeper darkness or be delivered from darkness and go into greater light in Christ Jesus. Now, those who go into deeper darkness could not withstand the fire and are burning in flames, and their torment and suffering is only the beginning because their hearts and deeds are not wrought in the love of God. But those who are going into greater light have been tested by the fire and have passed the tests because of the mercy and grace of God, for He has given them the victory, and they shall be clothed at the appointed time with power from on high. For they will be filled with the goodness of the Holy Spirit. For nothing will, by no means, harm them because they are filled with the glory of the Lord, for this is only the beginning of the works that God will do through them. Therefore, the ungodly will be consumed by darkness, but the redeemed of the Lord shall radiate with the glorious light of Christ.

Therefore, my beloved brothers and sisters in Christ Jesus who love the Lord your God, wait, I say, upon the Lord, and He will send you the right mate made specifically just for you in His divine timing. For your mate will be one that will help you go into greater light in Christ Jesus and not pull you down into deeper darkness. But I warn you, do not focus your mind on these things, beloved, lest (God forbid) you fall into a trap set up by Satan. For God already knows what you need even before you ask Him for it, trust in Him. And instead of worrying and trying to find a mate, I say unto you, first *seek the kingdom of God and all His righteousness,* and all these things shall be added unto you. Only God can give good gifts, and *He keeps those in perfect peace* whose minds are stayed on Him. Do not seek after mates, but instead, *grow in the love of God unto eternal life.*

June 10, 2021

The Separation of the Believers from the Unbelievers:

We are meant to be separated from unbelievers, but not disqualifying them nor the unsaved who have not chosen yet, nor push away those that desire to be saved and return back into the body of Christ. And within the body of Christ, there should not be divisions among us, neither contentions, lest it confuses those who are new in the Word of God and the salvation of the Lord, but instead, we should be all on one accord having one mind, and that is the mind of Christ in the love of God, submitting ourselves unto His divine will in every area of life agreeing with each other as brothers and sisters. We should not be looking to that of our own desires, puffed up with pride, becoming high-minded (thinking we are better than others) to where we are not receiving the Word of God correctly and distorting the Word of Truth.

For all the body of Christ with greater influence and lesser influence, higher position and lesser position must be together as one with all humility, humbleness, lowliness, and meekness with good intentions in the fruit of the Holy Spirit abiding in the love of God, looking to the will of Christ and not the will of our own selfish desires. For what God does through one it is meant for the good of all. For we, in the body of Christ, are all brothers and sisters and servants in many areas of life for the fulfilling of all things in the will of God, as Christ is the head of the body and no other. For all else are under Him, and we are all His disciples, brothers and sisters, and fellow servants of the Lord. No one else is greater, and God is the only Father, and we must be obedient unto His will with all agreement, not man's will. For whosoever does not agree with this in the body of Christ is still stuck in religion (fakeness and deceived) and is not yet a true disciple of Christ; they are still in the worldly mindset and not in the mind of Christ. If they desire to leave from the body because they are not having their own way, then let them go, but I warn all of you not to follow them, nor remain in the company of them, and neither entertain such a person. For that person is considered an unbeliever, mark him as such, and stay away from them, lest you become deceived by Satan with the blindfold of religion like them. For many are called, but only a few are chosen. For this reason, our only Shepherd, Jesus Christ said,

> "My sheep hear My voice, and I know them, and they follow Me. I give them eternal life. They shall never perish, nor shall anyone snatch them from My hand. My Father, who has given them to me, is greater than all. No one is able to snatch them from My father's hand, My father and I are one."

John 10:27-30 (MEV)

Therefore, whosoever remains in Jesus Christ's Word, to

obey it wholeheartedly, are His true disciples and are the real body of Christ because they don't obey man's will but only the will of God together as one. For Jesus Christ is also the one who said, "And a stranger will they not follow, but will flee from him: for they know not the voice of strangers" (John 10:5, KJV). But as for the blind leading the blind, they are not His sheep because of unbelief and desire, and will all fall into the pit because they were deceived and knew it not, nor did they know God.

June 11, 2021

An Unrenewed vs. A Renewed Mind:

If a person does not abide in the Word of God daily and is not in continuous prayer unto the Lord, know indeed that person's mind is not renewed and is set on earthly things. For I wouldn't advise anyone to trust in that person's counsel no matter if they are in a leadership position or not. Whosoever shifts their minds unto the things of this world instead of remaining in the Bible, based upon the things of the world will they counsel and act upon, for they are filled with desire and are deceived. But they that remain in the Word of God shall renew their minds within the mind of Christ and act upon His counsel and would advise others by His words.

For Jesus Christ's disciples know their Teacher's voice and a stranger they will not follow. Whosoever is of Christ will be in unity as one as brothers and sisters in humbleness and humility with all purity and goodness helping one another in love with all exhortation and edification and (not puffed up with pride nor conceitedness and neither for vainglorious ambitions) in accordance to the will of God and not the will of man, for they all have one mind, the mind of Christ. Therefore, there should be no controversy, problems, and divisions among the body of Christ, but instead, the love of God. For if there is controversy in the body, then there are some among them whose minds are not renewed. For they have not been abiding in the Word of God, nor have they been in prayer for their own relationship with God, but instead, been stuck under religion and never growing and should be silenced, for they seek after their own will and not the will of God.

Beware of these people, for they are wolves in sheep's clothing and snakes within the grass hiding and waiting for the strike to cast judgment and to condemn, being used by Satan. And many of them are high leaders of authority as well as people under them. You will know them by their fruit. For one that does not remain in the Word of God in order that they may obey the will of Christ is not a true disciple of Christ but only them of who always reads His Word and keeps (believe and remember) them by obeying it. For they are the true sheep of Christ, and they are always on one accord. For Jesus Christ said, "My sheep hear my voice, and I know them, and they follow me" (John 10:27, KJV).

June 11, 2021

Know Their Fruit:

You will know if a person has been in their Word and in prayer by how they treat and speak to their neighbors all around them, known and unknown, new and old, young and elderly, the rich and the poor, the well looking and the less attractive, the highly esteemed and the less influential. Know their fruit. Therefore, if you see error, do not be so quick to judge, but instead, go into your private dwelling and pray unto God for them in love and about those things of which you have observed, and God will give you answers by His Word. For there may need to be some great exhortation done to the pastor as well as the congregation, to the apostle as well as the leadership, to the prophet as well as the bishop, to the preacher as well as the evangelist, to the kings as well as to their subjects.

For no one is exhibited from the corrections and warning of the Lord, and God does not see one above another. For He is not a respecter of persons, nor is there found any partiality in Him. For God would use a poor person in rags to correct and warn a king set on high and use a saint without influence, title, nor position, neither status to correct and warn them of whom are "called" generals and fathers of the faith, and would even use a child to correct and warn their own father and mother. My true beloved brothers and sisters in Christ Jesus who love the Lord your God, let no one despise you because of your youth and look down on you because of your status in the world. Neither be afraid of their revealing of your past. For though we are not famous and well known in the world, God has called us His children who are written in the Lamb's Book of Life! We are the true disciples of Jesus Christ! And our redemption and righteousness are of Him, saith the Lord! For the lowly will be lifted up and the proud brought down low!

> For thus the Lord has spoken to me: Like the lion, and the young lion, roars over his prey, against which a multitude of shepherds is called out against him, he will not be afraid of their voice, nor disturbed at their noise, so shall the Lord of Hosts come down to fight for Mount Zion, and for its hill. Like flying birds, so the Lord of Hosts will defend Jerusalem. He will defend and deliver it; He will pass over and preserve it. Turn to Him whom you have deeply betrayed, O sons of Israel. For in that day every man shall cast away his idols of silver and his idols of gold which your own hands have made for you as sin.
>
> Isaiah 31:4-7 (MEV)

June 15, 2021

Full Revelation About Food:

I, Danyell Elder, have come into the revelation about food by the Word of God. For the truth is that it doesn't matter anymore about what you eat. Whether vegan or meat-eater, none sins in these cases unless they have doubts and do not eat what they eat by faith in Jesus Christ. And no one is better nor greater than the other concerning food. Therefore, everyone must eat what is allowed in their own conscience right for themselves personally to eat being persuaded by the Holy Spirit. For this reason, we must not tempt anyone to go against the conviction of their own conscience, lest they sin, and if they sin by our own influence, then we have sinned.

This is the reason why the Apostle Paul said, "Therefore, if food causes my brother to stumble, I will never eat meat, lest I cause my brother to stumble" (1 Corinthians 8:13, MEV). So let us not judge one another on what we eat and drink, lest we become judges and scorners, not remaining in the love Of God. Therefore, let us be careful of our words and thoughts concerning one another, beloved, so that we may remain abiding in God's love. Amen. For even Jesus Christ said,

> And he saith unto them, Are ye so without understanding also? Do ye not perceive, that whatsoever thing from without entereth into the man, it cannot defile him; because it entereth not into his heart, but into the belly, and goeth out into the draught, purging all meats? And he said, That which cometh out of the man, that defileth the man. For from within, out of the heart of men, proceed evil thoughts, adulteries, fornications, murders, thefts, covetousness, wickedness, deceit, lasciviousness, an evil eye, blasphemy, pride, foolishness: all

these evil things come from within, and defile the man.

Mark 7:18-23 (KJV)

Now our fellow disciples of Jesus Christ in Acts 15:19-20 confirmed that the only things that all must not eat and drink are food offered to idols, strangled animals, and blood. Other than these, there is no other decree that matters concerning food. Be blessed brothers and sisters in Christ Jesus, and may the peace of Christ Jesus, which surpasses all understanding, be within you. Praise God. Thank You, Jesus, for the revelation of truth.

June 17, 2021

He Will Not Fail Us; Continue the Great Fight of Faith:

My beloved brothers and sisters in Christ Jesus, I know that these days are trying times, but instead of trusting in our own strength, doubting, worrying, blaming one another, and complaining, let us put our trust and faith in Jesus Christ our Lord, Savior, and Redeemer. Let us wait upon God with patience, endurance, and all prayer with supplication for all, especially for the saints who love the Lord our God to do His divine will. Let us wait upon the Lord, believing in Jesus Christ. For with doubt and worry comes unbelief, and unbelief brings confusion, and confusion maketh one waver and go into a different direction we ought not to go. Therefore, beloved, as I said once, I will say again, *I pray that your faith does not fail you.* For they that believe in Jesus Christ shall not perish but have everlasting life!

Believe in Him, and your burdens will be released. Trust in Him, and He will not fail you. Wait upon Him, and He will renew your strength, and you will be mounted up on wings as eagles and will fly high; you shall run and not grow weary, you shall walk and not faint. Believe, have faith, wait, and be patient with all endurance being in the full armor of God. You will make it beloved, for the Great "I Am" has you in His hands. Just have faith, knowing that He does. Let us not give up on doing well in the love of God; we will reap if we faint not, and if you have tripped, get back in alignment with repentance and remain in His goodness. Believe in Jesus Christ, beloved, for He is with you in all things, and God is not a man that He shall lie nor the son of man that He should repent. His promises have been, shall be, and are being fulfilled in your life. Amen. Thank You, Jesus Christ, for and in all things, for our redeemer lives!

June 19, 2021

The fear of the Lord is to hate evil, for it is the beginning of wisdom. And the love of God is to keep His commandments. Whosoever loves the Lord and fears Him finds life. Only through Jesus Christ can these be fulfilled, and without faith, it is impossible to please God.

June 21, 2021

Exhortation and Edification Towards Children as Well as

Parents in These Last and Evil Days:

Children, obey and honor (respect) those of whom the Lord has made to be parents over you, concerning servitude and helping them in that of which they need help as service unto God, pleasing your heavenly Father in all your ways. Always pray unto God concerning your parents, and remain in the Bible so that you may know what the will of God is and abide by it. For God's Word is the only way that leads unto eternal life. Now, oh, little children, beware, do what your parents tell you, but if their lifestyle is ungodly and they oppress others, sowing iniquity and hardship upon their neighbors all around them for gain, observe them, and set it within your heart and mind not to be like them and do not do what they do, but instead, love your neighbors (everyone).

For they are your brothers and sisters of whom you have not known, love them, I say. Oppressing others is the way of hate and is indeed selfish and greedy and causes poverty and suffering upon those around them. But love gives to those in need and seeks nothing back in return, neither hold thy neighbors unto an account of debts to enslave them. Forgive all, have mercy on all, make peace with all, and love all in the love of God so that He may be pleased with your works. Lastly, beloved, beware of bad influences from everywhere you go; do not receive them within your heart but have wisdom and learn to understand the intent of everyone's heart (for many are wicked and manipulative in these last and evil days and are used by Satan and demonic spirits) so that you may not be tricked into doing the abominations, perversions, and witchcrafts that they influence.

For they are used by Satan to trap and ensnare by false teachings and practices, but you, oh little one, keep your innocence and purity and do not receive the ways of darkness and destruction but instead hold onto the teachings of Jesus Christ from the Bible, believe in it and walk in that way all the days of your life, beloved. For Jesus Christ will be with you always, listen to me, even if you are alone and as an outcast. Know that God our Father and Jesus Christ have you in His hands. You are not alone, beloved, for though the whole world may hate you, the Great "I Am" will never leave you nor forsake you, and He will protect you and save you, and eternal life in paradise with Him forever shall be your inheritance, you faithful servant of God. Remember to always love and forgive, and love will be with you always, even when you don't think it is. I pray for you most of all, beloved, that you may not be swayed to the dark side, but instead, come and remain in the light of Christ. Blessed indeed are the little ones who are in the light, for they are covered in the shadow of the Almighty.

> Hear the word of the Lord, you who tremble at His word: Your brothers who hate you, who cast you out for My name's sake, said, "Let the Lord be glorified that we may see your joy." Yet they shall be ashamed.
>
> Isaiah 66:5 (MEV)

Now, oh, ye parents, watch yourselves on how you treat and teach these little ones. Do not let your wicked ways and lack of care for what they do lead them down the wrong path, lest you condemn their souls into everlasting hellfire. Beware, oh, ye parents, teach your children with more than just your words, practice what you preach. For your children watch and learn from everything you do and speak out of your own mouth. Remember, oh, ye parents, treat and teach your children rightly and justly in the ways of our Lord who is Jesus Christ. Let your children learn the Word of God, get baptized, and teach them how to pray early in their youth, letting them know why they are getting baptized, and teaching them to walk in the ways and teachings of Jesus Christ so that they may be saved as His true disciples in purity and innocence with all integrity without wavering in the midst of a crooked and perverse generation unto the coming of the Lord. In this, oh, ye parent, of whom God has entrusted with the souls of His children, will you have then done your best to save their soul from the lake of fire. And if you do this, sacrificing your time to sow seeds in the hearts of your children daily, God sees you and will honor you because of this.

Now, woe unto you unfaithful and ungodly parents who have taught and influenced your children to hate, the sowing of oppression, manipulation, lies, selfishness, ignorance, wrath, perversion (homosexuality), sexual immorality (fornication, adultery, and incest), transgenderism (which is defiance of ones own identity and intended function), abomination (bestiality, drinking of blood, and cannibalism), witchcraft and sorcery, idolatry (the worship of false gods, myths, idols, and demonic spirits), and other unnatural and unholy dark works that should never be spoken of. For, oh, ye ungodly parents, do you not see that all of these things go against and destroys God's true intended purpose of creation? Look at the condition of the earth because of these dark actions. For I say unto you, these influences, temptations, and enticements are not from God. To even speak that these are God's fault is blasphemous! But I say unto you, these things have come to pass because you, ungodly generation, have loved the lies and deceit of Satan, and you have followed him faithfully.

Woe unto you, ungodly who love darkness, for your own children will even cast judgment upon you and condemn you. Woe unto you, ungodly, see, for the guardian angels of your children are always before the face of God, giving unto account how you are treating and teaching these little ones. And if their souls (God forbid) are condemned unto eternal death because of your own influence, their blood will be on your hands, and on the day of judgment, you will pay the ultimate price for the forsaking of your soul and their souls. Woe, indeed woe unto you, for reasons like this, Jesus Christ is calling many unto repentance so that they and their children may be saved from eternal fire.

A parent that truly loves their children does not give them what they want nor let them do whatever they want to do, lest their soul suffers eternal fire. For the Word of God says, "Foolishness is bound in the heart of a child; but the rod of correction shall drive it far from him" (Proverbs 22:15, KJV). And, "Chasten thy son while there is hope, and let not thy soul spare for his crying" (Proverbs 19:18, KJV). Therefore, blessed are those wise parents that come unto Christ Jesus with repentance, get baptized, and learn from His ways (by the Bible with prayer) so that in turn, they may be used by God to train their newborns and older children in the ways of the Lord also giving them what they need to help them reach for eternal life also.

"Train up a child in the way he should go: and when he is old, he will not depart from it" (Proverbs 22:6, KJV). Whosoever teaches their children in the ways of darkness (the world/Satan) hateth them because they are guiding them straight unto the lake of fire. But whosoever comes unto Christ Jesus with true repentance and becomes baptized and, therefore, baptized their children also in the name of the Father, the Son (Jesus Christ/the Word), and the Holy Spirit, teaching them in the way of light (the Bible/the teachings of Jesus Christ/the Word of God), loves them with a love that lasts forever. For God is love, Whoever does not have God, knows not love.

June 22, 2021

The Parable of the Servant of the Father:

One day, there was a servant whom the Father had divinely chosen to go and send out food unto all the people that were starving and hungry because they had no food and were close to death. So, the man went to fulfill the will of the Father with an abundance of meals. When the servant got to the people, he saw them all lying on the ground and crawling because they were weak and famished. So, the servant quickly ran to them with haste, grabbing the food, and said, "Here, quickly eat, our beloved Father has made food for you so that you may live and be filled." Some of the people received it and ate it and were filled with joy, glorifying the Father.

Others quickly grabbed the Food and ate it, thanking the Father for the food. Then the servant came to others who were a little indecisive on receiving the food and about eating it because they weren't sure if they should trust in the Father or not, thinking that the food might kill them, for they did not know their Father. But then the servant said, "Please eat, for our Father cares for your well-being and spent a great amount of time and hard work making sure it was just right for you. For see, if He did not love you, He would not have bothered on sending the food and would have left you to starve and died and be gone forever, but look, here the food is, and yay, I would not even be here giving it to you if He did not love you but yet, see, here I am." When they heard the word of the servant, they began to believe, but they started feeling death coming upon them, and they quickly, with haste, grabbed the food one by one and ate it and was revived in an instant, and they all wept with conviction because of their past unbelief in their Father and His food. Then the servant seeing them, said, "Look, it's okay, our Father is a forgiving and patient one, and you are forgiven this day and are made new. See, even your pulse of blood flow is regulated. Therefore, for now on, trust and believe in the food of the Father, and you shall live. For only His food can save you, and it is made perfect by Him and is able to save." So, they were comforted, and the servant went on to the others.

Now when the servant came to the last ones that were left and had not eaten, grabbing food for them and said, "Here, eat the food, and you shall live." When they saw it, they were offended by it and knocked it out of the servant's hands and cursed it with their mouths, coughing hard with blood, for these people were very sick and were dying as they said, "We don't like that mess nor do we want it, leave us be, we are gonna die anyway." So, the servant quickly ran to go get more food and came back to them and saw that they were even in a worse condition than before and said, "Please, eat the food, quickly, lest you perish and die. The Father wants to save you, not kill you, believe and trust in His food!" Then again, when they saw the food, they found offense by it and again hit the food out of the servant's hands as the food fell to the ground. And they said, "Leave us alone; we don't trust in that food nor believe in the Father!" Then the servant became angry with them and said, "Why are you treating the food this way? It was sent to save you, but you keep turning it away! Do you not see your condition? You are sick and at the gates of death and are faint, if you do not eat the food, you will surely die, and it will be an everlasting death!" Then they said unto the servant, "We are going to perish, and we don't care. Let us die and get away from us!"

Then the servant quickly ran back to the Father and cried out unto Him and said, "Why are they not listening and so stiff-necked towards Your food? If they would just eat it, they would see that it is good and would live. But no, they treat me and those that also eat Your food with scornings and hate and make us suffer their blasphemy against us, the food, and You, oh, Father." Then after the Father comforted His servant with the food, He said unto the servant, "Look, I am coming quickly unto them myself, and those that I see that are dead, I will put them in an everlasting furnace for eternity, but for the ones that I see that are living and are vibrant, I will take them to a new home because they ate of My food and continued to eat it and saw that it was good. Therefore, they shall live with Me in My house forever, and My food will be there, and they shall never hunger nor thirst ever again." So, the servant was then lifted up in his spirit and took the food also to the people once again, and the people that ate before grew to love the food and received it joyfully and with thanksgiving unto the Father, they sang and danced and were merry in their hearts.

But when the servant saw the ones that rejected the food before, many of them were already dead and perished, and there were only a few of them left. And the last was on their last string of life. So, the servant shed tears because of it and quickly gotten the food and urged it to some of them and said, "Please, please, eat quickly, for the Father is coming to take us home forever, and you need to be well, lest you perish and not be with us in paradise, but instead, burning in the fiery furnace for eternity." After hearing this and knowing that they were on their last breath, some believed with fear and trembling and much weeping because, within their own hearts, they truly did not want to die as like some of those that have already died. Therefore, they said with fear, "Please, feed me." So, quickly, the servant put the food in their mouths as they ate it, and immediately their hearts were regulated, and blood rushed to their bones, and they were strengthened and began to stand, and they were astonished, so they said, "We want more of the food, please." And so, they grabbed more of the food for themselves and ate it whole and were made alive and went over to rejoice with the living in the name of the Father and the food.

But when the servant got to the last dying, they said with bitterness to the servant, "We hate you, the food, and the Father. We don't care that we are on our last breath. Go away! Let us die. We don't want Him nor the food!" After they said that, a heart attack so severe came upon them, and they died instantly. Then all the living along with the servant looked up over the horizon and saw the Father coming to them, and they all said, "Look, the Father has come to take us home!" And all His children ran to Him, and as they were coming to Him, He was looking upon all who were dead, and He was furious with great and fiery wrath against them because they all denied the food that came to save them. For the amount dead was many, and He threw all the dead into the great fire, and they remained there forever. But as for the living, the Father remained with them in their own land for one thousand years, and He smiled upon them because they believed in Him and His food, and after that, He took them home, and the living remained with the Father and the food forevermore, and all things were made new.

June 22, 2021

Know Wisdom:

The Word of God is wisdom, blessed are they that cherish it and hold on to it, for they eat of its delicacies and be filled, they shall drink of its living water and shall live forever, for this is the water of life, yes, eternal life indeed. Drink of it, and it shall keep you vibrant; drink of it, and it shall keep you youthful. Whosoever remains in wisdom and receives it shall receive of its riches, yes, great treasures that are filled up unto eternal life. Yes, for the Word of God is greater than silver and gold, money, objects, and jewelry. Yes, indeed, see, for all those things will burn, perish, and cease to exist and those that wholeheartedly love them will die along with it. But look, the Word of God is set up for eternity, and those that love and remain in His goodness, are set up for eternity with Him.

For the Word of God is wisdom, yes, wisdom incarnate. And wisdom is the Word of God. Wherever there is wisdom, understanding, discernment, and knowledge is present. Whosoever does not believe in the Word of God to obey Him knows not wisdom because faith was not found within them. Where there is no faith in Jesus Christ, wisdom is not, only foolishness and lies. Know the difference between wisdom and foolishness. Whoever does not love wisdom loves foolishness, and with foolishness comes death. But whosoever loves wisdom and considers it shall live forever.

June 23, 2021

This Is the Wrath of God within This Generation: Romans 1:18-32.

Come unto Christ and repent, ye ungodly, turning away from your wicked ways so that you may be saved from the day of destruction to come because of Romans chapter one, verses eighteen to thirty-two; read it and know the truth! Repent, beloved, God loves you, but your sins will not save you! The only way into salvation is by believing in Christ Jesus with confession from the heart speaking out of the mouth.

> But what does it say? "The word is near you, in your mouth and in your heart." This is the word of faith that we preach: that if you confess with your mouth Jesus is Lord, and believe in your heart that God has raised Him from the dead, you will be saved, for with the heart one believes unto righteousness, and with the mouth confession is made unto salvation. For the Scripture says, "Whoever believes in Him will not be ashamed."
>
> Romans 10:8-11 (MEV)

Become baptized, and remain in His Word to obey His will with prayer and fasting! For Jesus Christ is the only way that leads to life. Deny yourselves and follow Him!

June 24, 2021

The Fire Has Now Come:

Correction is a part of the love of God, for this is called exhortation. This is needed so that one may know to do the will of God. We must not compromise with the ungodly, lest (God forbid) we give them the go-ahead to continue sinning, and in turn, we begin to sin because we have not upheld the standards of the Word of God so that they may be saved. No one who is in Christ Jesus and has been washed by His precious blood will continue sinning, but instead, by salvation in Christ Jesus with the fire of the Holy Spirit, He helps us to sin no more, but we must first desire not to sin anymore for this to happen. And then that leads them to finally believe that Jesus Christ can and will save them from their sins, and if they believe in Him with faith, then He will free them from sinning ever again, being made into a new creature, holy and acceptable in the sight of God.

Therefore, correction must come. Whoever does not want to listen and obey but instead despise, grumble against, and hate the Word of Truth is not truly a disciple of Jesus Christ (not truly saved) because they do not believe in the truth, and who is the truth? Jesus Christ is the truth and the Word of God; whoever despises His Word is not of Him because they love their own sins more than they love God. Jesus Christ said that if you love Him, then keep His commandments. Now, concerning forgiveness of sins, it also says in Hebrews 10,

> For if we willfully continue to sin after we have received the knowledge of the truth, there no longer remains a sacrifice for sins, but a fearful expectation of judgment and fiery indignation, which will devour the adversaries. Anyone who despised Moses' law died without mercy in the presence of two or three witnesses. How much more severe a punishment do you suppose he deserves, who has trampled under foot the Son of God, and has regarded the blood of the covenant that sanctified him to be a common thing, and has insulted the Spirit of grace? For we know Him who said, "Vengeance is Mine," says the Lord, "I will repay." And again He says, "The Lord will judge His people." It is a fearful thing to fall into the hands of the living God.
>
> Hebrews 10:26-31 (MEV)

This is not judgment and scorning; this is warning and correction, which is exhortation so that one may repent turning away from their wicked ways with fear and trembling and be saved. This is not an "opinion," this is the truth. Now, I am not saying that we do not nor have not sinned, for I would be a liar if I did. I am saying that Jesus Christ gave salvation and redemption so that, through Him, we become perfected to not sin again. This is to save us from the day of destruction and the eternal lake of fire that burns and shall come upon the ungodly suddenly. Yes, everyone has sinned and fallen short of the glory of God, but that does not give us the right to continue sinning. For this reason, Jesus Christ said,

> Jesus answered them, "Truly, truly I say to you, whoever commits sin is a slave of sin. Now a slave does not remain in the house forever, but a son remains forever. Therefore if the Son sets you free, you shall be free indeed.
>
> John 8:34-36 (MEV)

Therefore, we must look to Jesus Christ believing in Him to free us from our sins and desire to be freed beloved. This has everything to do with mercy and grace; they are meant to grow us, not leave us where we are at. To perfect us in holiness and righteousness, not keep us condemned. I hope you understand, beloved. God's Word is not a liar, for, with Christ Jesus, all things are possible unto them that believe in Him, and with God, nothing is impossible. Remember, beloved, what the Word of God said in Matthew 22:14, "For many are called, but few are chosen." And that the Word of God also said in Luke 12,

> I have come to send fire upon the earth and wish that it were already kindled! But I have a baptism to be baptized with, and how pressed I am until it is accomplished! Do you suppose that I have come to give peace on earth? No, I tell you, but rather division. For there will be from now on five divided in one house, three against two and two against three. They will be divided, father against son and son against father, mother against daughter and daughter against mother, and mother-in-law against her daughter-in-law and daugh-

ter-in-law against her mother-in-law.

Luke 12:49-53 (MEV)

And I tell you this; the fire has now come! Now please, don't misunderstand me, beloved; I did not come to cause a debate nor argue with you about "opinions." For that is vanity and a waste of time to me. I come in the love of God to reveal the Word of Truth unto all that will listen to Him. Now, however you receive, it is between you and God. I love you, my beloved brothers and sisters, and may the peace of God be with you that you may receive the truth with all understanding and not lukewarm religious Christianity Satan had created to deceive the true disciples of Jesus Christ from off the path of righteousness in Christ Jesus our Lord and Savior. Be blessed, beloved.

Whosoever remains in His Word and truly believes and abides by Him with prayer and fasting are truly Jesus Christ's disciples and are laid up for eternal life and are written in the Lamb's Book of Life. But whosoever does not believe in Him becomes laid up for destruction and devastation on every side unto eternal damnation in the lake of fire. I pray, may all come unto true repentance desiring the divine will of God to fulfill it in Christ Jesus' mighty name. Nevertheless, oh Lord, my heavenly Father, let Your will be done, not my will but Your will, for You know who will come unto You and who will not. Thank You, Jesus Christ, Selah.

June 24, 2021

Indeed, we are supposed to live every day as if the rapture will come at any moment, but also know that it will come at a time that no one knows. Therefore, let us do the will of God with the time on earth that we do have remaining in the Word of God and prayer and fasting with the fear (to hate evil works and stay away from them) and the love (keep His commandments which is to love everyone without partiality) of God. This is all that He asks of us, remaining in the truth and doing His will. Pray and remain watchful of the coming of the Lord.

June 28, 2021

Fear the Lord, Ye Ungodly:

If you do not fear the Great "I Am," you should! For even Satan and the demons know Him, and they quake with fear at the sound of His voice, screech at His presence, and tremble even at the mention of His name! He is not a fairy-tale, He is not a religion, He is not a myth, nor is He a theory! He is real, He is alive, He speaks, He hears everything, He sees everything, and He knows everything, nothing is hidden from Him and knows us all personally, inside and out! How is it that you did not know that even your breath is His! For He is God alone! Therefore, repent, ye ungodly, and turn away from your wicked ways, lest ye fall into His wrath! It is a terrible thing to fall into the hands of an angry God!

> Thus says the Lord: Let not the wise man glory in his wisdom, and let not the mighty man glory in his might,

let not the rich man glory in his riches; but let him who glories glory in this, that he understands and knows Me, that I am the Lord who exercises lovingkindness, justice, and righteousness in the earth. For in these things I delight, says the Lord. The days are surely coming, says the Lord, that I will punish all who are circumcised and yet uncircumcised—Egypt, Judah, Edom, the children of Ammon, Moab, and all who dwell in the wilderness who clip the hair on their temples; for all these nations are uncircumcised, and all the house of Israel are uncircumcised of heart.

Jeremiah 9:23-26 (MEV)

June 28, 2021

Conversion of Purification Fulfilled:

True change goes deeper than just the physical appearance of a thing. For the true change is found within one's heart proceeding to their own soul. The conversion thereof towards life is only through Jesus Christ and His Word believing in Him with the desire for change. One must have the desire to change with patience and endurance, having faith in Jesus Christ so that, at the time appointed, their change will be made manifest. For by the fire of the Holy Spirit shall they then be made new, holy, and acceptable in the sight of God for His good use for the saving of His people that He may be glorified. For indeed, He is worthy to be praised because He is the redemption of His people that love Him and desires His divine will.

> Therefore if any man be in Christ, he is a new creature: old things are passed away; behold, all things are become new. …For he hath made him to be sin for us, who knew no sin; that we might be made the righteousness of God in him.
>
> 2 Corinthians 5:17, 21 (KJV)

July 4, 2021

The Just Shall Live by Faith:

The work of faith in God is foolish in the sight of the world. But, will that same who believed it to be foolish before not indeed later on also marvel with wonder at the good it produces? And also, while watching, question within their ignorance (because of unbelief, therefore, then producing confusion) wonder, "How did these people who had nothing now have everything?" For indeed, they will, and, because of jealousy, begin to hate (woe unto them for whatever they do next). But the just shall walk and live by faith and not by sight and are made to be above and not beneath, the heads and not the tails. Because of their faith in Jesus Christ, God favored them.

July 5, 2021

Blessed be the name of our Lord and Savior, Jesus Christ, for God my Father has kept me from the strange women in order so that He may soon bring a divine helper that is worthy and honorable in His sight to be united with me in this walk of faith that He has me on. Blessed be my Father for holding me for the right one to be with me in His divine will for our lives. Glory be unto God for the love that He has given me, indeed, oh, my beloved Abba, you have been a good, good Father, and no one can take Your place. My love, my God, and my King, the Great "I Am." I humbly and patiently wait on Your divine timing, Father. Therefore, in the meantime, I shall keep my mind stayed on You, Jesus Christ, in Your divine will. I must remain focused, for only in You does my heart trust. For You have made me as a prince in waiting for my princess. And, oh Lord, You have been molding me well for Your good purposes. In You, oh God, my life will always remain, Selah.

July 6, 2021

Jesus Christ is the only one and true superhero; He is real, alive, and the greatest of them all. By no other name can one be saved. God has even made His name the name above every name. Whosoever puts their faith in false gods, false christs, and idols condemn their own souls, but whosoever puts their whole trust and believes in Jesus Christ shall be saved. For whosoever the Son sets free, is free indeed!

July 7, 2021

Wait, Watch, and Pray:

The best is yet to come for those who wait upon the Lord. Therefore beloved, be patient with endurance, having great faith in the Lord. For the best is yet to come, and it shall not tarry. Wait, I say, upon the Lord. Be of good courage, for He is faithful unto them of whom He has promised. The greatest gifts come unto those that love the Lord. Give up not in well-doing, for you shall reap if you faint not. May Jesus Christ our life and strength sustain and maintain you in His goodness, not detouring from the path of righteousness unto His coming. *You will make it, beloved;* trust and believe in Jesus Christ. For He is even our Redeemer, and He lives.

July 9, 2021

No one can argue with the Word of Love, For He is absolute!

July 9, 2021

Above all revelations and prophecies that have ever been written, spoken, and fulfilled, this one thing is certain. In the end, only love and His Word will remain. And He will preserve all those that believe in His Word and abide in Him, for this is an everlasting unto everlasting covenant that shall never be abolished. All glory, all honor, and all praise be unto the Lamb of God who sits upon the throne! Hallelujah!

July 10, 2021

Let Jesus Christ Be the Captain of Your Soul:

God has written the story of mankind from the beginning to the end, but concerning the story of your own soul's salvation, He has given you the pen. So, the question is, what will your own soul testify on the judgment scrolls concerning your story personally, before the throne room of God? For you are what guide your souls' destination. Blessed are they that make Jesus Christ the captain of their ship, for He will lead us into an eternal home of paradise. But woe unto the ungodly, for they do not desire for Jesus Christ to take the lead because they love their own control. Therefore, they suffer many shipwrecks, and it will be the cause of great and eternal deaths. For if they do not give their souls into the hands of Christ Jesus, then instead, they will give it into the hands of Satan. For this reason, shipwrecks come upon the ungodly. Therefore, beloved, let Jesus Christ be the captain of your own soul so that you may be saved and preserved. For His yoke is easy, and His burden is light upon those that believe in Him.

> Surely the day is coming, burning like an oven; all the proud, yes, all evildoers will be stubble. The day that is coming will burn them up, says the Lord of Hosts, so that it will leave them neither root nor branch. But for you who fear My name, the sun of righteousness will rise with healing in its wings. You will go out and grow up like calves from the stall. And you will tread down the wicked, for they will be ashes under the soles

> of your feet, on the day when I do this, says the Lord of Hosts. Remember the Law of Moses, My servant, the statutes and judgments which I commanded him at Horeb for all Israel.

Malachi 4:1-4 (MEV)

July 15, 2021

Relentless pursuit must come back into the hearts of God's people knowing that whether I must live for God or die for God, nevertheless, my life is preserved in Jesus Christ!

August 24, 2021

Beware of Gluttony:

My beloved brothers and sisters, saved and unsaved, beware of gluttony. For though it matters not about what we eat, it still matters about how we are eating. For this is the truth of this matter, gluttony is the coveting of food and the manifestation thereof is overeating. Overeating destroys the body. As being the temple of the Holy Spirit, this is a sin and a part of the lust of the flesh. For this is what causes stubborn fat and obesity. Therefore, I warn us all by the wisdom of God, stop overeating and your body will begin to heal itself, eat small portions not large throughout the day, and eat unto satisfaction but not full. For a just balance and good amount is well pleasing unto the Lord. Now, if it is a certain type of food that causes you to overeat, having lack of self-control and discipline then I would advise you to let it be far from your mist and choose foods that would help you eat less.

For it is better that one of your members should perish and not that your whole entire body be thrown into hell. And if going to a restaurant causes you to sin, then I say unto you, never go to a restaurant. For it is better to be in the house of mourning than the house of feasting. For the Word of God used king Solomon saying,

> Hear, my son, and be wise; and guide your heart in the way. Do not be among winebibbers, among riotous eaters of meat; for the drunkard and the glutton will come to poverty, and drowsiness will clothe a man with rags.
>
> Proverbs 23:19-21 (MEV)

And even Jesus Christ said in Luke 12:23 (MEV), "Life is more than food, and the body is more than clothes." Beware beloved of gluttony.

September 5, 2021

The Fulfillment of Perfect Love:

My dearly beloved brothers and sisters in Christ Jesus, It is essential for one to give love just as it is also essential to receive love. And it is essential for one to receive love just as it is also essential to give love, lest that one becomes partial in the way that they love and in turn sin. For if we give but do not desire to receive, we are sinning. And likewise, if we receive but do not desire to give, then we are still yet sinning. For beloved, even this is partial in the sight of God and a false balance of love. Let us therefore remember the word of God spoken through Paul in 1Corinthians 13:7, for he explained that love bears all things, believes all things, hopes all things, and endures all things. Therefore, beloved, as you give (without expecting anything in return), also be open to receive (without Criticism and judgment but instead, have a grateful heart). And as you receive, always also be open to give without complaining and grumbling against one another but instead have a humbled and submissive heart with all compassion and support. Freely do these in the love of God unto all creation in purity and innocence. For this is the fulfillment of perfect love.

Now, also lastly beloved, in these last and evil days, do not be ignorant to the devices of Satan but instead, be as wise as a serpent and as harmless as a dove. If anyone being used by Satan comes to you in the way of deceit, falsehood, and fakeness to try and put you in bondage and chains, be aware quickly, and make sure that you don't receive any gift from this person neither submit yourself unto them, lest you fall into a deep trap. Be sure that you are spiritually woke and aware to discern these things rightly in the Holy Spirit beloved with the wisdom of God that you may not be deceived because of ignorance towards the Truth.

See then that you walk carefully, not as fools, but as

wise men, making the most of the time because the days are evil. Therefore do not be unwise, but understand what the will of the Lord is. Do not be drunk with wine, for that is reckless living. But be filled with the Spirit. Speak to one another in psalms, hymns, and spiritual songs, singing and making melody in your heart to the Lord. Give thanks always for all things to God the Father in the name of our Lord Jesus Christ, being submissive to one another in the fear of God.

Ephesians 5:15-21 (MEV)

CONCLUSION

All of these words of warning, revelation, exhortation, and edification given by God (not man) are not to condemn you but to push you towards true repentance and receiving the salvation of the Lord, becoming true disciples of our Lord and Savior Jesus Christ, abiding and remaining in the Word of God with all prayer and fasting, praying with supplication for all people and saints on the earth and their souls. Let us not become of the mind of the world, but instead, let us be of (one mind) the mind of Christ, being renewed by the Word of God, daily remaining in the truth and holding, standing fast onto it, receiving no other wind of doctrine unto the coming of the Lord! May all the saints say, "Amen, amen!"

Now, Jesus Christ speaks unto you, saying,

> Abide in me, and I in you. As the branch cannot bear fruit of itself, except it abide in the vine; no more can ye, except ye abide in me. I am the vine, ye are the branches: He that abideth in me, and I in him, the same bringeth forth much fruit: for without me ye can do nothing. If a man abide not in me, he is cast forth as a branch, and is withered; and men gather them, and cast them into the fire, and they are burned. If ye abide in me, and my words abide in you, ye shall ask what ye will, and it shall be done unto you. Herein is my Father glorified, that ye bear much fruit; so shall ye be my disciples. As the Father hath loved me, so have I

loved you: continue ye in my love. If ye keep my commandments, ye shall abide in my love; even as I have kept my Father's commandments, and abide in his love. These things have I spoken unto you, that my joy might remain in you, and that your joy might be full. This is my commandment, That ye love one another, as I have loved you. Greater love hath no man than this, that a man lay down his life for his friends. Ye are my friends, if ye do whatsoever I command you. …Ye have not chosen me, but I have chosen you, and ordained you, that ye should go and bring forth fruit, and that your fruit should remain: that whatsoever ye shall ask of the Father in my name, he may give it you. These things I command you, that ye love one another. If the world hate you, ye know that it hated me before it hated you. If ye were of the world, the world would love his own: but because ye are not of the world, but I have chosen you out of the world, therefore the world hateth you.

John 15:4-14, 16-19 (KJV)

CPSIA information can be obtained
at www.ICGtesting.com
Printed in the USA
LVHW081054121221
705947LV00032B/1097

9 781637 698440